Ch
P9-AFL-768

INSIDE RUNNING: BASICS OF SPORTS PHYSIOLOGY

DAVID L. COSTILL

Director, Human Performance Laboratory
Ball State University
Muncie, Indiana

Benchmark Press, Inc.
Indianapolis

Copyright © 1986, by Benchmark Press, Inc.

ALL RIGHTS RESERVED.

Reproduction or translation of any part of
this work beyond that permitted by Sections
107 and 108 of the 1976 United States
Copyright Act without the permission of the
copyright owner is unlawful. Requests for
permission should be addressed to Publisher,
Benchmark Press, Inc.

Library of Congress Cataloging in Publication Data:

COSTILL, DAVID L.   1936–
INSIDE RUNNING: BASICS OF SPORTS PHYSIOLOGY

Library of Congress Catalog Card number: 85-73461
ISBN: 0-936157-00-3

Printed in the United States of America
10 9 8 7 6 5 4 3 2 1

Contents

FOREWORD

There came a time last year when I was fed up with conducting medical clinics for runners. That weekend, as so often in the past, I was on a program with Dr. David Costill. My role was to discuss injuries. His was to show how the exercise physiologist could help the runner.

When I saw Dave, I told him, "There must be something better we can do with our time than saying the same old things one meeting after another."

Dave looked at me, smiled and said, "George, they're hungry out there."

He's right. They are hungry. Distance running is more than a sport. It is a way of life. And the running life requires more and more knowledge of the workings of the human body. Distance runners are hungry for any information they can get. I should not need to be reminded of that. Runners ask more questions than a three-year-old. Their questions are just as basic and just as difficult. I'm as hungry as the next one— and just as likely to be at Dave Costill's lecture, taking notes.

Dave has the last word on physiology for me. He is one of the few scientists I have been associated with who has a complete grasp of his subject. When Dave says, "I don't know," I realize nobody knows. Most runners feel the same. For us, Costill has become the Answer Man.

Costill also is that rare academic individual—the exceptional scientist who is also an exceptional teacher. When he takes his six feet, one inch, 162 pound frame up to the podium, he commands a quality of attention you rarely find in school. People who last attended classes only under duress vie for front-row seats. Students who never were true students can be seen busily checking their notes. Others who cut more classes than they attend eagerly follow Costill's intricate and sophisticated outlines of body functions.

Costill didn't come to this level of acceptance by accident. He has gilt-edged credentials as an exercise physiologist. If there were an exercise physiology hall of fame, he would make it on the first ballot. The literature is filled with significant work that has come out of his laboratory at Ball State University in Muncie, Indiana.

His standing with his colleagues is indicated by his election as president of the American College of Sports Medicine and his recent medal for the application of science to sport. This regard reflects not only his professional competence but his modesty as well. He is the academic counterpart of Bill Rodgers. He is so unself-conscious about his achievements and takes them so lightly, you begin to wonder whether this relaxed person in front of you is really the number one running physiologist in the country, if not the world.

When I first met Dave, I was overwhelmed by the range and depth of his knowledge. He moved around the Krebs Cycle, for instance, like I moved around my own home. So for some time I restricted my conversation to "Yes," "No," and "Where's the bathroom?" It wasn't long, however, before I discovered that like most "biggies," (as he calls those he admires), Dave was more concerned about his own ignorance than mine. He treats everyone as another searcher after truth with something to contribute.

There is another reason why we distance runners admire Costill and flock to hear him. What he offers is practical. It works. We can take it out the next day and use it. In this sense he is a throwback to the clinical professors I had in medical school. Unlike the academics, these men were actually in the day-to-day practice of medicine. What they taught could be applied to the next patient.

Costill is a clinical exercise physiologist. When he performs a biopsy on a muscle, it is a runner's muscle. When he studies the emptying of a stomach, it is a runner's stomach. When he tests a replacement solution's effect on rectal temperature, it is a runner's rectal temperature.

And the truth is that Dave Costill is as hungry to teach as we runners are hungry to learn. Perhaps that is why Dave and I still go around the country giving clinics, saying the same things time and again. It isn't often that you face students as eager to be taught as you are to teach.

This book has been written for those runners David Costill cannot reach in person. It contains the full ranges of his lectures and the slides he uses to illustrate them.

It is the next best thing to sitting at the master's feet.

George Sheehan, M.D.

PREFACE

It has been 20 years since I did my first research with distance runners. Over that period I have had the good fortune to study some of the world's best runners and to collaborate with a number of the world's best sports scientists. Although much of the research we have conducted has been aimed at gaining a greater understanding of the physiological responses to exercise and training, I have always found it enjoyable to apply the findings to improve performance. The problem is that converting scientific fact to usable information is not always easy. Scientists are often guarded in drawing conclusions from their research. They prefer to qualify their results and are seldom willing to draw practical conclusions. Athletes and coaches, on the other hand, aren't interested in the minute details of scientific information. They simply want the "bottom-line."

This book has been written in a effort to bring the most objective information available to bear on the problems and questions facing runners and other athletes. Since coaching and running publications are often based on traditional and intuitive ideas, I have attempted to substitute fact for fiction. Hopefully, such information will help the athlete evaluate his/her training and performance. Achieving one's full potential is seldom a matter of luck. Success by "trial and error" is an inefficient system, resulting in many who fail and few who reach their peak performance.

Every effort has been made to describe the body's responses to exercise and training in terms that can be understood by individuals who are unfamiliar with exercise physiology. With some concentrated effort the coach and athlete are certain to gain a greater appreciation for the role of heredity, training, and nutrition on performance, an important step toward athletic success.

Finally, I want to express my appreciation to my friends and colleagues, Mike Flynn, Bill Fink, John Kirwan, Darrell Neufer, Larry Stewart and Joel Mitchell, for their editorial assistance. A special thanks must go to Butch and Joanne Cooper, and Kendal Gladish, for the hours they have spent in bringing this book into its final form.

Muncie, Indiana   David L. Costill
January, 1986

CHAPTER 1

The Running Body

In *The Right Stuff*, the best-selling book and popular movie about the Mercury space program, certain pilots had just what it takes to succeed as astronauts. Similarly, the superstars of sport must have the right qualities and combination of characteristics to be the best. But what is the right stuff in distance running? What natural physical traits enable one person to perform better than another? What qualities can be changed to improve performance?

This chapter will summarize the physical qualities that experts have identified as important for success in distance running. Although science has focused much of its attention on the most elite runners, the findings are also of value to less talented athletes. It is important to realize that many of the physical characteristics of the elite runner are controlled by hereditary factors. Even the ability to adapt to the stresses of training may be determined by genetics. Nevertheless, some of the factors described in this chapter can be improved through proper training and diet. Each runner has a unique profile that enables him or her to succeed.

BODY COMPOSITION

In most major sports, successful athletes come in all shapes and sizes, but distance runners have one common trait—the good ones are skinny. Regardless of variations in their structures, successful distance runners are characterized by a low body fat content (10). Since a large part of the energy used during running is needed to overcome the pull of gravity, the addition of excess body fat simply makes running more costly.

On the average, the body fat content of normally active men and women between 18 and 24 years old ranges from 14 percent (men) to 22 percent (women). Distance runners, on the other hand, have repeatedly been reported to have less than 10 percent fat. At the 1968 Olympic Marathon trial, the men had an average body fat of 7.5 percent. Studies of elite female distance runners have reported body fat contents that range from 6.1 to 18.1 percent (3, 14, 43). In 1980, the great Norwegian marathoner Grete Waitz had a fat content of 9 percent.

Although measured values of less than 4 percent have been reported for some world class male runners, namely Frank Shorter, Gary Tuttle, and Alberto Salazar, such measurements of body fat are subject to the errors of instruments and can only be accurate to within roughly 2 to 3 percent.

Since excessive body fat and bone structure serve as dead weight for the runner, it is easy to understand the advantage held by the runner with small bones and minimal body fat. One might ask the question, *"What is the ideal body fat content for optimal distance running performance?"* Current research findings do not present a clear answer. However, data obtained from a variety of studies suggest that men and women are in their best running form when their body fat contents are slightly below 10 percent (men) and 15 percent (women) (14, 43).

For an overweight runner, weight loss often results in improved performance. As an example, in 1967 we studied a male runner who weighed 175 pounds (19 percent fat) and had a best 10-mile performance of 80 minutes:20 seconds. When his body weight was reduced to 165 pounds (14 percent fat), performance in the 10-mile decreased to 70 minutes:50 seconds. A further reduction in weight to 154 pounds (7.7 percent fat) resulted in a best time of 67 minutes:13 seconds. Measurable improvements in performance can be expected with relatively large reductions in body weight, but it is unlikely that small daily variations have a noticeable effect on running.

The idea that major weight losses will immediately produce dramatic improvements in performance may oversimplify the situation. There is always the risk that extreme and sudden weight loss will produce some loss of the body's lean tissue, its muscle. As a result, sudden weight losses may weaken the runner, drain his or her energy reserves, and result in poorer performances. A few runners may become so obsessed with the idea of being skinny to perform that they may become anorexic. Body fat plays an important role for normal body functions. Complete or even partial starvation may initially impair performance. For that reason, it is wise to monitor your percentage of body fat and total body weight at regular intervals.

Some laboratory methods for the determination of body fat use the physical principles of Archimedes, involving the measurement of body density by comparing an individual's weight on land and under water. Since fat is lighter per unit volume than water, it floats. Individuals who have more than their share of body fat have a low density and are good floaters.

Most laboratories or fitness facilities can give a relatively good estimate of your body fat content using skinfold measurements. In the hands of a trained, experienced tester, this method will be sufficiently accurate to help judge major changes in body composition. Such body fat measurements should, however, be used only for monitoring individual changes rather than attempting to make direct comparisons between athletes. In most cases the error of measurement is too large to substantiate such judgments. Regular monthly measurements are particularly important for young runners who are confronted with rapid growth and the stresses of endurance training.

If you have had your body fat measured by underwater weighing or skinfold estimates, use the table below to rate yourself.

In the past, standard height and weight charts have been used to describe the *"ideal body weight."* Unfortunately, these tables are relatively useless for runners since they assume a much higher body fat content than that normally found among trained athletes. The Metropolitan Life Insurance chart says that a 5 foot, 11 inch tall male who has a "medium frame" should weigh between 150 and 165 pounds. Alberto Salazar, previous holder of the world's best marathon time (2 hours:8 minutes:18 seconds), stands 5 feet, 11 inches, weighs 148 pounds, and has 5.7 percent fat. He would appear to be far from ideal when compared to the standard tables.

TABLE 1-1. Indications of too much or too little body fat. The rating of "Good" represents the range of values we have observed in topflight distance runners.

RATING	MALES	FEMALES
Too Thin . . . . below 4%		below 8%
Good . . . . 5 to 10%		9 to 14%
Average . . . . 11 to 15%		14 to 18%
Excess Fat . . . . above 15%		above 18%
**Normal . . . . 14 to 16%		20 to 25%**

**denotes the average values for normally active young men and women (18 to 24 years).

As early as 1899, the qualities of height and weight have been recognized as important for successful marathon performance (*Philadelphia Medical Journal*, 3:12–33, 1933). Although early investigations suggested that "as the distance increases the runners become smaller," more recent evidence indicates that this is not the case (33). Whereas the average height for all the Boston Marathon champions from 1897 to 1965 was 5 feet, 7 inches, the winners from 1968 to the present have averaged over 6 feet tall (28). Derek Clayton, who is 6 feet, 2 inches (13) and posted a marathon time of 2 hours:8 minutes:33 seconds, typifies the current trend toward taller men excelling in endurance running.

The range in body stature among elite distance runners is wide. In a study of 20 nationally ranked male distance runners, their heights ranged from 5 feet, 6 inches to just over 6 feet (33). Likewise, topflight female runners range in height from 5 feet, 1 inch to 6 feet (43). It appears that success in distance running is unaffected by body height, but may be greatly affected by weight.

MUSCLE CHARACTERISTICS

The runner's endurance and speed during competition depends to a large part on the muscles' ability to produce energy and force. Individual differences in performance can, in some ways, be related to these characteristics in the runner's leg muscles.

Thanks to technological advances it is now possible to obtain samples of muscle tissue from runners before, during, and after exercise. This has allowed us to study the makeup of the muscle cells and gauge the effects of exercise and training. Microscopic and biochemical analyses are used to identify the muscle's machinery for energy production.

One characteristic of muscle that has gained considerable attention from the "world of sport" is the muscle composition of *fast and slow twitch fibers*. The following discussion will focus on the fiber types and their relationship to distance running performance.

The microscopic photograph of human muscle in Figure 1-1 illustrates the different types of fibers. Those fibers that stain black in this method of staining are the slow twitch fibers (ST). There are two types of fast twitch fibers: fast twitch type "a" (FTa) and fast twitch type "b" (FTb). In this photograph the fast twitch *a* fibers are unstained and the fast twitch *b* fibers appear gray.

The nerves that control these fibers determine whether they will be slow twitch or fast twitch. The muscle fiber and its connecting nerve system are referred to as a motor unit. A slow twitch motor unit may include one relatively small nerve cell connected to a cluster of 10 to 180 fibers (Figure 1-2). Fast twitch motor units, on the other hand, comprise

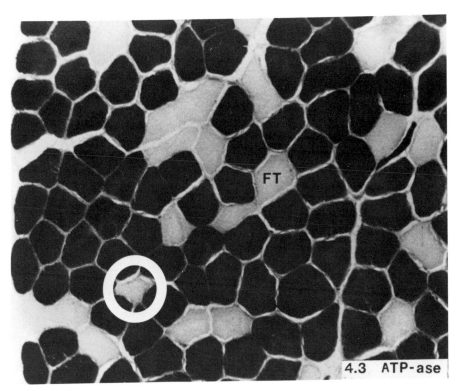

A microscopic view of Frank Shorter's leg muscle fiber type. The black fibers represent the slow twitch (type I) type, whereas the unstained cells are the fast twitch (FT, type II) fibers. Shorter's muscle was 80 percent slow twitch.

a larger nerve cell and from 300 to 800 fibers per nerve cell.

In general, the slow twitch motor units are characterized as having good aerobic endurance and are, therefore, recruited most often during low-intensity distance running. The fast twitch *a* motor units develop considerably more force than a slow twitch motor unit, though they fatigue rather easily. Thus, these fast twitch *a* fibers are used during shorter, faster races. Although the significance of the fast twitch *b* fibers is not fully understood, it appears that these fibers are not easily turned on by the nervous system and are used rather infrequently.

Figure 1-3 attempts to illustrate the relationship between the speed of running and the recruitment of the different fiber types. During slow, easy running most of the muscle force is generated by slow twitch fibers. As the muscle tension requirements increase at faster speeds, the fast twitch *a* fibers are added to the work force. Finally, at sprinting speeds, where maximal strength is needed, even the fast twitch *b* fibers are turned on.

Figure 1-1. Microscopic view of muscle from the calf of an untrained woman. The black-stained fibers are the slow twitch (ST), while the fast twitch type "a" (FTa) fibers are unstained. The gray fibers are the fast twitch "b" (FTb) type. In general, slow twitch fibers demonstrate higher aerobic and lower anaerobic potential than do fast twitch fibers.

During long-distance events, we begin running at a submaximal or slow pace, so the nervous system recruits principally the muscle fibers best adapted to endurance activity, that is slow twitch and some fast twitch *a* fibers. Gradually, as they become fatigued, the nervous system calls upon other fibers to maintain muscle tension and running pace. It

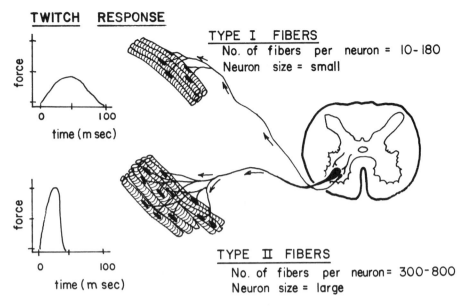

TWITCH RESPONSE

TYPE I FIBERS
No. of fibers per neuron = 10-180
Neuron size = small

force

0　　　　100
time (m sec)

force

0　　　100
time (m sec)

TYPE II FIBERS
No. of fibers per neuron = 300-800
Neuron size = large

Figure 1-2. Characteristics of the type I (slow twitch) and type II (fast twitch) motor units. Each motor unit consists of a nerve cell and the muscle fibers it innervates. Note the difference between the duration and height of a muscle twitch for the type I and II motor units.

recruits more fast twitch *a* fibers. As more slow twitch and fast twitch *a* fibers become exhausted, the fast twitch *b* fibers are called upon in a final effort to continue running. This may explain why fatigue seems to come in stages during the race, and why it takes great mental concentration to maintain a given pace near the finish. Much of that mental effort is probably used to activate muscle fibers that are not easily recruited.

Figure 1-4 indicates that male and female track athletes have varied percentages of slow twitch fibers in their calf muscles (gastrocnemius). In other studies there is considerable evidence that successful distance runners have relatively more slow twitch than fast twitch fibers in their leg muscles (16, 17, 19, 26). An average individual has roughly 50 percent slow twitch, 25 percent fast twitch *a*, and 25 percent fast twitch *b* fibers in his leg muscles. Studies of elite male and female distance runners have revealed that some had calf muscles composed of more than 90 percent slow twitch fibers (17). Alberto Salazar's calf muscle, for example, has 93 percent slow twitch fibers, 7 percent fast twitch *a* fibers, and no fast twitch *b* fibers.

In contrast, world class sprinters' muscles are composed predominantly of fast twitch *a* fibers (19, 26). This may explain why Salazar had trouble sprinting. Although there is a marked difference in the compo-

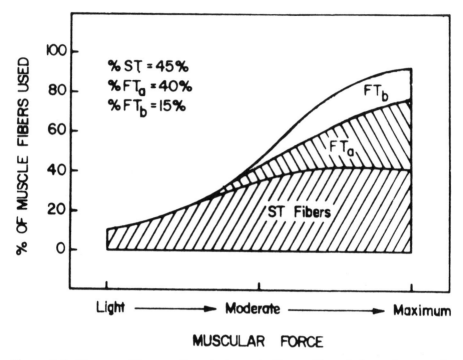

Figure 1-3. The ramp-like recruitment of muscle fibers with varied running speeds. Very slow running and walking may only use the slow twitch fibers, whereas high speed running or sprinting will require the recruitment of all three types of muscle fibers.

sition of fibers in the muscles of sprinters and distance runners, fiber composition alone is not a reliable predictor of distance success.

While previous studies have shown that training may increase the endurance capacity of muscle, there is little evidence to suggest that the percentage of slow twitch and fast twitch fibers changes with endurance training (22, 25). This fractional composition of muscle appears fixed and unaffected by training, suggesting that at least this quality of the champion may be inherited. Studies have shown that identical twins (from the same egg) have identical fiber compositions (33). Fraternal twins (those from separate eggs) differ in their fiber profiles as well as in other physical characteristics. Muscle composition is established soon after birth during the process of natural development and remains relatively unchanged throughout life.

One exception to this rule is that the sub-types of fast twitch fibers may show some modification with training. The fast twitch *a* fibers are generally described as being a bit more aerobic, able to use oxygen for energy production, than the fast twitch *b* fibers. With endurance training

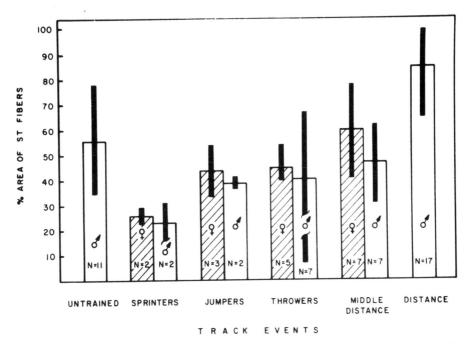

Figure 1-4. Percentage of the calf muscle (gastrocnemius) composed of slow twitch fibers in male and female track athletes. The untrained subjects shown in the far left column were an age-matched group of sedentary men. The number of subjects tested in each group is indicated by "N." The black vertical bar represents the range of scores observed within each group.

the fast twitch *b* fibers begin to take on the characteristics of the fast twitch *a* fibers. This suggests that these fibers are used more heavily during training and gain greater endurance ability. Though the full significance of this change of fast twitch *b* fibers to fast twitch *a* fibers is not known, it may explain why we find very few, if any, fast twitch *b* fibers in the leg muscles of highly trained distance runners.

The diameter of the muscle fibers varies markedly among elite distance runners (16, 19), but on the average slow twitch fibers are some 22 percent larger than fast twitch fibers in elite male and female runners' gastrocnemius muscles (16). Experts have proposed that training for endurance or strength may result in selective enlargement or hypertrophy of the slow twitch and fast twitch fibers, respectively.

Some runners wonder if the percentage of slow twitch and fast twitch fibers is the same in all the muscles of the body. Generally, the muscles of the arms and legs have similar fiber compositions, though there are some exceptions. The soleus, a muscle near the bone in the calf area, is almost completely slow twitch in everyone. Someone with a predominance of slow twitch fibers in his thigh or gastrocnemius muscles will likely have a high percentage of slow twitch fibers in his arm muscles as well.

AEROBIC QUALITIES

In order for the muscles to continuously produce the force needed for distance running, they must have a steady supply of energy. The form of energy used for all the muscles' operations is a special compound produced inside the fibers, adenosine triphosphate (ATP). There are three possible sources of ATP: (1) that stored in the muscles as ATP and creatine phosphate (CP), (2) that produced from the oxidative or aerobic breakdown of carbohydrates and fats, and (3) that produced anaerobically from muscle glycogen.

Each muscle fiber has a quantity of ATP stored for immediate use. This supply is very limited and can only provide enough energy for three to five seconds of all-out effort, hardly enough for a distance race.

The energy bound into the ATP molecule is derived from the breakdown of the foods we eat: carbohydrates, fats, and protein. When this process of disassembling fuels is conducted in the presence of oxygen, it is said to be "*aerobic.*" Although the muscle can produce ATP anaerobically, or without oxygen, this method is quite inefficient and alone is too limited for exercise lasting more than 20 to 60 seconds. Consequently, aerobic energy production (metabolism) is the primary method of energy production during distance running, which places great demands on the runner's capacity to deliver oxygen to the exercising muscles.

Within the muscles, there are special powerhouse-like structures called mitochondria, which use the foodstuffs and oxygen to produce large amounts of ATP. To speed the rate of energy production and to perform this task efficiently, mitochondria employ specialized proteins called enzymes. Since these enzymes are used in aerobic energy production, they are often called *oxidative enzymes.* Measurements of oxidative enzymes levels are used to indicate the capacity of the muscle to do aerobic work.

Numerous studies have shown a close relationship between the ability of a muscle to perform prolonged exercise and the amount of oxidative enzymes present (23, 31). The muscles of elite distance runners, for example, have nearly 3.5 times more oxidative enzymes than those of untrained men and women (18, 19). Figure 1-5 illustrates that the runner's endurance is, in part, due to the aerobic capacity of his muscles (Q_{O_2}).

Since elite runners possess more slow twitch fibers, which generally have more mitochondria and oxidative enzymes, we might expect that distance runners are endowed with a greater capacity for adapting to

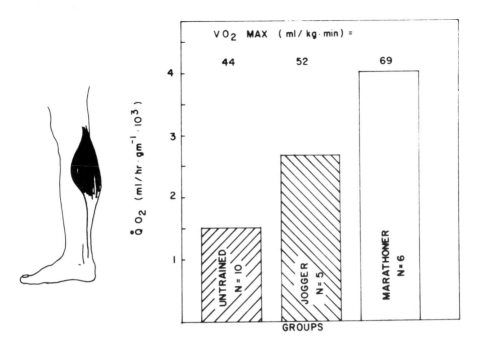

Figure 1-5. Aerobic capacity (Q_{O_2}) of the gastrocnemius (calf) muscle in untrained, moderately trained (joggers), and highly trained (marathon) men. Note that the Q_{O_2} values somewhat paralled the subjects' state of training. The number of individuals tested is indicated by "N."

endurance training. Current research findings do not support this idea. A poor relationship has been found between the percentage of slow twitch fibers and the amount of oxidative enzymes in the muscle (19). Certainly, endurance training can enhance the oxidative capacity of all fibers, especially the fast twitch fibers, which naturally have few mitochondria and aerobic enzymes in an untrained state. Even individuals having a small percentage of slow twitch fibers can increase the aerobic capacity of their muscles with endurance training, but it is our general impression that an endurance-trained fast twitch fiber will not have the endurance capacity of a well-trained slow twitch fiber (16).

One of the factors responsible for exhaustion during distance running is the rapid depletion of the muscle's carbohydrate stores or glycogen. Training enables muscles to store more glycogen and also rely more on fat for energy during running. The apparent advantage of performing long runs in training is to improve the muscle's capacity to burn fat, thereby reducing the demands placed on the body's limited carbohydrate supply.

The leg muscles are seven times more capable of burning fat after marathon training than untrained muscles (18). The amount of improvement in the ability of muscles to burn fat depends, for the most part, on the amount of aerobic work (distance running) performed during training. It is essential for the marathoner to perform extremely long runs in training, for only with such work will the muscles develop the mechanisms necessary to use fat as a major fuel.

Since the 1920s, exercise physiologists have associated the limits of human endurance with the ability to use large volumes of oxygen during exhaustive exercise (27). The oxygen absorbed by the blood as it passes through the lungs matches the amount being used by the muscles. When the energy demands are at maximum, as during exhaustive running, the muscles attain their highest level of oxygen use.

In the laboratory, we can measure the gases that are breathed by the runner while he or she runs on a motor-driven treadmill (Figure 1-6). In this way, it is possible to determine how much oxygen is being taken by the blood as it passes through the lungs and is delivered to the exercising muscles.

The maximal amount of oxygen that can be consumed by the body is commonly referred to as "V_{O_2} max," and most exercise physiologists consider it the best single indicator of endurance potential. This point is confirmed by studies on distance runners (2, 10, 12, 15, 34, 39, 40). While

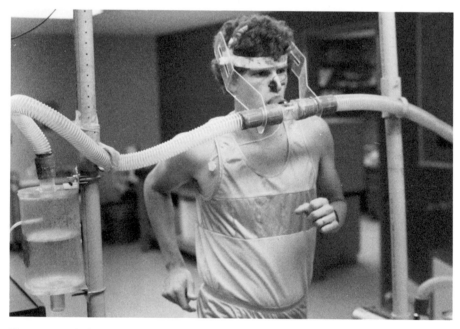

Figure 1-6. Laboratory testing for oxygen uptake during treadmill running.

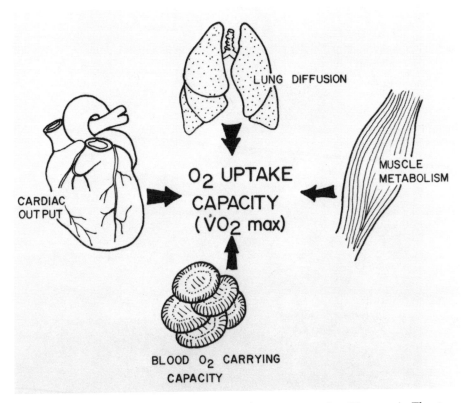

The major factors that determine maximal oxygen uptake (Vo_2 max). The two major contributors appear to be the ability of the heart to pump blood (cardiac output) and the muscles' ability to use oxygen and produce energy.

the normally active 20-year-old male has a Vo_2 max of 44 to 47 milliliters of oxygen per kilogram of body weight per minute (ml/kg × min), trained distance runners commonly have values in excess of 70 ml/kg × min. Alberto Salazar and Bill Rodgers, for example, were found to have values of 78 ml/kg × min. (14). The late Steve Prefontaine, previous American record holder for the 5,000 meters, recorded a Vo_2 max of 84.4 ml/kg × min. (61).

Although this ability to consume, transport, and utilize large volumes of oxygen is critical for distance running success, it frequently fails to predict the winner when a group of similarly talented runners compete (14). Topflight runners may have similar running performances but markedly different Vo_2 max values. This was true in the case of Frank Shorter, 1972 Olympic Marathon Champion, and Steve Prefontaine. Both men had posted times of 12 minutes:52 seconds for three miles. Yet, the highest Vo_2 max value recorded for Shorter was only 71.4 ml/kg × min,

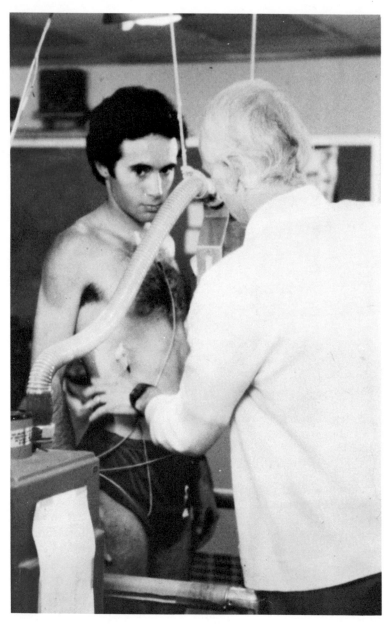

Alberto Salazar being prepared for a treadmill test at the Human Performance Laboratory in 1980. Salazar recorded a Vo_2 max of 78 ml/kg × min, nearly identical to that of Bill Rodgers.

13 ml/kg × min lower than for Prefontaine. It is interesting to note, however, that Shorter's value is quite similar to Derek Clayton's, one of history's best marathon performers (13). Despite Clayton's ability to run at an average speed of 4 minutes:54 seconds per mile for the marathon, his VO_2 max was only 69.7 ml/kg × min. These findings make it clear that a high VO_2 max, in itself, does not automatically make a runner great.

Given your **best current time** for different distances we can estimate VO_2 max, with the use of a little mathematics. The equations for estimating VO_2 max from your best **competitive** performances in the mile, two-mile, six-mile, and/or 10-kilometer events are as follows:

$$VO_2 \text{ max} = 133.61 - (13.89 \times T1)$$

where T1 is your time for one mile in minutes

$$VO_2 \text{ max} = 128.81 - (5.95 \times T2)$$

where T2 is your time for two miles in minutes

$$VO_2 \text{ max} = 120.62 - (1.59 \times T6)$$

where T6 is your time for six miles in minutes

$$VO_2 \text{ max} = 120.8 - (1.54 \times T0)$$

where T0 is your time for 10 kilometers in minutes

Example: Convert time for distance from minutes and seconds (5 minutes:30 seconds) to total minutes (5.5 minutes). Thus, VO_2 max bases on the mile performance would be:

$$VO_2 \text{ max} = 133.61 - (13.89 \times 5.5)$$

$$= 133.61 - 76.40$$

$$= 57.2 \text{ ml/kg} \times \text{min}$$

If you have competitive performances for all of the distances, calculate the respective VO_2 max values and average them. Remember, your ability to perform well during distance running depends on the capacity to produce energy aerobically. Elite runners have aerobic capacities above 65 (female) or 70 (male) ml/kg × min; world class male mile runners are above 80 ml/kg × min.

The table below will give you a rough estimate of your current potential for distance running success. Of course, this value can be improved with training, so do not be discouraged if your rating is less than you hoped for.

In addition to the aerobic capacity, other factors are instrumental in determining a winning performance. The ability to exercise at an intensity near one's VO_2 max is of equal importance. Although most distance

TABLE 1-2 Ratings of maximal oxygen uptake (ml/kg × min) for young men and women. The values in the right hand column (Potential 10-kilometer Time) offer an estimate of the runner's running potential (min:sec).

Aerobic Capacity	Potential 10-km Time (min:sec)
above 70 ml/kg × min	33:00 or faster
65 to 69 ml/kg × min	36:15 to 33:40
60 to 64 ml/kg × min	39:30 to 36:50
55 to 59 ml/kg × min	42:45 to 40:10
50 to 54 ml/kg × min	46:00 to 43:25
45 to 49 ml/kg × min	49:15 to 46:40
40 to 44 ml/kg × min	52:30 to 49:50
below 39 ml/kg × min	53:10 or slower

runners perform at 75 to 80 percent of their Vo_2 max values during a marathon, Salazar, Rodgers, and Waitz are able to run rather comfortably at 86 to 90 percent of their Vo_2 max values (14, 18, 35).

Normally, intense exercise will result in a large accumulation of lactic acid from energy production without enough oxygen to keep the process aerobic. In one study, Derek Clayton ran for 30 minutes on the treadmill at a 4 minute:54 second per mile pace, a speed that required him to consume oxygen at a level equal to 88 percent of his Vo_2 max. Throughout the run he was able to carry on a conversation with our laboratory staff and even suggested that he could easily run another hour at that pace. Blood samples taken from him immediately after the treadmill run revealed that he had accumulated no lactic acid, indicating that he had remained completely aerobic during the run. This ability to exercise at a high percentage of one's Vo_2 max for long periods without accumulating lactic acid is not fully understood, though it appears that this quality is a function of the muscular adaptations during training (15).

HEART AND LUNGS

The preceding discussion concerning the aerobic qualities of muscle makes it clear that the key to success in distance running rests on the capacity to deliver oxygen to the muscles. This task is the responsibility of the heart and arteries that serve as the oxygen transport system.

The amount of blood that can be pumped out of the heart each minute (cardiac output) during exercise determines, in part, the capacity of the muscles to carry on aerobic energy production. It is not surprising

Grete Waitz being tested on the treadmill in Oslo, Norway in 1980. She recorded one of the highest Vo_2 max values (73.5 ml/kg × min) ever observed for a woman.

that elite distance runners are noted for their efficient, and often enlarged hearts (38). Highly trained distance runners have frequently been described as having enlarged left ventricles, from which the heart chamber ejects the oxygen-laden blood into the arteries. This hypertrophy of the heart appears to result from endurance training, and it serves to increase the amount of blood that can be pumped from the heart with each contraction.

Studies in 1962 used the electrocardiograph (EKG) to examine the heart function and size of marathon runners at the British Commonwealth Games (41). These investigators noted high voltage from the left ventricle (QRS complex) of these runners, indicative of a large muscle mass. Similar studies in 1966 of 46 endurance athletes showed that a large percentage of them had enlarged hearts (1).

These findings of ventricular hypertrophy have been confirmed by x ray shadow estimates of heart size (20). Paavo Nurmi, seven-time Olympic distance running champion, was found to have a heart nearly three times larger than normal (4). We have noted similar x ray characteristics in our studies of elite distance runners, though not all world class runners show such hypertrophy.

The contrast in heart size between untrained and elite distance runners is illustrated by the chest x ray of Hal Higdon, a world champion veteran runner (2 hours:29 minutes for marathon at age 49), and an untrained man of similar age, height, and weight (Figure 1-7). The lateral dimension of Higdon's heart (15.5 centimeters) is roughly 50 percent greater than that of the less active man's.

Since the hypertrophied heart of the distance runner ejects more blood than normal with each beat, it is not surprising that the heart will beat much less frequently at rest than the heart of an untrained individual. Consequently, the distance runner's heart accomplishes its work at rest

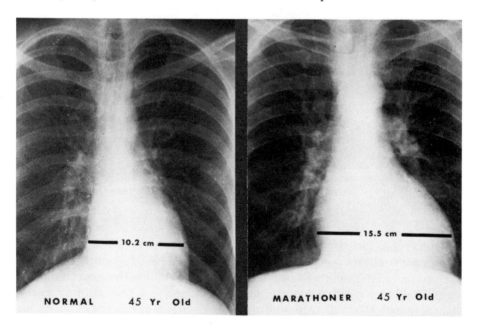

Figure 1-7. Chest x ray showing the shadows of the hearts of two men. The measured lines denote the horizontal width of the hearts. The marathoner's (Hal Higdon) heart is roughly 50 percent larger than that of the untrained man.

and during exercise with considerably greater efficiency than the heart of an untrained person. Higdon had a resting heart rate, while standing, of only 32 beats per minute, compared to a rate of 76 to 80 beats per minute in the untrained man. If we assume that at rest these men had similar oxygen demands and cardiac outputs, then Higdon's heart must eject nearly 2.5 times as much blood with each beat as the untrained man.

Twenty elite distance runners studied in Dallas in 1974 were found to have a number of EKG abnormalities (24). Twenty-five percent of these athletes exhibited significant changes (ST segment depressions) in their EKG during treadmill running, suggesting that they might have coronary artery disease. Although such ST segment depressions immediately following exercise have previously been reported in distance runners, these observations are rare and generally occur in populations that include runners over the age of 40. Though coronary disease might be more likely in this older age group, its presence in the young (21 to 32 years) Dallas group seems highly unlikely. None of these men had any known cardiovascular disease, nor did they experience any symptoms suggestive of heart disease. Further cardiovascular examination revealed no additional abnormalities that might indicate an impairment in coronary blood flow. Although no invasive studies of the coronary arteries were done in these runners, it seems unlikely that the ST segment depressions could be interpreted in the same manner as they would be for the general population. These and other apparently non-functional abnormalities in the EKG lead us to doubt that such interpretations in exercising, endurance-trained athletes can be of clinical significance.

We have limited access to the results of post-mortem examinations of the hearts of deceased distance runners. However, findings in the case of Clarence DeMar, who competed in more than 1,000 long-distance races and won the Boston Marathon seven times, revealed a significantly enlarged heart with relatively clean coronary arteries (21). DeMar was diagnosed as having peritoneal carcinomatosis (intestinal cancer), but he continued to train to within two weeks of his death. His heart upon examination weighed 340 grams, compared to the normal male heart weight of roughly 300 grams. The left ventricular wall was 18 millimeters thick, (normal thickness is 10 to 12 millimeters), and the right wall was eight millimeters thick (normal thickness is three to four millimeters). The valves of his heart were normal, but the coronary arteries were estimated to be two to three times normal size. The very large coronary vessels, other things being equal, would have insured an adequate supply of oxygen to the cardiac muscle during the most strenuous muscular effort. The physicians who examined DeMar's heart concluded by stating, "The evidence in DeMar's case, after 49 years of strenuous physical training, was one of notable compensatory change."

Although there is considerable evidence that training for distance running strengthens the heart and improves the efficiency of the cardiovascular system, there is no direct evidence that such activity will reduce or prevent the development of atherosclerosis, a degenerative disease of the coronary arteries. Myocardial infarctions and sudden deaths in older, well-trained distance runners have been reported with increasing frequency in recent years. Though the energy demands on the heart during distance running are great, natural safeguards prevent overstressing it. Only individuals with heart disease or cardiac abnormalities are at risk during such exercise.

It is our experience that the frequency of these heart abnormalities are small (less than one in 1,000) in men and women below the age of 35 years. The likelihood of having these problems increases with age. For that reason, it seems prudent for runners to have an annual cardio-

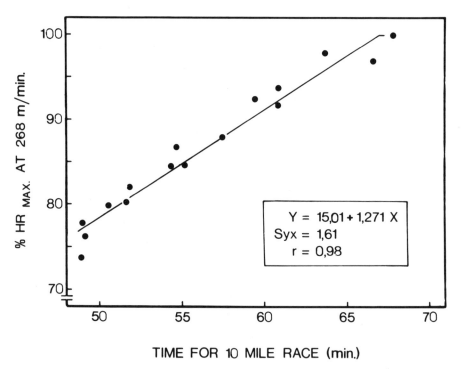

TIME FOR 10 MILE RACE (min.)

Figure 1-8. Relationship between performance in a 10-mile (16.1 kilometer) race and the percentage of the runner's maximal heart rate recorded while running at a six-minute per mile pace (268 meters per minute). We can predict time in the 10-mile run by drawing a horizontal line across the graph at the 90 percent level to the point where it intercepts the diagonal line, then drop a perpendicular line from that point to the bottom of the graph. The point at which it intercepts the scale of time for the 10-mile run is your estimated potential for that distance.

vascular examination, including an exercising EKG. Caution should be used, however, in generalizing about the cardiac characteristics of elite distance runners. What may appear abnormal in untrained, sedentary people, might be insignificant in the highly trained runner.

While there are few non-invasive cardiovascular measurements that predict running potential, various circulatory measurements and physical fitness tests have been used with some success (7). For example, trained cross-country runners score significantly higher than other trained athletes on the Harvard Step Test and the Bruce Physical Fitness Index (10, 37). As one might anticipate, treadmill running time to exhaustion correlates quite highly with distance running success (20).

Probably the best single circulatory measure for predicting distance running performance is the percentage of maximal heart rate (% HR max) reached during treadmill running at 10 miles per hour (six-minute mile). If you know your maximal heart rate (measured at the end of a four- to five-minute exhaustive run) and your rate while running a six-minute mile, it is possible to predict your potential time in a 10-mile run (Figure 1-8). If, for example, your maximal heart rate was 200 beats per minute and your six-minute mile heart rate was 180 beats per minute, then your percentage of maximal heart rate would be 90 percent (% HR max = 100 × (180/200)).

Figure 1-8 demonstrates the relationship between performance in a 10-mile (16.1 kilometer) race and the percentage of the runner's maximal heart rate recorded while running at a six-minute per mile pace (268 meters per minute).

Several studies have shown that indirect blood pressure measurements at rest are not related to endurance capacity (10, 20). Since training has been found to lower some athlete's diastolic blood pressure, it is not surprising to find studies that report normal systolic pressures of 120 to 122 millimeters of mercury (mm Hg) during systole (during heart contraction) and 50 to 60 mm Hg during diastole (between heart contractions) (10). Pulse pressure waves, measured in the arteries, also have no value in predicting distance running performance (36).

While the capacity of the elite runner's heart to pump blood is markedly greater than that of the untrained individual's, there are fewer, less dramatic differences in the structure and function of the lungs. The maximal volume of air that can be expelled from the lungs in a single breath (vital capacity) appears to increase with years of training (5). It is not surprising to find that distance runners are significantly above average for vital capacity. One study observed vital capacities of 5.7 liters for 17 cross-country runners (1), compared to the average of 4.8 liters for a group of untrained men of similar age (8). When computed on the basis of body size (height, weight, or body surface area), distance runners score even higher as a result of their smaller dimensions.

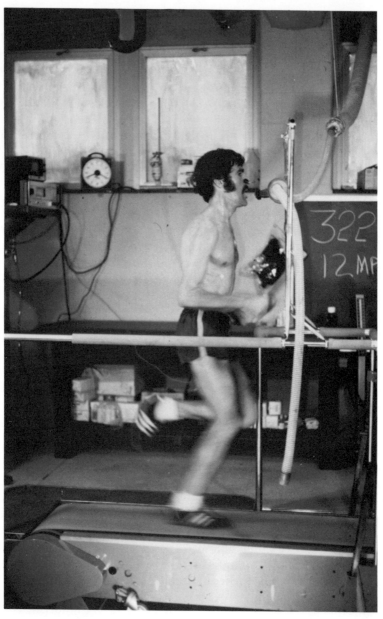

Derek Clayton, a 2 hour:8 minute:33 second marathon runner during laboratory testing in 1970.

Training for distance running develops respiratory muscle endurance and strength. Maximum breathing capacity (MBC) is the volume of air that can be forced in and out of the lungs per minute (10). While the normal male is said to have a maximum breathing capacity of from 125 to 170 liters per minute, a group of 10 college cross-country runners were found to have a mean maximum breathing capacity of 207.5 liters (6). One might theorize that well-trained distance runners have developed exceptional endurance in their respiratory muscles and/or reduced the resistance to air movement, enabling them to keep breathing during heavy exercise without overtaxing their respiratory muscles. During exhaustive running, highly trained distance runners have been able to breathe more than 120 liters per minute for more than 20 minutes (9), an amount most individuals can only sustain for a few seconds.

Measurements of lung function among marathon runners have shown that gases are exchanged between the lung and the blood more rapidly than would be predicted (32). Experts assume that this capacity for diffusion is facilitated by an increase in total body hemoglobin (30). This explains, at least in part, the superior oxygen transport system possessed by highly trained distance runners.

BLOOD: THE TRANSPORT TISSUE

Measurements of various blood constituents offer no explanation for the superior endurance abilities of the elite distance runner. There are, however, a number of differences seen when blood samples taken from nonrunners are compared to samples from good and elite runners (35).

In hematocrit measurements, which indicate the percentage of blood composed of red blood cells, good and elite distance runners had values of between 43.6 and 43.8 percent, compared to 47.2 percent for nonrunners (35). These results are somewhat surprising, since one of the primary functions of the red blood cells and hemoglobin is to transport oxygen. Chapter 4 will discuss the theory that the lower hematocrit values in runners are probably caused by an increase in plasma volume due to intense training. The percentage of red blood cells is thereby diluted.

Most runners are aware that hemoglobin plays a key role in oxygen transport and are concerned that hard training may cause blood cell destruction and subsequent anemia. While it is true that the ratio of red blood cells to whole blood may be a bit low in trained distance runners, the concentration of hemoglobin is quite normal: 15.5 to 15.6 grams per 100 milliliters of blood (35). The red blood cells of runners have unusually large amounts of hemoglobin. Whereas endurance training causes an increase in plasma volume, the runner seems to possess a greater number of red blood cells and a normal concentration of hemoglobin.

During repeated days of heavy training, plasma volume may increase 15 to 30 percent as a result of sodium and water retention by the kidneys. It is not uncommon, therefore, to observe unusually low (less than 39 percent) hematocrits and hemoglobin concentrations in trained distance runners. This condition seems to be only temporary, since the runner will void the excess body water with 24 to 48 hours of rest. Despite these unusually low values, it may be inaccurate to describe the runners as "anemic," since we do not fully understand the influence of such hemodilution on the ability of the blood to carry oxygen during exercise.

There are of course some exceptions and variations in the production and loss of red blood cells. Some investigations have reported an increased rate of red cell destruction during heavy exercise, but they agree that this is rather unusual and unlikely to explain the lowering of hemoglobin and hematocrit.

Female runners who experience excessive menstrual flow may become mildly anemic. Though the body's normal mechanism of red cell production should compensate for this red cell loss, there are a number of reports confirming an anemic status in a relatively large percentage of female runners. Serum ferritin, the stored form of iron for hemoglobin formation, has been found to be low in female runners, which has led to a recent suggestion that they should use iron supplements.

Another major function of blood is to transport fuels (glucose and free fatty acids) to the muscles and to remove the by-products of metabolism. Under resting conditions, the concentrations of fuels and waste products in the blood of runners do not differ from those in untrained men and women. The only exception to this point is the alteration in the blood fat (lipid) profile seen in the endurance athlete.

For the most part, endurance training tends to lower plasma triglyceride values. It also initiates a shift in the composition of lipoproteins, the fat- and cholesterol-carrying proteins, toward a greater content of high density lipoprotein cholesterol (HDLC), sometimes referred to as "good cholesterol." Physical training seems to have little effect on plasma cholesterol concentration, though distance runners are generally characterized by a low level of cholesterol. This may be the result of their high metabolic turnover of ingested fuels or simply the fact that they consume foods lower in cholesterol. Nevertheless, a lowering of plasma triglyceride and cholesterol, and an increase in high density lipoprotein cholesterol, have been closely correlated with a lower incidence of heart disease. These changes in the plasma lipid profile suggest a reduction in the risk of heart disease in distance runners. This point has not, however, been clearly elucidated.

Since heavy training tends to alter a number of the items in blood, it is important that the values for blood constituents in runners be viewed with some caution. One example is the change in serum enzymes, special proteins used by cells to facilitate their internal workings. Clinically, such enzymes as lactate dehydrogenase (LDH), serum glutamic oxaloacetic transaminase (SGOT), and creatine phosphokinase (CPK) are used as indicators of cardiac and skeletal muscle damage. Some muscle membrane damage does occur during endurance running, releasing these enzymes into the blood. Consequently, it is not surprising that these enzymes are in rather high concentrations in the blood following a long, hard run or after several days of intense training (35). Though the presence of elevated enzymes in blood may be a reasonable indication of very stressful training, the findings should not be viewed with any clinical concern. Some sports physiologists recommend that these enzymes be monitored to determine the runner's status of training stress and overtraining.

STRENGTH AND SPEED

On most tests of strength and reaction time, distance runners tend to be below average (10, 42). Whereas an average group of male college students were found to have a dominant hand grip strength of 117.3 pounds (53.2 kilograms), 38 cross-country runners scored only 106.1 pounds (48.1 kilograms) of force. We might anticipate that the runners would score better in a test of leg strength. Surprisingly, distance runners perform poorly in tasks requiring explosive leg strength. When tested for vertical jump, the average, untrained individual can jump 20.9 inches (53.1 centimeters), compared to a mean jump of 13.5 inches (34.3 centimeters) for a group of elite marathon runners (10, 11).

Although it might seem logical that such runners, known to have a predominance of slow twitch fibers in their leg muscles, might inherit this inability to jump, some individual cases suggest that this is not the case. For example, Lou Castagnola, a 2 hour:17 minute marathoner in 1967, was found to have a vertical jump of only 11.5 inches (29.2 centimeters). Following the 1968 U.S. Olympic marathon trial he stopped training and led a rather sedentary life. Three years later we reexamined him and found that while his Vo$_2$ max had declined from 72.4 ml/kg $\times$ min to 47.6 ml/kg $\times$ min, his vertical jump had increased to 20.3 inches (51.5 centimeters). Despite a lack of physical activity, his explosive leg strength had increased 77 percent.

These findings suggest that endurance running and the presence of a high percentage of slow twitch fibers in the leg muscles may impair explosive leg strength, which could have a negative effect on sprinting speed. Although the mechanisms for this response remain unexplained, recent evidence concerning the recruitment of muscle fibers and our knowledge of the specificity of training suggests that endurance training may lead to a selective reduction in the number of motor units or contractile elements that can be activated. Our studies have shown that the muscle fiber composition has little bearing on one's ability to perform explosive jumping or sprint running.

DO YOU HAVE THE RIGHT STUFF?

The preceding discussion may have led you to think that the major determinants of distance running success are controlled by genetics, and that you cannot be a topflight runner without inheriting the right physical characteristics. To the contrary, the body has an exceptional capacity to improve its endurance with training. The champion distance runners show no unusual talents for endurance exercise when they are untrained. Only with weeks, months, and years of training do they develop the circulatory and muscular qualities necessary to achieve their full potential. Regardless of your inherited capacities, you can be better than you are! The following chapters will give you the facts, as we know them, that will allow you to make the right choices in your efforts to perform your best.

BIBLIOGRAPHY

1. Arstila, M. and A. Koivikko. Electrocardiographic and vectorcardiographic signs of left and right ventricular hypertrophy in endurance runners. *J. Sports Med. and Phys. Fit.*, 6:166–174, 1966.
2. Astrand, P.-O. New records in human power. *Nature*, 176:922–923, 1955.
3. Behnke, A. R. and J. Royce. Body size, shape, and composition of athletes. *J. Sports Med. and Phys. Fit.*, 6:75–78, 1966.
4. Boardman, R. World's champions run to type. *J. Hlth. and Phys. Educ.*, 4:32, 1933.
5. Bock, A. V. The circulation of a marathoner. *J. Sports Med. and Phys. Fit.*, 3:80–86, 1963.
6. Bowers, R. W. and D. L. Costill. Some physiological characteristics of distance runners. *Presentation at A.C.S.M. Meeting*, 1967.
7. Bramwell, C. and R. Ellis. Some observations on the circulatory mechanism in marathon runners. *Quart. J. Med.*, 24:329–334, 1931.
8. Comroe, J. H. *The Lung*. Chicago:Yearbook Medical Publishers, 1963.
9. Costill, D. L. Metabolic responses during distance running. *J. Appl. Physiol.*, 28:251–255, 1970.
10. Costill, D. L. The relationship between selected physiological variables and distance running performance. *J. Sports Med. and Phys. Fit.*, 7:61–66, 1967.
11. Costill, D. L. and E. L. Fox. Energetics of marathon running. *Med. Sci. Sports*, 7:81–86, 1969.

12. Costill, D. L. and E. Winrow. Maximal oxygen intake among marathon runners. *Arch. Phys. Med. Rehab.*, 51:317–320, 1970.
13. Costill, D. L., G. Branam, D. Eddy and K. Sparks. Determinants of marathon running success. *Int. Z. Angew. Physiol.*, 29:249–254, 1971.
14. Costill, D. L. and H. Higdon. The perfect running body. *The Runner*, 12:45–50, 1980.
15. Costill, D. L., H. Thomason and E. Roberts. Fractional utilization of the aerobic capacity during distance running. *Med. Sci. Sports*, 5:248–252, 1973.
16. Costill, D. L., J. Daniels, W. Evans, W. Fink, G. Krahenbuhl and B. Saltin. Skeletal muscle enzymes and fiber composition in male and female track athletes. *J. Appl. Physiol.*, 40:149–154, 1976.
17. Costill, D. L., P. D. Gollnick, E. D. Jansson, B. Saltin and E. M. Stein. Glycogen depletion pattern in human muscle fibers during distance running. *Acta Physiol. Scand.*, 89:374–383, 1973.
18. Costill, D. L., W. J. Fink, J. L. Ivy, L. H. Getchell and F. A. Witzmann. Lipid metabolism in skeletal muscle of endurance trained males and females. *J. Appl. Physiol.*, 47:787–791, 1979.
19. Costill, D. L., W. J. Fink and M. Pollock. Muscle fiber composition and enzyme activities of elite distance runners. *Med. Sci. Sports*, 8:96–100, 1976.
20. Cureton, T. K. *Physical fitness of champion athletes*. Urbana: University of Illinois Press, 1951.
21. Dill, D. B. Marathoner DeMar: Physiological Studies. *J. Nat. Cancer Inst.*, 35:185–191, 1965.
22. Eriksson, B. O., P. D. Gollnick and B. Saltin. Muscle metabolism and enzyme activities after training in boys 11–13 years old. *Acta Physiol. Scand.*, 87:231–239, 1972.
23. Foster, C., D. L. Costill, J. T. Daniels and W. J. Fink. Skeletal muscle enzyme activity, fiber composition and Vo_2 max in relation to distance running performance. *Europ. J. Appl. Physiol.*, 39:73–80, 1978.
24. Gibbons, L. W., K. H. Cooper, R. P. Martin and M. L. Pollock. Medical examination and electrocardiographic analysis of elite distance runners. *Ann. N.Y. Acad. Sci.*, 301:283–296, 1977.
25. Gollnick, P. D., R. B. Armstrong, B. Saltin, C. W. Saubert, W. L. Sembrowich and R. E. Shephard. Effects of training on enzyme activities and fiber composition of human skeletal muscle. *J. Appl. Physiol.*, 34:107–111, 1973.
26. Gollnick, P. D., R. B. Armstrong, C. W. Saubert, K. Piehl and B. Saltin. Enzyme activity and fiber composition in skeletal muscle of untrained and trained men. *J. Appl. Physiol.*, 33:312–319, 1972.
27. Hill, A. V. and H. Lupton. Muscular exercise, lactic acid and the supply and utilization of oxygen. *Quart. J. Med.*, 16:135–171, 1923.
28. Hirata, K. Physique and age of Tokyo Olympic champions. *J. Sports Med. and Phys. Fit.*, 6:207–221, 1966.
29. Holloszy, J. O. Biochemical adaptations in muscle. *J. Biol. Chem.*, 242:2278–2282, 1967.
30. Holmgren, A. et al. D_L and the dimensions and functional capacities of the 02 transport system in humans. *J. Appl. Physiol.*, 21:1463–1468, 1966.
31. Ivy, J. L., D. L. Costill and B. D. Maxwell. Skeletal muscle determinants of maximum aerobic power in man. *Europ. J. Appl. Physiol.*, 44:1–8, 1980.
32. Kaufmann, D. A., E. W. Swenson, J. Fencl and A. Lucas. Pulmonary function of marathon runners. *Med. Sci. Sports*, 6:114–117, 1974.
33. Komi, P. V. and J. Karlsson. Physical performance, skeletal muscle enzyme activities, and fiber types in monozygous and dizygous twins of both sexes. *Acta. Physiol. Scand.*, Suppl., 462:28, 1979.
34. Lindsay, J. E. et al. Structural and functional assessments on a champion runner—Peter Snell. *Res. Quart.*, 38:355–365, 1967.

35. Martin, R. P., W. L. Haskell and P. D. Wood. Blood chemistry and lipid profiles of elite distance runners. *Ann. N.Y. Acad. Sci.*, 301:346–360, 1977.

36. Montoye, H. J., W. Mack and J. Cook. Brachial pulse wave as a measure of cross-country running performance. *Res. Quart.*, 31:174–180, 1960.

37. Pierson, W. R. and P. J. Rasch. Bruce physical fitness index as a predictor of performance in trained distance runners. *Res. Quart.*, 31:77–81, 1960.

38. Pollock, M. L. Submaximal and maximal working capacity of elite distance runners. *Ann. N.Y. Acad. Sci.*, 301:310–322, 1977.

39. Robinson, S., H. T. Edwards and D. B. Dill. New records in human power. *Sci.*, 85:409–410, 1937.

40. Saltin, B. and P.-O. Astrand. Maximal oxygen uptake in athletes. *J. Appl. Physiol.*, 23:347–352, 1967.

41. Smith, W. G., K. J. Cullen and I. O. Thorburn. Electrocardiograms of marathon runners in 1962 Commonwealth games. *Brit. Heart J.*, 26:469, 1964.

42. Westerlund, J. H. and W. W. Tuttle. Relationship between running events in track and reaction time. *Res. Quart.*, 2:95–100, 1931.

43. Wilmore, J. H. and C. H. Brown. Physiological profiles of women distance runners. *Med. Sci. Sports*, 6:178–181, 1974.

CHAPTER 2

The Demands of Distance Running

Feats of human endurance have piqued the curiosity of physiologists since at least 1870, when long-distance runner Edward Payson Weston was studied during his efforts to walk 400 miles (644 kilometers) in five consecutive days (29). Although the rate at which Weston burned energy was relatively low compared to those of competitors in shorter events, the data obtained provide us with an appreciation of man's physiological and psychological limits. This chapter will describe many more studies of the body's response to the stress of distance running.

NEED FOR ENERGY

The runner's ability to maintain an extremely high rate of energy production for two hours or more is impressively demonstrated by world class marathoner Alberto Salazar, whose 2 hour:18 minute marathon (26.2 miles) performance was estimated to cost him 2,700 kilocalories (kcal) (8). In order to run at such speeds, all distance runners must increase the rate of muscular energy production by more than 15 times the testing level. On the average, distance runners use 95 to 100 kilocalories per mile (kcal/mile).

A number of sports scientists have shown that the total energy required to run a given distance on level ground is constant, regardless of the speed. Only the rate of energy expenditure will differ. As noted in Figure 2-1, when Grete Waitz ran a mile in eight minutes, she used 35 milliliters of oxygen per minute for each kilogram of her body weight (ml/kg × min), approximately 8.9 kilocalories per minute, or 71.2 calories per mile. At a six minute per mile pace, she would use 47 ml/kg × min, 12.0 kilocalories per minute, or 72 kilocalories per mile.

This is not to say that all runners use energy at the same rate or that the cost of running each mile is the same for all runners. A heavier runner would expend more energy because it costs more to carry the added weight. Derek Clayton, for example, weighed 73.4 kilograms compared to Waitz's 51.7 kilograms. Although Clayton had about the same level of efficiency (per kilogram of body weight), it was more expensive for him to run the mile. Where Waitz might expend only 72 kilocalories per mile, Clayton might use 102.

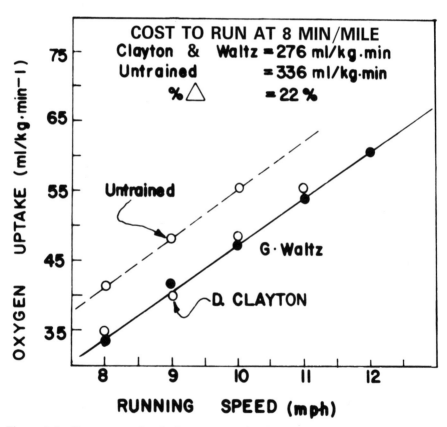

Figure 2-1. Oxygen uptake during running for Grete Waitz, Derek Clayton, and a group of untrained subjects.

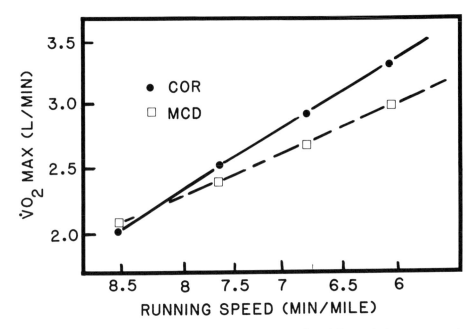

Figure 2-2. Oxygen requirements (Vo_2; ml/kg × min) for McDonagh (open squares) and Corbitt (closed circles) while running at various speeds. Though they had similar Vo_2 max values, McDonagh was the more efficient and, therefore, the faster runner.

Although most elite distance runners are quite efficient at running, some runners are mechanically wasteful, expending more energy than needed to run at a given speed. Differences in running efficiency are well illustrated in Figure 2-2, which shows the test results for two middle-aged distance runners, Ted Corbitt (49 years) and Jim McDonagh (45 years), who were studied in 1968 (14). At all running speeds faster than eight minutes per mile (200 meters per minute), McDonagh used significantly less oxygen than Corbitt. Since these men had similar Vo_2 max values (64 to 65 ml/kg × min), it is obvious that McDonagh's use of less energy provided him with a decided advantage during competition.

Since these two men competed on numerous occasions, it is interesting to examine these encounters. We estimated that during marathon races these men ran at paces requiring them to use energy at 85 percent of their Vo_2 max values. Table 2-1 indicates that, on the average, McDonagh's running efficiency gave him a 13-minute advantage in marathon and ultra-marathon races. Since these men had similar Vo_2 max values but markedly different energy needs during distance running, a large part of McDonagh's advantage in competition can be attributed to his greater running efficiency. Unfortunately, we have no explanation for the

TABLE 2-1. Performance data (hr:min:sec) for two middle-aged distance runners (3).

MON/YR	DISTANCE	CORBITT	PLACE	McDONAGH	PLACE
2/67	42.2 km	2:51:40	8	2:46:21	6
4/67	42.2	2:45:20	81	2:29:55	22
5/67	42.2	2:48:08	11	2:30:06	1
5/67	60.4	4:48:08	4	3:36:52	1
6/67	42.2	3:08:42	14	2:43:42	2
2/68	42.2	2:51:33	8	2:44:40	4
4/68	42.2	2:52:00	43	2:39:34	19
5/68	42.2	2:45:37	6	2:36:35	2
5/68	60.4	4:29:17	3	3:50:11	1
6/68	42.2	3:02:54	10	2:46:51	1
8/68	42.2	2:55:01	8	2:36:36	1
2/69	42.2	2:42:40	9	2:37:25	6
4/69	42.2	2:42:02	56	2:29:07	13
5/69	60.4	3:57:01	2	3:48:11	1
5/69	42.2	2:49:41	5	2:39:34	3

underlying causes of these differences in efficiency.

Various studies with sprint, middle-distance, and distance runners have shown that marathon runners are more efficient than other trained runners (9, 14, 15, 21, 23). In general, these ultra-long distance runners tend to use 5 to 10 percent less energy than middle-distance and sprint runners. Since this economy of effort has only been studied at relatively slow speeds of five to 10 minutes per mile, it seems reasonable to assume that distance runners are less efficient at sprinting than those runners who train specifically for the short, faster races. Though the difference in energy use between the distance and sprint runners may seem small, it becomes a serious consideration during events lasting several hours. Variations in running form and the specificity of training for sprint and distance running probably account for differences in running economy. Film analyses reveal that middle-distance and sprint runners have significantly greater vertical movement when running at seven to 12 miles per hour than marathoners. Such speeds are well below those required during middle-distance races and probably do not represent the running efficiency of competitors in shorter events of 1,500 meters or less. It is interesting to note that the oxygen consumption at a given running speed is also less for world class middle-distance runners than it is for less successful middle-distance runners (23, 24, 45, 50).

Although it is important for runners to be efficient, the upper limits of energy expenditure are determined by one's capacity for oxygen consumption. The discussion in Chapter 1 indicated that successful distance runners are characterized by the ability to consume large amounts of oxygen during exhaustive running (Vo_2 max). Higher Vo_2 max levels enable runners to use lower percentages of those levels to meet the aerobic energy demands of distance competition and avoid heavily taxing their oxygen transportation systems.

If, for example, two runners having Vo_2 max values of 60 ml/kg $\times$ min (Runner A) and 70 ml/kg $\times$ min (Runner B) were asked to run at a six minute per mile pace, both runners would consume about 50 milliliters of oxygen per minute for each kilogram of body weight. Because of the difference in their aerobic capacities (60 vs 70 ml/kg $\times$ min), the demands placed on their cardiovascular and muscular systems would be markedly different. Runner A, for example, would be working at 83 percent of his Vo_2 max, whereas runner B would only use 71 percent of his aerobic capacity. Runner B could sustain that pace for a longer period and feel less distress than runner A.

The fractional use of the aerobic capacity (percent Vo_2 max) for runners competing at distances of five to 84 kilometers (3.1 to 52.2 miles) has been estimated from treadmill testing (13, 16). Figure 2-3 illustrates that as the distance of the race increases, runners must work at lower percentages of their Vo_2 max. Although there are differences in the shape of this curve, marathoners generally run at speeds that require them to

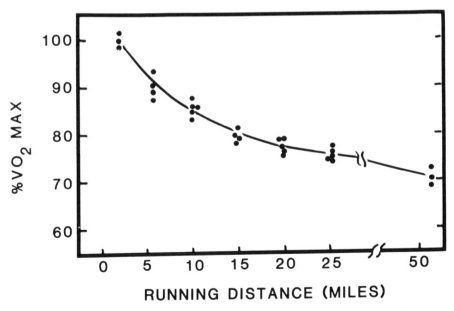

RUNNING DISTANCE (MILES)

Figure 2-3. The average percentage of maximal oxygen uptake (percent Vo_2 max) used during races of from 1,500 meters to 84,000 meters (0.93 to 52.2 miles).

use 75 to 80 percent Vo_2 max during competition (9). As mentioned earlier, however, elite runners Grete Waitz, Frank Shorter, and Derek Clayton were estimated to use between 85 and 90 percent Vo_2 max during the marathon (8, 55). Most runners can tolerate this level of effort for distances of only 10 miles or less.

The ability to judge just the right pace depends on a number of sensory inputs, such as muscle tension, respiratory rate, and the visual sensation of speed. Through experience, the runner learns to match these sensations with just the right level of energy expenditure.

In 1973, we studied 16 distance runners in Salford, England (16) and observed that their percent Vo_2 max levels during a 10-mile (16.1 kilometer) race ranged from 82 to 92 percent with the average being 86 percent. Table 2-2 lists some of the average values for these runners during the 10-mile race. The runners' times in the 10-mile run were not related to either their percent Vo_2 max or the amount of lactate in the blood after the run.

The level of blood lactic acid (lactate) during submaximal exercise may be a good indicator of endurance capacity (26, 43). Terms such as "anaerobic threshold," "aerobic threshold," and the "onset of blood lactate accumulation," (OBLA) describe the sudden change in respiration and lactate accumulation during progressive increments in running speed. Since lactate tends to be produced by the muscles when they are unable to acquire sufficient oxygen to produce energy aerobically, its accumulation in the blood is considered to be a good indicator of the pace that the runner can tolerate during long runs.

Figure 2-4 illustrates the relationship between blood lactate levels and running speeds for an elite marathoner and a good collegiate cross-country runner. Whereas the cross-country runner is able to run comfortably at speeds below six minutes per mile with little accumulation in lactate, the marathoner can run at nearly five minutes per mile before there is any appreciable lactate accumulation. Such laboratory measurements have been used to predict performance and to select an optimal training pace (26). Additional attention will be given to this topic in the discussion on training in Chapter 4.

TABLE 2-2. Mean (range) values for oxygen consumption, %Vo_2 max, and blood lactate during a 10-mile race (16).

10-MILE TIME (MIN)	Vo_2 (ML/KG × MIN)	%Vo_2 MAX	LACTATE (MMOL/L)
56.3 (48.9–67.8)	51.1 (72–46)	86.1 (92–82)	7.7 (5.6–9.8)

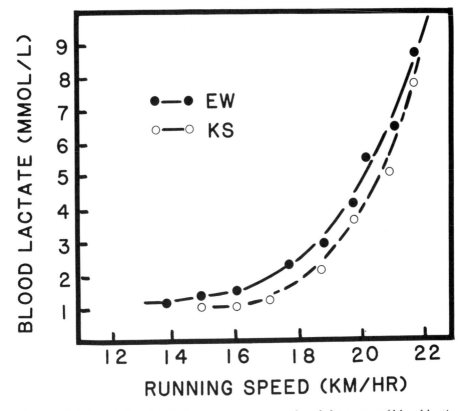

Figure 2-4. The relationship between running speed and the onset of blood lactic acid accumulation (OBLA). Note that lactate changes very little at the slower speeds, but begins to rise rapidly when the runner's pace exceeds 16 kilometers per hour (six minutes per mile).

Runners seldom maintain a steady pace throughout a race, especially when the terrain is hilly. Estimates of average energy expenditures during competition are a bit misleading, because it is logistically difficult to obtain measurements from runners during competition. One exception was a Swedish study in 1972, which measured oxygen consumption in runners during a 30-kilometer cross-country race (20). The results revealed that the percent Vo_2 max varied from 76 percent during downhill running to 90 percent during uphill running. During those same periods heart rates averaged 174 and 180 beats per minute, respectively, compared to the subjects' maximal heart rate of 189 beats per minute.

Despite the runner's option to reduce pace to compensate for variations in terrain, a hilly course may be more costly than a level one. This fact was confirmed by a study in 1970, which demonstrated that when men ran on a 6 percent incline (six meters of vertical climb per 100 meters of horizontal distance) at an eight minute per mile pace, they consumed 35 percent more energy than they did during level running. Running down a similar grade, however, only reduced the energy demands by 24 percent. Despite a potential balance between uphill and downhill running, a hilly course will cost significantly more than level running.

Some runners, however, are considerably more efficient in running up and down various inclines than their competitors. In the same study, the individual oxygen requirements varied from 50 to 61 ml/kg × min on the incline, and from 27 to 34 ml/kg × min on the downslope. Simply because a runner is efficient while running on the level, does not mean that he or she will be efficient while running uphill or downhill.

Variations in terrain can also affect the stress placed on the different leg muscles. When a runner was made to run uphill or downhill on a treadmill at 70 percent Vo_2 max for two hours, we noted that the thigh muscle (vastus lateralis) was notably more active than it was during level running (12). This suggests that it is important to include hill running in training programs to prepare for the specific demands of road and cross-country competition.

The cost of running also is compounded by variations in air resistance. Early studies suggested that during distance running, roughly 5 to 8 percent of the energy spent is needed to overcome the resistance to movement through the air (39, 56). The energy cost of running at a constant speed against the wind was found to increase as the head wind increased. When someone runs on a track in calm air, the difference in oxygen uptake will increase with the cube of the running velocity (56). The difference in oxygen consumption can, therefore, be computed by the equation:

$$Vo_2 = 0.002 \times V^3$$

where Vo_2 is the increase in oxygen uptake in liters per minute

and V is the velocity of the air in meters per second.

As an example, running into a 10 miles per hour (4.44 meters per second) headwind would mean an increase in oxygen uptake of 0.18 liters per minute ($0.002 \times 4.44^3 = 0.18$). If the runner were traveling at eight minutes per mile where the oxygen requirements were about 2.50 liters per minute in still air, the added headwind would increase the cost of running to 2.68 liters per minute, a 7 percent increase in energy demand.

At the highest running speeds, variations in body contour and clothing have a dramatic effect on air resistance and energy expenditure. These findings demonstrate that a considerable advantage is gained by runners who select to run in the "aerodynamic shadow" (drafting) of their competition.

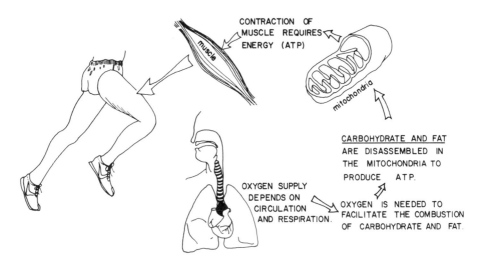

Figure 2-5. The interaction of respiration, circulation, and the energy-producing mechanisms needed by the muscle during distance running. The oxygen transported to the muscle is used by the mitochondria of the cell to breakdown fat and carbohydrate, producing ATP for contraction.

FUELS FOR THE FIRE

The production of energy by the leg muscles depends on the availability of carbohydrates and fats. In Figure 2-5 these fuels are broken down in the presence of oxygen by the mitochondria, the powerhouses of the cell, to produce the ATP for muscular work. These fuels are stored in the muscles and liver as glycogen (carbohydrate) and in the fat cells as triglyceride. The storage of body fat is very large, but the supply of carbohydrates is limited.

The electronmicrograph in Figure 2-6 offers a view inside a single muscle fiber, exposing the contractile filaments that make the muscle shorten (C), the mitochondria (A), and glycogen granules (B). During exercise the number of glycogen granules is gradually reduced, and at exhaustion they may be completely used.

As early as 1934 experts knew that carbohydrates are the preferred fuel for muscles during distance running (25). Although the muscles generally use a mixture of carbohydrates and fats to produce the energy for muscular effort, greater demands are placed on blood glucose and muscle glycogen than on the body's stored fat.

At the onset of exercise, muscle glycogen is the primary source of carbohydrate used for energy. This point is illustrated by the data in Figure 2-7, which show the change in muscle glycogen content during three hours of treadmill running at a pace that equalled the runners' best mar-

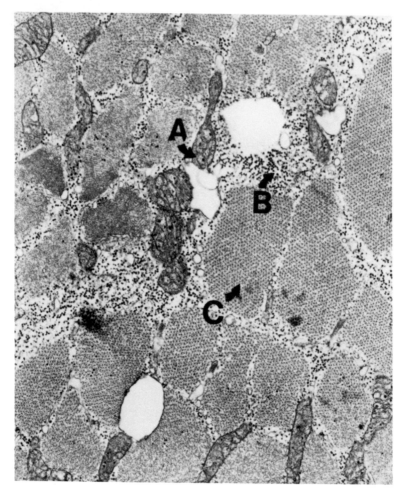

Figure 2-6. Electronmicrograph looking inside a single muscle fiber. If the contractile filaments, actin and myosin (C), are to perform the work of contraction, then they must be provided with ATP which is produced within the mitochondria (A). The carbohydrate stored in the muscle fiber is glycogen (B).

athon speed. Although the test was run at a steady pace, the rate of muscle glycogen use from the calf muscle was greatest during the first 90 minutes of running. Thereafter, the use of glycogen slowed as it approached zero. The runner felt only moderately stressed during the early part of the run, when his rate of muscle glycogen use was most rapid. Not until glycogen was nearly depleted did he experience severe fatigue (note: and demand considerable financial reward before agreeing to finish the trial).

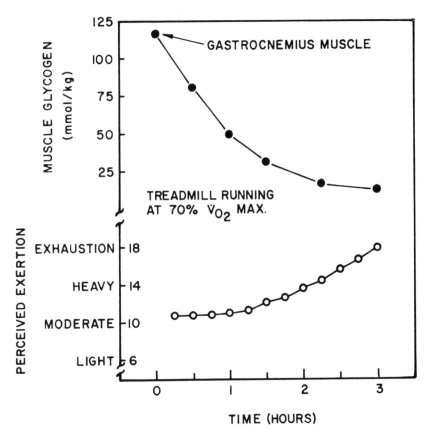

Figure 2-7. Muscle glycogen content and the subject's rating of effort during a three-hour treadmill run at marathon pace. Note that during the first half of the run glycogen was used at a higher rate than during the last 90 minutes of exercise. The runner's perception of exertion did not approach exhaustion until the muscle glycogen was nearly depleted.

Runners have no way of knowing what type of fuels their muscles are using or how rapidly the muscles are depleting glycogen. Since the rate of muscle glycogen use increases somewhat in proportion to running speed (Figure 2-8), a fast pace in the early part of a race may lead to glycogen depletion and premature exhaustion. A runner must carefully choose the correct pace for the length of the run. When muscle glycogen levels are very low, the runner must reduce his or her speed and is easily exhausted (4, 5, 20, 18).

Early studies by Christensen and Hansen (7) showed that at exercise levels below 95 percent of the runner's V_{O_2} max, both carbohydrates and fats are used as fuels. Above this intensity, however, carbohydrates are used almost exclusively.

Figure 2-8. Effects of running speed on the rate of muscle glycogen use. The rate of muscle glycogen use may be 40 times faster during sprint running than during walking.

Although studies with cyclists showed that muscle glycogen was depleted from the thigh muscles after one hour of exercise at 80 percent V_{O_2} max, runners have shown that total depletion of muscle glycogen seldom occurs at the end of races which demanded the same intensity of effort (38, 66). After a 10-mile run of roughly 60 minutes, for example, glycogen was still available in the thigh muscles (vastus lateralis) (18, 38). We could interpret this to mean that exhaustion in running is not related to the depletion of muscle glycogen, but there are two other possible explanations for the discrepancy between muscular exhaustion in cycling and running.

First, the thigh muscles may be more heavily used during cycling than running. Exhaustion in distance running may deplete other leg muscles more than is reflected by the samples taken from the vastus la-

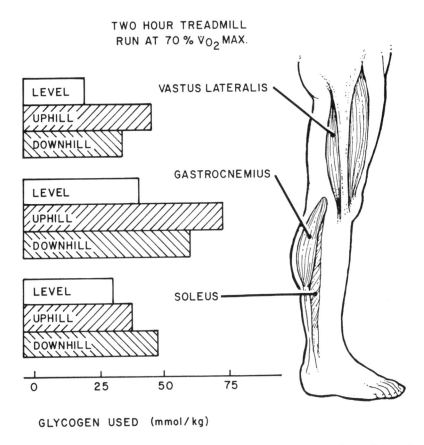

TWO HOUR TREADMILL
RUN AT 70 % V_{O_2} MAX.

VASTUS LATERALIS

LEVEL
UPHILL
DOWNHILL

GASTROCNEMIUS

LEVEL
UPHILL
DOWNHILL

SOLEUS

LEVEL
UPHILL
DOWNHILL

0   25   50   75

GLYCOGEN USED (mmol/kg)

Figure 2-9. Amount of glycogen used from the thigh (vastus lateralis) and calf (soleus and gastrocnemius) muscles during level, uphill, and downhill running for two hours at 70 percent of Vo_2 max (12).

teralis. To test this theory, we had men run on the level, uphill, and downhill for two hours and obtained biopsies from the vastus lateralis, soleus (deep calf) and gastrocnemius muscles at rest and after 70 and 120 minutes of running (12). As can be seen in Figure 2-9, greater amounts of glycogen were used from the gastrocnemius and soleus than the vastus lateralis. This suggests that the thigh muscles are not a representative muscle group for study during exhaustive running. Only during uphill and downhill running is the vastus lateralis required to use glycogen at rates approximating those used by the muscles of the lower leg (12, 34). Even under these circumstances, the glycogen content in the vastus lateralis did not approach zero, despite extreme exhaustion.

A second possibility might explain the lack of complete muscle glycogen depletion at exhaustion during distance running. In 1972, we stud-

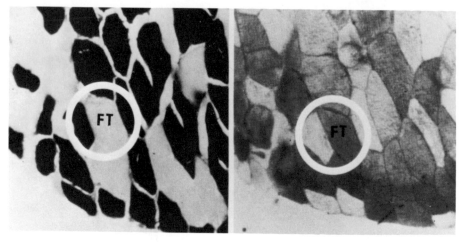

Figure 2-10. Selective muscle glycogen depletion from slow twitch (ST) and fast twitch (FT) fibers during a 30-kilometer distance race. The unstained fiber inside the circle is fast twitch. The muscle section on the left shows the fiber types (black are slow twitch and white are fast twitch), whereas the glycogen content for the same fibers is shown in the right panel. Dark fibers have glycogen, while white fibers are empty of glycogen.

ied the use of glycogen in slow twitch (ST) and fast twitch (FTa and FTb) muscle fibers in runners before and after a 30-kilometer cross-country race (20). Microscopic examination of these muscle samples (Figure 2-10) revealed that the glycogen content of the slow twitch fibers was nearly exhausted, while the fast twitch fibers still contained considerable quantities. This demonstrates that the slow twitch fibers are the muscle cells most heavily used during this type of running. When the slow twitch fibers have relinquished their glycogen stores, the fast twitch fibers are apparently unable to generate enough tension and/or cannot be easily recruited to compensate for the exhausted slow twitch fibers. As a result, the runner finds each stride progressively more difficult. This selective depletion of muscle glycogen is undoubtedly the cause of the muscle distress often described by runners during the final stage of races like the marathon.

Muscle glycogen alone cannot provide all of the carbohydrate needed for a long-distance run. The liver breaks down glycogen to provide a constant supply of glucose in the blood. In the early stages of exercise, energy production uses relatively small amounts of blood glucose, but in the later stages, blood glucose may make a large contribution. The longer the exercise period, the greater the glucose output from the liver (64).

Exercising muscles also show a greater uptake and use of glucose with increasing periods of exercise (70). Since the liver has a limited supply of glycogen and is unable to produce glucose rapidly, blood glucose levels may begin to decrease when the muscle uptake becomes greater than the liver's output. We have sampled blood from runners at each five-mile point in a marathon and observed that glucose gradually declined until the level was clinically abnormal near the finish of the race. Similar findings were reported as early as 1924, which led to the generalization that low blood glucose may be one of the factors responsible for exhaustion during distance running (47).

Recent studies do not show consistent support for this concept. Measurements of blood glucose during 1.5 to 4.0 hours of treadmill running have shown a number of cases of extremely low blood glucose without symptoms of fatigue or exhaustion (17, 19). This does not mean that low blood glucose is not a cause for fatigue. On the contrary, when the glucose supply from the blood is low, muscles must rely more on their own carbohydrate reserves (35). As a result, muscle glycogen is depleted more rapidly, which leads to inevitable exhaustion.

Both lipids (fat) and amino acids (protein) have been shown to serve as significant energy sources during long runs. Although protein is the major building block of body tissues, it also contributes to the muscles energy needs as a source of fuel for glucose production. Estimates of protein use during exercise suggest that as much as 9 percent of the total energy expended during a marathon race may be derived from amino acids. Some of the amino acids like alanine may be used by the liver to form glucose, which is subsequently used by the muscles (27, 28). Though the muscles may use protein in this indirect way to get energy, they do not have the capacity to burn amino acids directly.

Runners draw on fat deposits inside and outside the muscle fibers during races longer than 10 kilometers (6.2 miles). Up to that distance, runners probably use carbohydrates exclusively, since they are working at more than 90 to 95 percent of their Vo_2 max values (65). By measuring the exchange of carbon dioxide and oxygen in a runner's respired air, we can estimate the percentage of energy derived from both fat and carbohydrates.

During a two-hour treadmill test at 65 percent Vo_2 max, we have observed a decrease in the ratio between carbon dioxide and oxygen (RER) from 0.88 at 10 minutes of exercise to 0.80 at 120 minutes (9). This indicates that fats contributed 39 percent of the total energy for running at 10 minutes and 67 percent during the final minutes of exercise. This increase in fat use seems to be related to a rise in blood free fatty acids (FFA), a simple form of fat released from the breakdown of triglyceride in the fat cells (37).

This shift toward a greater reliance on fat as an energy source was profoundly demonstrated in our studies with an ultra-distance runner,

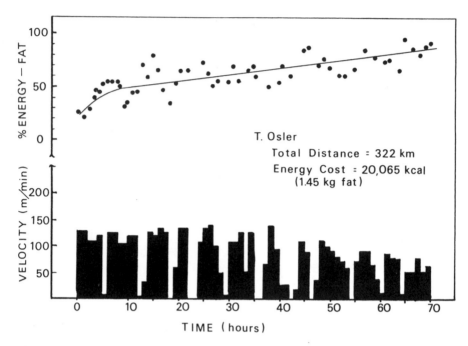

Figure 2-11. Results of a 70-hour run-walk-rest trial by Tom Osler, an ultra-marathoner. Top panel illustrates the percentage of the total energy derived from fat, whereas the lower panel shows his rate of running and walking.

Tom Osler, who ran-walked-rested for 70 hours. Although he consumed food *ad libitum* throughout the trial, there was a gradual shift toward greater and greater use of fat (Figure 2-11). Over the final hours of the exercise, fat was contributing 90 to 100 percent of all the energy he needed.

Although it is well known that fats are stored in the skeletal muscles as triglyceride, the importance of fat during distance running is not fully understood. Studies in the early 1970s demonstrated that muscle triglyceride is a major energy source during exercise (31, 32). The unique ability of slow twitch muscle fibers to use oxygen allows them to derive a larger part of their energy from fat than the fast twitch fibers. Since slow twitch fibers are the ones most frequently used during endurance training and competition, it is not surprising to find that they also have larger storages of triglyceride. In Chapter 4 we will discuss how endurance training tends to increase the storage of both triglyceride and glycogen.

CARDIOVASCULAR RESPONSES

Since distance running is primarily an aerobic form of exercise, great demands are placed on the cardiovascular system, which transports oxygen and fuels to the working muscles and removes wastes produced during energy production. As a measure of the stress imposed on the heart and vascular system, experts have estimated that marathoners performing a 2 hour:26 minute marathon would maintain an average cardiac output of 26.5 liters per minute (30). Since their maximal cardiac output was estimated to be 28.8 liters per minute, it seems that these highly trained runners can exercise for nearly two and one-half hours while working their cardiovascular systems at 92 percent of their full capacities. The amount of blood being pumped with each beat (stroke volume) averaged 149 milliliters per beat and the heart rates averaged 178 beats per minute, which were also near the runners' maximums of 153 milliliters per beat and 188 beats per minute, respectively.

These average values obtained during prolonged exercise may be somewhat misleading. Cardiac output, stroke volume, and heart rate are not constant throughout a race. Saltin and Stenberg (67) have shown that during more than three hours of exercise at 75 percent Vo_2 max (approximate marathon pace), cardiac output rose 10 percent with a 5 percent increase in oxygen uptake. The major circulatory changes during this exercise were a 15 percent progressive rise in heart rate and a 12 percent fall in stroke volume. The causes for these changes are not known, though Rowell (60) has speculated that the rise in heart rate and fall in stroke volume may be caused by a rise in body temperature with an increase in blood flow to the skin. When body temperature is elevated, as is the case in distance running, central blood volume and stroke volume fall, thereby forcing heart rate to rise in an effort to keep the runner's cardiac output constant (61, 62).

To complicate the issue even more, during the initial minutes of running, the water in blood plasma decreases. This change in plasma volume is due to a rise in the pressure of the small blood vessels within the muscle, which results in a shift in fluids from the blood into and around the muscle fibers (49, 48). The effect of this plasma water loss is a relative increase in hematocrit (percent of blood composed of red blood cells) and hemoglobin concentration.

The major change in the cardiovascular system during long-distance races appears to be a gradual increase in the distensibility of the peripheral vessels, causing blood volume shifts from the central vessels to the periphery. Cardiac filling pressure, central blood volume, and stroke volume are reduced, so cardiac output must be maintained by an increased heart rate. It is difficult to state whether oxygen transport is limited by fatigue of the heart muscle. Nevertheless, with exhaustion, stimulation of the smooth muscles surrounding the arterial vessels may constrict the vessels and reduce blood flow to less active regions of the body such as the digestive organs (3). This may explain the pallor and gastrointestinal distress sometimes seen at exhaustion.

From a practical point of view, the simplest method for monitoring the stress of exercise is to measure your heart rate during or immediately after running. Since modern technology has created several commercial monitors, runners can observe their heart rates during training runs and competition.

Although several formulas have been suggested to indicate the "ideal" heart rate to achieve optimal conditioning, the preferred heart rate during training is usually in the range of 130 to 150 beats per minute for men, and 150 to 170 beats per minute for women. Of course these values will vary widely, depending on the running pace, physical condition, and individual differences in maximal heart rate. Individuals with unusually low or high maximal heart rates may be proportionately lower or higher during training runs. Although there are prediction tables to estimate your maximal heart rate based on age, these tables can be grossly in error for some individuals. If you have a method of monitoring your heart rate during exercise, maximal heart rate can be determined by performing a four- to-five-minute maximal run. The heart rate recorded during the last 30 to 60 seconds of the run or within 15 seconds after the end of the run will reflect the maximal rate. Such information will help to judge the optimal stimulus for training and to prevent overtraining. These matters will be discussed in Chapter 4.

RESPIRATION: A BREATHTAKING EVENT

To accommodate the high rate of oxygen consumption demanded during distance running, large volumes of air must be delivered to the lungs (9). Breathing is probably the most obvious subjective indicator used by the runner to judge his or her pace and level of distress. Although the volume of air breathed per minute is not directly proportional to the amount of oxygen being consumed by the body, most runners adjust the running pace to permit a tolerable level of respiratory distress.

The air we breathe is a mixture of gases, 21 percent of which is oxygen. After we inhale the gases into the lungs, some of the oxygen is taken up by the blood to replace that being used by the body tissues. At the same time, carbon dioxide (CO_2), the by-product of aerobic energy production, is released into the lungs' gases to be exhaled. Consequently, the air leaving the lungs has less oxygen (15 to 17 percent) and more carbon dioxide (3 to 5 percent).

While the average person may breathe approximately five to six liters of air per minute at rest, the volume may exceed 150 liters per minute during intense running (44). In the late 1960s we studied a group of runners during a simulated 10,000-meter run (9). These runners were able to breathe between 120 and 145 liters of air per minute for more than 20 minutes of the run. Such values are unusually large, since these men were relatively small, averaging 143 pounds in weight. Other non-endurance trained athletes are only able to breathe such large volumes for one or two minutes of voluntary effort or during the final seconds of an exhaustive exercise bout. One of the unique adaptations to training among distance runners is the ability of the respiratory muscles to sustain a high breathing rate and volume for prolonged periods.

One might ask the question, "Does breathing become a limiting factor during long-distance running?" At least two points should be considered in answering.

First, the work of breathing places heavy demands on the muscles that expand and contract the chest wall. Though the oxygen consumed by the respiratory muscles under resting conditions is small (about 1 percent of the body's total energy need), the cost of breathing becomes progressively greater with increasing levels of effort. Since the actual efficiency of the respiratory muscles cannot be measured, it is impossible to be precise in estimates of the energy needed to ventilate the lungs. During distance races, where the respiratory volume may average 100 to 120 liters per minute, as much as 9 percent of the energy used by the body will be needed for respiration (52). In any event, though the work of breathing increases with increased effort, respiratory ventilation is probably not a limiting factor in long-distance races except perhaps at high altitude.

The second consideration is the problem of maintaining normal oxygen and carbon dioxide concentrations in the blood. Previous studies have demonstrated that arterial oxygen content remains relatively constant at various levels of exercise (1). However, in athletes with breathing volumes of 120 to 150 liters per minute, a fall in arterial oxygen content has been observed at exhaustion (63, 68). Since long-distance runners or marathoners seldom tax their respiratory systems to the maximum during competition, it is unlikely that the diffusion of gases between the lung and blood will become limiting. This may not be the case, however, in shorter races of 5,000 to 10,000 meters. Little scientific evidence is available to determine the effects of such high-intensity running on the arterial oxygen content during the final stages of such competition, when many runners experience extreme respiratory distress.

Subjective reports of breathing distress near the end of marathon and longer races are not uncommon. Considering the constant, intense demands placed on the respiratory muscles throughout such events, these muscles may simply be experiencing the order of fatigue confronting the leg muscles, glycogen depletion. The task of ventilating the lungs may become more difficult, leading to a sensation of respiratory resistance. After many hours of intense respiratory effort, there also may be some swelling of the bronchioles in the respiratory pathway, which would cause some resistance to breathing and lead to additional respiratory muscle fatigue. Further studies are needed on the importance of breathing to distance running performance.

Most runners monitor various senses of effort, especially breathing, in order to judge their pace. Aside from the visual clues of the speed of movement and the sensations of muscular effort, the runner has little to directly indicate the rate of energy expenditure.

Breathing rate and depth are the best physiological guides to pace. Even during running in hot weather or at high altitude, the signs of labored breathing reflect the level of stress imposed on the cardiovascular and energy system and serve as a warning of overstress.

BY-PRODUCTS OF RUNNING

In the process of using fuels to produce energy aerobically, the muscles generate a number of waste products, including carbon dioxide, heat, and lactic acid (lactate). Since excessive amounts of these by-products can impair normal muscle function, they must be eliminated constantly.

Some of these items diffuse rapidly out of the cells and into the blood. When an individual runs at an easy submaximal pace, the circulatory system is able to transport carbon dioxide and heat to the lungs and skin where they can be dissipated, minimizing build-ups in the blood.

By-products such as lactic acid, however, are not so easily eliminated and accumulate rapidly during intense effort. Since lactic acid is formed only when the muscles produce energy anaerobically, one would not expect it to accumulate to any degree in distance running. Although this is the case in most relatively easy training runs and long races, a sizeable amount of lactate may appear in the blood and muscles during shorter events of 10 miles or less.

During the initial seconds or minutes of a race, a runner's circulatory and respiratory systems cannot adjust to the sudden burst of energy. The immediate oxygen requirements may be far greater than the circulatory system can supply, forcing the muscles to derive some energy anaerobically. Consequently, the runner incurs an oxygen debt with significant lactate accumulation. The muscles and blood become more acid, a condition incompatible with the operation of the cells.

The scale used to assess the acidity of body fluids is pH. A solution that is neither acid nor alkaline, such as water, has a pH of roughly 7.0, whereas more acid solutions have lower values.

Arterial blood and resting muscles normally have pH values of 7.4 and 7.1, respectively, somewhat on the alkaline side. During hard running, muscle pH may drop to 6.8 or lower, which results in a lowering of blood pH to approximately 7.1. In exhaustive sprint events of 400 meters, muscle lactate may rise from a resting level of 1.0 millimoles of lactate per kilogram of muscle to 25, with a concomitant decrease in muscle pH to 6.5. Subsequent diffusion of this lactate into the blood causes the blood pH to drop from 7.4 to 6.9 (11).

Since body tissues can only operate optimally within a very narrow range of pH, such large changes in muscle and blood lactate and pH have a dramatic effect on performance. Increased acidity impairs the operation of the mitochondria, limiting the muscle's ability to produce energy. In addition, the contractile processes of the muscle begin to fail, reducing the tension developed by the muscle. Such changes result in a shortening of the runner's stride and an inability to maintain even a slow speed. It is important to realize, however, that such drastic changes in muscle and blood pH only occur in events that result in large accumulations of lactic acid.

Figure 2-12 illustrates that blood lactate at the end of various distance races is only slightly above the resting levels after the marathon, but ex-

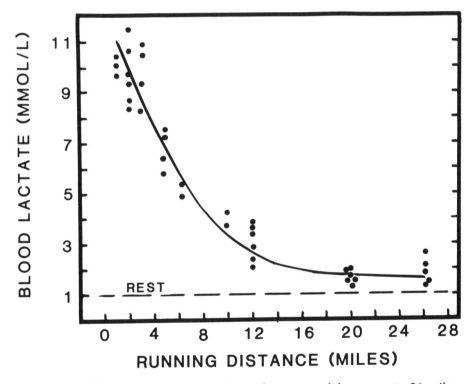

Figure 2-12. Blood lactate concentrations after races of from one to 26 miles. Note the greatest lactate levels are in the shorter events, whereas the values after the marathon are only slightly above the resting level.

tremely high after races as short as one mile. There are two possible explanations.

First, the longer the race, the smaller the percent Vo_2 max used during the run. Consequently, energy can be produced almost exclusively by aerobic means, with little lactate production. Secondly, the lactate produced in the early stages of a long run may be removed by less active tissues, including the liver, kidney, and inactive muscles, even during the exercise (6, 36, 40, 48). It has been shown that the lactate produced during an hour of exercise reaches a peak concentration in the blood during the first 10 minutes of running (59). Approximately half of that, however, is removed by the end of 30 minutes of running. This suggests that changes in blood lactate levels and pH are seldom responsible for the fatigue commonly experienced during races longer than 10 kilometers (2).

Another common misconception of some runners is that lactic acid causes muscle soreness. In light of the knowledge that little or no lactate is produced during the marathon, an almost purely aerobic event, the leg soreness cannot be attributed to lactate. Theoretically, there is no justification for this belief, since lactate has no properties that could induce pain and tightness. Some new theories concerning muscle soreness and tissue damage will be discussed in Chapter 4 under "Overtraining."

Exercising muscles consume greater amounts of glucose during longer running periods (58, 70). (You will recall that the longer the period of exercise, the greater the liver's glucose output.) When the muscles' demands for glucose are greater than the liver's output, however, blood glucose levels may fall from the normal level of 5.0 millimoles per liter of blood to less than 3.0 (10). Since blood glucose serves as the primary source of energy for the nervous system, low blood glucose (hypoglycemia) may be one factor responsible for intolerable sensations experienced during the final stages of very long races.

As mentioned earlier, free fatty acids provide a large part of the energy during long races like the marathon. Runners do not reap the full benefits of fat energy until they have been running for 30 minutes or longer. This shift toward the use of fat is indicated by a rising level of free fatty acids in plasma, with a concomitant increase in plasma glycerol, a by-product of the breakdown of triglyceride. Fat provides an alternate source of energy and spares the potential exhaustion of muscle glycogen stores during endurance exercise.

There are a number of other changes in the composition of blood during distance running, but none of them seem to impose any risk to the runner's health. Despite relatively large changes in serum enzymes during distance running, there is no evidence to suggest that they are of any clinical significance (41, 57, 63, 71). Although these special proteins play important roles in the energy mechanisms of the muscle, the significance of their increases in serum following long periods of running are not fully understood. Recent evidence, however, has linked increases in serum GOT (glutamic oxaloacetic transaminase), LDH (lactate dehydrogenase), and CPK (creatine phosphokinase) with muscle tissue damage (42, 69). As we will discuss in Chapter 4, there is substantial evidence indicating some damage to the muscle membranes during long runs, which seems to explain how these enzymes leak into the blood. The significance of this muscle trauma, however, has not been fully explained.

As previously discussed, there is a rapid movement of water from plasma into the working musculature (49). This loss of water from the blood causes many of the plasma constituents to become concentrated, since most of them do not move out of the vessels as rapidly as water. We may see a marked increase in the concentration of such plasma particles as cholesterol and protein, even though the total amount of these items in circulation does not change.

RUNNING A FEVER

Probably no single factor poses a greater threat to the distance runner's health and performance than overheating. Since much of the energy generated by a muscle is not used for contractions, most of the energy is degraded to the lowest form of energy, heat. Consequently, the internal heat of the muscle rises rapidly during exercise, reaching temperatures of 106 to 108 degrees Fahrenheit. In order to cool the muscle, the internal heat is transferred to the blood passing through the capillaries, which surround the muscle fibers. As a result, the muscle heat raises the temperature of the blood and the internal temperature of the body.

While moderate changes in body temperature are tolerated, fevers of 104 degrees Fahrenheit or higher can affect the nervous system and the body's mechanisms of temperature regulation. The removal of heat from the body is regulated by the hypothalamus, a small mass of nervous tissue seated in the base of the brain. Functioning as a thermostat, the hypothalamus triggers a sweating response and directs blood flow to the skin in an effort to dissipate the excess body heat. Although surprisingly effective, this system of cooling is not without limitations, and often it is no match for the high rate of heat produced during running.

One of the primary responsibilities of the circulatory system is to transport heat from the muscles to the surface of the body where the heat can be transferred to the environment. Since the volume of blood is limited, exercise poses a complex problem for the circulatory system. During exercise, a large part of the cardiac output must be shared by the skin and working muscles. An increase in the demand for flow to one tissue will automatically decrease flow to the other.

Any factor that tends to overload the cardiovascular system or interfere with the transfer of heat from the body to the environment will drastically impair the distance runner's performance and increase the risk of overheating. Running at a fast pace, for example, will require more oxygen and blood flow to the muscles, with a concomitantly greater rate of muscle heat production. Despite this increase in heat production, blood flow to the skin must decrease, resulting in an inability to move the heat to the shell of the body. Fast running in warm weather also tends to overload the circulatory system, produce greater heat, and reduce the ability to deliver muscle heat to the skin. This causes greater rise in body temperature.

Under resting conditions the amount of heat produced by the body is relatively small (about 1.5 kilocalories per minute) compared to that generated during distance running (about 20 kilocalories per minute). Whereas excess heat loss at rest is accomplished via radiation or infrared rays, conduction and convection, roughly 80 percent of the heat loss during exercise is accomplished through sweat evaporation. With as little as a one hundredth of a degree increase in blood temperature, the hypothalamus stimulates the sweat glands in the skin to release sweat, moistening the skin surface. Using the heat delivered to the skin by the blood, sweat is converted from a liquid into a gas. Unless this conversion takes place, little or no heat can be dissipated, and the body begins to store heat at a dangerous rate. When the air is humid, for example, it is nearly saturated with water and cannot absorb the water of sweat. As a result, little body heat can be lost and the runner may develop a dangerously high fever.

A number of studies have reported rectal temperatures higher than 104 degrees Fahrenheit after marathon races conducted on moderately warm days (22, 72). Following a 10,000-meter race in the heat (85 degrees Fahrenheit, 80 percent relative humidity, and bright sun) we recorded a rectal temperature of 109.5 degrees Fahrenheit in a 40-year-old man who collapsed only 100 yards from the finish. Without proper medical attention, such fevers result in permanent brain damage and in some cases death. Fortunately, this man was rapidly cooled with ice and recovered without complications. Body temperature during distance running is directly dependent on running speed, gross body weight, or both. Heavier individuals would run a higher risk of overheating than lighter athletes when they are running at the same pace.

There is little we can do about the environmental conditions, but it is obvious that runners must slow down to reduce heat production and the risk of overheating. All runners and race promoters should be able to recognize the symptoms of a high internal fever. There is a fair relationship between subjective sensations and the runner's body tempera-

TABLE 2-3. Subjective symptoms associated with overheating.

RECTAL TEMPERATURE	SYMPTOMS
104–105°F	Throbbing pressure in head, cold sensation over stomach and back.
105–106°F	Muscular weakness, disorientation, and loss of postural equilibrium.
Above 106°F	Diminished sweating, loss of consciousness.

ture (Table 2-3). Although we are seldom concerned with rectal temperatures of 101 to 104 degrees Fahrenheit at the end of prolonged exercise, a runner who has a throbbing pressure in his head and chills should realize that he is rapidly approaching a dangerous stage that could prove fatal if he continues to run.

Heat stroke, the result of a high internal temperature, is the major threat to the well-trained, highly motivated distance runner. Some guidelines[1] to follow for the prevention of such heat-related injuries are as follows:

1. Distance races of greater than 10 kilometers should not be conducted when the combination of air temperature, humidity, and sun raise the WBGT temperature above 82 degrees Fahrenheit.

$$WBGT = 0.7(TWB) + 0.2(TG) = 0.1(TDB)$$

where TWB = temperature of wet bulb; TG = temperature of

black globe; and TDB = temperature of dry bulb

2. Summer events should be scheduled before 8 A.M. or after 6 P.M. to minimize the heat of the sun.

3. An adequate supply of water or other fluids should be available before the race and at two- to three-kilometer intervals during the race. Runners should drink 100 to 200 milliliters at each feeding station.

4. Runners should train adequately for fitness and become heat-acclimatized (33, 51, 53, 54).

5. Runners should be aware of the early symptoms of heat injury, including dizziness, chilling, headache, and awkwardness.

6. Race sponsors should make prior arrangements with medical personnel to care for heat injuries. Responsible and informed personnel should supervise each feeding station. Organizational personnel should reserve

---

[1]Modified from "Prevention of Thermal Injuries During Distance Running," *Med. Sci. Sports Exer.,* 16:ix–xiv, 1984.

the right to stop runners who exhibit clear signs of heat stroke or heat exhaustion.

Heat exhaustion, although not usually life-threatening, is characterized by dizziness, nausea, weakness, and pale skin that is cool and moist. Unconsciousness often accompanies these symptoms, induced by a sudden pooling of blood in the skin and a drop in blood flow to the brain.

The frequency of **muscle cramping** increases during distance running in the heat. Although such cramping may be the consequence of large water and mineral losses in sweat, the precise cause is not fully understood. As a matter of fact, no conclusive explanations or objective data are available to explain the cause of muscle cramping. Since cramps occur under a wide variety of conditions, during sleep and in exercise, there are probably a number of possible causes.

EXPENSE OF RUNNING

The preceding discussion has pointed out some of the costly aspects of distance running and factors that may limit one's performance. Though body weight is one of the most important factors determining the amount of energy needed to run at a given speed, there are marked individual differences in running efficiency. It costs some runners more to run at a given speed than it does others with better technique.

This leads us to wonder why so little effort is made to improve the runner's mechanics. In nearly every other sport, at least part of each training session is directed toward the improvement of skill. This is not the case in distance running. Few runners ever attempt to analyze or improve their running techniques. When we consider the fact that even a 1 percent decrease in the energy cost of running would improve a three-hour marathoner's time by nearly two minutes, it is surprising that more attention is not given to this aspect of training. Although the biomechanical aspects of running are outside the scope of this book, it is obvious that skill and energy expenditure are important determinants of success in long-distance events.

BIBLIOGRAPHY

1. Asmussen, E. and M. Neilsen. Alveolar-arterial gas exchange at rest and during work at different o2-tensions. *Acta Physiol. Scand.*, 50:153–166, 1960.
2. Astrand, P. O. and others. Blood lactates after prolonged severe exercise. *J. Appl. Physiol.*, 18:619–622, 1963.
3. Barger, A. C., R. J. Greenwood, J. R. DiPalma, J. Stoker III and L. H. Smith. Venous pressure and cutaneous reactive hyeremia in exhausting exercise and certain other circulatory stresses. *J. Appl. Physiol.*, 2:81–96, 1948.

4. Bergstrom, J. and E. Hultman. A study of the glycogen metabolism during exercise in man. *Scand. J. Clin. Lab. Invest.*, 19:218–228, 1967.
5. Bergstrom, J., L. Hermansson, E. Hultman and B. Saltin. Diet, muscle glycogen and physical performance. *Acta Physiol. Scand.*, 71:140–150, 1967.
6. Carlsten, A. and others. Myocardial metabolism of glucose, lactic acid, amino acids, and fatty acids in healthy human individuals at rest and at different work loads. *Scand. J. Clin. Lab. Invest.*, 13:418–428, 1961.
7. Christensen, E. H. and O. Hansen. I. Zur Methodik der Respiratorischen Quotient-Bestimmungen in Ruhe und bei Arbeit. II. Untersuchungen uber die Verbrennungsvorgange bei langdauernder, schwerer Muskelarbeit. III. Arbeitsfahigkeit and Ernahrung. *Skand. Arch. Physiol.*, 81:137–171, 1939.
8. Costill, D. L. Salazar and Clayton: A physiological comparison of the marathon record holders. *The Runner*, 20, March, 1982.
9. Costill, D. L. Metabolic responses during distance running. *J. Appl. Physiol.*, 28:251–255, 1970.
10. Costill, D. L. Muscular exhaustion during distance running. *Physician and Sportsmedicine*, 36–41, October 1974.
11. Costill, D. L., A. Barnett, R. Sharp, W. Fink and A. Katz. Leg muscle pH following sprint running. *Med. Sci. Sports Exer.*, 15:325–329, 1983.
12. Costill, D. L., E. Jansson, P. D. Gollnick and B. Saltin. Glycogen utilization in leg muscles of men during level and uphill running. *Acta Physiol. Scand.*, 91:475–481, 1974.
13. Costill, D. L. and E. L. Fox. Energetics of marathon running. *Med. Sci. Sports*, 1:81–86, 1969.
14. Costill, D. L. and E. Winrow. A comparison of two middle aged ultra-marathon runners. *Res. Quart.*, 41:135–139, 1970.
15. Costill, D. L., G. Branam, D. Eddy and K. Sparks. Determinants of marathon running success. *Int. Zeitschift fur angerwandte Physiol.*, 29:249–254, 1971.
16. Costill, D. L., H. Thomason and E. Roberts. Fractional utilization of the aerobic capacity during distance running. *Med. Sci. Sports*, 5:248–252, 1973.
17. Costill, D. L. and J. M. Miller. Nutrition for endurance sport: Carbohydrate and fluid balance. *Int. J. Sports Med.*, 1:2–14, 1980.
18. Costill, D. L., K. E. Sparks, R. Gregor and C. Turner. Muscle glycogen utilization during exhaustion running. *J. Appl. Physiol.*, 31:353–356, 1971.
19. Costill, D. L., P. Cleary, W. Fink, C. Foster, J. Ivy and F. Witzmann. Training adaptations in skeletal muscle of juvenile diabetics. *Diabetes*, 28:818–822, 1979.
20. Costill, D. L., P. D. Gollnick, E. D. Jansson, B. Saltin and E. M. Stein. Glycogen depletion pattern in human muscle fibers during distance running. *Acta Physiol. Scand.*, 89:374–383, 1973.
21. Costill, D. L., R. Bowers, G. Branam and K. Sparks. Muscle glycogen utilization during prolonged exercise on successive days. *J. Appl. Physiol.*, 31:834–838, 1971.
22. Costill, D. L., W. F. Kammer and A. Fisher. Fluid ingestion during distance running. *Arch Environ. Health.*, 21:520–525, 1970.
23. Daniels, J. and N. Oldridge. The effects of alternate exposure to altitude and sea level on world-class middle-distance runners. *Med. Sci. Sports*, 2:107–112, 1970.
24. Dill, D. B. Oxygen used in horizontal and grade walking and running on the treadmill. *J. Appl. Physiol.*, 20:19–22, 1965.
25. Edwards, H. T., R. Margaria and D. B. Dill. Metabolic rate, blood sugar and the utilization of carbohydrate. *Am. J. Physiol.*, 108:203–209, 1934.
26. Farrell, P. A., J. H. Wilmore, E. F. Coyle, J. E. Billing and D. L. Costill. Plasma lactate accumulation and distance running performance. *Med. Sci. Sports*, 11:338–344, 1979.
27. Felig, P. and J. Wahren. Amino acid metabolism in exercising man. *J. Clin. Invest.*, 50:1702–1711, 1971.

28. Felig, P., T. Pozefsky, E. Morliss and G. F. Cahill. Alanine: Key role in gluconeogenesis. *Science,* 167:1003–1004, 1960.
29. Flint, A. Physiological effects of severe and protracted muscular exercise. *3, 1872.*
30. Fox, E. L. and D. L. Costill. Estimated cardiorespiratory responses during marathon running. *Arch. Environ. Health,* 24:316–324, 1972.
31. Froberg, S. O. and F. Mossfeldt. Effect of prolonged strenuous exercise on the concentration of triglycerides, Phospholipids and glucogen in muscle and man. *Acta Physiol. Scand.,* 82:167–171, 1971.
32. Froberg, S. O., L. A. Carlsson and L.-G. Eklund. Local lipid stores and exercise. *Muscle Metabolism During Exercise,* B. Pernow and B. Saltin, ed. New York: Plenum Press, 11:307–313, 1971.
33. Gisolfi, C. V. and J. Cohen. Relationships among training, heat acclimation and heat tolerance in men and women: the controversy revisited. *Med. Sci. Sports,* 11:56–59, 1979.
34. Gregor, R. A comparison of the energy expenditure during positive and negative grade running. *Master's Thesis, Ball State University, Muncie, Indiana, 1970.*
35. Hargreaves, M., D. L. Costill, A. Coggan, W. Fink and I. Nishibata. Effect of carbohydrate feedings on muscle glycogen utilization and exercise performance. *Med. Sci. Sports Exer.,* 16:219–222, 1984.
36. Harris, P. M. and others. The regional metabolism of lactate and pyruvate during exercise in patients with rheumatic heart disease. *Clin. Sci.,* 23:545–560, 1962.
37. Havel, R. J. Influence of intensity and duration of exercise on supply and use of fuels. *Muscle Metabolism During Exercise,* B. Pernow and B. Saltin, ed. New York: Plenum Press, 11:315–325, 1971.
38. Hermansen, L., E. Hultman and B. Saltin. Muscle glycogen during prolonged severe exercise. *Acta Physiol. Scand.,* 71:129–139, 1967.
39. Hill, A. V. The air resistance of a runner. *Proc Roy Soc London,* 102:380–385, 1928.
40. Himwick, H. E., Y. D. Koskoff and L. H. Nahum. Studies in carbohydrate metabolism. I.A., glucose-lactic acid cycle involving muscle and liver. *J. Biol. Chem.,* 85:571–584.
41. Kew, M. C., I. Bersohn, H. C. Seftel and G. Kent. Liver damage in heat stroke. *Am. J. Med.,* 49:192–202, 1970.
42. Kielblock, A. J., M. Manjoo and J. Booyen. Creatine phosphokinase and lactate dehydrogenase levels after ultra long-distance running: an analysis of isoenzyme profiles with special reference to indicators of myocardial damages. *S. Afr. Med. J.,* 55:1061–1064, 1979.
43. Kindermann, W. G. and J. K. Simon. The significance of the aerobic-anaerobic transition for the determination of work load intensities during endurance training. *European J. Appl. Physiol.,* 42:25–34, 1979.
44. Kollias, J., D. L. Moody and E. R. Buskirk. Cross-country running: Treadmill simulation and suggested effectiveness of supplemental treadmill training. *J. Sports Med.,* 7:148–154, 1967.
45. Kollias, J., D. L. Moody and E. R. Buskirk. Cross-country running: Treadmill simulation and suggested effectiveness of supplemental treadmill training. *J. Sports Md. and Phys.,* 7:148–154, 1967.
46. Leithead, C. S. and A. R. Lind. Heat stress and heat disorders. *1964.*
47. Levine, S. A., B. Gordon and C. L. Derick. Some changes in the chemical constituents of the blood following a marathon race. *J. Amer. Med. Assoc.,* 82:1778–1779, 1924.
48. Levy, M. N. Uptake of lactate and pyruvate by intact kidney of the dog. *Amer. J. Physiol.,* 202:302–308, 1962.
49. Lundvall, J. Tissue hyperosmolality as a mediator of vasodilatation and transcapillary fluid flux in exercise skeletal muscle. *Acta Physiol. Scand. Suppl.,* 397:1–142, 1972.

50. Margaria, R., P. Cerretelli and P. Aghems. Energy cost of running. *J. Appl. Physiol.*, 18:367–370, 1963.

51. Minard, D. Prevention of heat casualties in Marine Corps Recruits. *Milit. Med.*, 126:261–265, 1961.

52. Nielsen, M. Die Respirationsarbeit bei Korperruhe und bei Muskelarbeit. *Skand. Arch. Physiol.*, 74:299–366, 1936.

53. Pandolf, K. B., R. L. Burse and R. F. Goldman. Role of physical fitness in heat acclimatization, decay and reinduction. *Ergomoics*, 20:399–408, 1977.

54. Piwonka, R. W., S. Robinson, V. L. Gay and R. S. Manalis. Preacclimatization of men to heat by training. *J. Appl. Physiol.*, 20:379–384, 1965.

55. Pollock, M. L. Submaximal and maximal working capacity of elite distance runners. *Ann. N.Y. Acad. Sci.*, 301:30–44, 1977.

56. Pugh, L. G. C. Oxygen uptake in track and treadmill running with observations on the effect of air resistance. *J. Physiol.*, 207:825–835, 1970.

57. Rose, K. I., J. E. Bousser and K. H. Cooper. Serum enzymes after marathon running. *J. Appl. Physiol.*, 29:355–357, 1970.

58. Rowell, L. B. Circulation. *Med. Sci. Sports*, 1:15–22, 1969.

59. Rowell, L. B. and others. Splanchnic removal of lactate and pyruvate during prolonged exercise in man. *J. Appl. Physiol.*, 21:1773–1783, 1966.

60. Rowell, L. B., H. J. Marx, R. A. Bruce, R. D. Conn and J. Kusumi. Reductions in cardiac output central blood volume with thermal stress in normal men during exercise. *J. Clin. Invest.*, 45:1801–1816, 1966.

61. Rowell, L. B., H. L. Taylor, Y. Wang and W. S. Carlson. Saturation of arterial blood with oxygen during maximal exercise. *J. Appl. Physiol.*, 19:284–286, 1964.

62. Rowell, L. B., J. A. Murray, G. L. Brengelmann and K. K. Kranning II. Human cardiovascular adjustments to rapid changes in skin temperature during exercise. *Circulat. Res.*, In Press.

63. Rowell, L. R., E. J. Masoro and M. J. Spencer. Splanchnic metabolism in exercising man. *J. Appl. Physiol.*, 20:1032–1037, 1965.

64. Rowell, L. R., E. J. Masoro and M. J. Spencer. Splanchnic metabolism in exercising man. *J. Appl. Physiol.*, 20:1032–1037, 1965.

65. Saltin, B. Metabolic fundamentals in exercise. *Med. Sci. Sports*, 5:137–146, 1973.

66. Saltin, B. and J. Karlsson. Muscle glycogen utilization during work of different intensities. *Muscle Metabolism During Exercise*, B. Pernow and B. Saltin, ed. New York: Plenum Press, 11:289–300, 1971.

67. Saltin, B. and J. Stenberg. Circulatory responses to prolonged severe exercise. *J. Appl. Physiol.*, 19:833–838, 1964.

68. Shephard, R. H. Effect of pulmonary diffusing capacity on exercise tolerance. *J. Appl. Physiol.*, 12:487–488, 1958.

69. Siegel, A. J., L. M. Silverman and B. L. Holman. Elevated creatine kinase MB isoenzyme levels in marathon runners. *JAMA* 246, :2049–2051, 1981.

70. Wahren, J., P. Felig, R. Hendler and G. Ahlborg. Glucose and amino acid metabolism during recovery after exercise. *J. Appl. Physiol.*, 34:838–845, 1973.

71. Wyndham, C. H., M. C. Kew, R. Kok, I. Bersohn and N. B. Strydom. Serum enzyme changes in unacclimatized and acclimatized men under severe heat stress. *J. Appl. Physiol.*, 37:695–698, 1974.

72. Wyndham, C. H. and N. B. Strydom. The danger of an inadequate water intake during marathon running. *S. Afr. Med. J.*, 43:893–896, 1969.

CHAPTER 3

Nutrition: Eating to Succeed

Aside from the limits imposed by heredity and the physical improvements associated with training, no single factor can play a greater role in optimizing performance than diet. Despite the wealth of published information dealing with "proper nutrition," few efforts have been made to describe the nutritional needs and best dietary regimen for the distance runner. Most distance runners have at one time searched for the "magic food" that would produce a winning performance. Unfortunately, most efforts to manipulate diet have been prompted by suggestions from more successful performers, poorly designed research studies, invalid commercial advertising claims, and the misinterpretation of facts. The following discussion will take an objective look at the body's nutrient needs and present the more recent research findings which have direct bearing on running performance.

NUTRIENT STATUS OF MUSCLE

Discussions in the preceding chapters pointed out that the energy used for all cellular operations is derived from the splitting of a powerful chemical compound known as adenosine triphosphate, or ATP. The energy stored in the ATP molecule is obtained from such fuels as carbohydrates, fats, and protein. The energy needed to make the muscle fibers shorten cannot be obtained directly from fuels like sugar and fat, since they release only small quantities of energy when they are broken down. Instead, each cell uses the energy stored in ATP as the immediate energy for its operation. Without carbohydrates and fats, however, the muscle cannot maintain adequate levels of ATP. Since the mid-1930s we have known that both carbohydrate and fat contribute the primary energy for endurance exercise. Though protein may contribute 6 to 9 percent of the energy during a long run of 20 miles or more, it is not considered a limiting factor in running performance.

As noted earlier, the fraction of energy derived from carbohydrates during distance running depends on a number of factors including running speed, physical conditioning, environmental temperature, and the preexercise diet (9, 27). Early studies by Christensen and Hansen (9) demonstrated that subjects who were fed diets rich in carbohydrates tended to derive a larger fraction of their energy from carbohydrate during exercise. Although the underlying cause for this shift toward a higher carbohydrate use following a diet rich in carbohydrates has not been fully explained, this diet regimen may inhibit the use of fat. Since depletion of muscle and liver glycogen limits performance during distance running, one might question the wisdom of eating a high-carbohydrate diet, which accelerates the combustion of glycogen (45). This apparent disadvantage is probably offset by the enlarged glycogen reserves that result from the carbohydrate diet, a point to which we will return later.

Blood glucose also serves as a major contributor to the carbohydrate pool. At rest, the uptake of glucose accounts for less than 10 percent of the total energy used by muscles (1). During steady running, however, the net glucose uptake by the leg muscles may increase 10 to 20 times the resting level (49). As the duration of exercise is extended, the fraction of energy derived from blood glucose grows and may account for 75 to 90 percent of the muscles' carbohydrate use (49). This large drain on blood glucose necessitates a concomitant increase in liver glucose output to lessen the risk of hypoglycemia. Since the liver is the major contributor of glucose to blood, the increased demands by muscular activity rapidly reduce liver glycogen stores. During four hours of slow running at 50 percent of Vo_2 max, 75 percent of a runner's liver glycogen may be removed (25, 48). As a result, runners who compete in races lasting three or more hours may become hypoglycemic (38).

As we will discuss later, one of the major adaptations to endurance running is developing a greater capacity to use fat as an energy source (30). Marathon runners, for example, get more than 75 percent of their energy from fat oxidation during 60 minutes of running at 70 percent Vo_2 max (22). Since fat serves as an alternative source of energy for the muscles, factors that enhance its use during distance running will spare muscle glycogen and improve endurance performance (14, 15).

Optimal distance running performance is strongly influenced by the availability of both carbohydrate and fat. Nutrition plays a central role in both the storage and use of these substances. Though stores of body fat exceed the amounts needed for the longest distance races even in the runner with just 4 or 5 percent fat, carbohydrate (glycogen) reserves in the liver and muscles are limited and may not be able to accommodate the requirements of races lasting two to four hours. The distance runner must focus on the intake of carbohydrates to replace tissue glycogen used during training and to promote glycogen storage prior to competition.

DIETARY CARBOHYDRATES AND TRAINING

Early studies demonstrated that when men ate a diet containing a normal amount of carbohydrates, about 55 percent of total calories, their muscles stored approximately 100 millimoles of glycogen per kilogram of muscle (5). Diets low in carbohydrate, containing less than 15 percent of calories, resulted in storage of only 53 millimoles per kilogram of muscle, whereas a rich carbohydrate diet produced a muscle glycogen content of 205. When these subjects were asked to exercise to exhaustion at 75 percent Vo_2 max, their exercise times were proportional to the amount of glycogen present in the muscles before the test (Table 3-1). Carbohydrate in the diet clearly has a direct influence on muscle glycogen stores and the runner's ability to train and compete.

Studies from Scandinavia in the mid-1960s indicated that muscle glycogen was restored to muscle within 24 hours after exhaustive exercise if athletes ate a rich carbohydrate diet (4). Continuing this diet for two additional days elevated the glycogen to twice the preexercise level.

More recent studies have shown that glycogen replacement and storage is not so simple. We have observed that seven days after a marathon race in which muscle glycogen dropped from 196 to 26 millimoles per kilogram of muscle, replacement processes had restored the glycogen only to 125 (46) (Figure 3-1). We have recorded similarly slow glycogen restorage after exhaustive treadmill running.

This delayed recovery of muscle glycogen seems to be characteristic

TABLE 3-1. Effects of dietary carbohydrate on muscle glycogen stores and endurance performance.

CHO INTAKE (GM/24 HR)	GLYCOGEN CONTENT (MMOL/KG MUSCLE)	EXERCISE TIME TO EXHAUSTION (MIN)
100 gm	53 mmol/kg	57 min
280 gm	100 mmol/kg	114 min
500 gm	205 mmol/kg	167 min

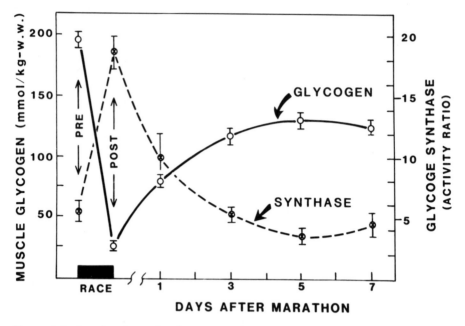

Figure 3-1. Levels of muscle glycogen and synthase activity ratios before and for seven days following a marathon (46). Note that when muscle glycogen is low (post-marathon), the stimulus for glycogen storage (synthase) is high.

of distance running, since it does not occur after exhaustive cycling or swimming. Although the cause has not been fully explained, the muscle trauma which occurs in distance running may inhibit the mechanisms normally responsible for the uptake and storage of glucose by the muscle.

Although the amount of carbohydrate in the diet determines, to a large extent, the rate of muscle glycogen storage, there are also special enzymes, glycogen synthase, that facilitate the conversion of glucose molecules into glycogen. The activity of glycogen synthase is very high when the muscle glycogen is low. The enzymes are promoting glycogen storage. As the glycogen reserves begin to fill up, the synthase activity declines, lessening the drive for further glycogen formation. Even in the presence of a high glycogen synthase activity, muscle glycogen replacement is slow and incomplete unless the dietary intake is rich in carbohydrate.

Figure 3-2 demonstrates that when runners trained heavily and ate low-carbohydrate diets (40 percent of total calories), they had a day-to-day decline in muscle glycogen. When the same subjects ate high-car-

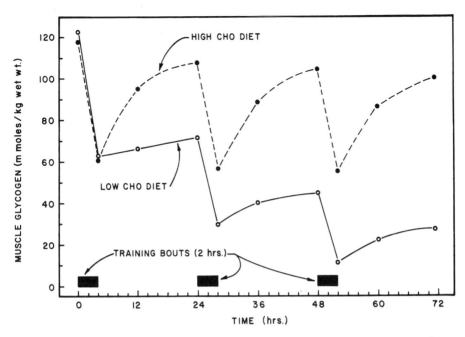

Figure 3-2. Muscle glycogen content of the vastus lateralis (thigh) during three successive days of heavy training with diets with caloric compositions of 40 percent carbohydrate (Low CHO) and 70 percent carbohydrate (High CHO).

bohydrate diets (70 percent of total calories) of equal caloric content, muscle glycogen replacement was nearly complete within the 22 hours separating the training bouts. The runners perceived the training as much less difficult when they ate the high-carbohydrate diet. Actually, few of the runners could complete the full two hours of effort on the third day of the low-carbohydrate diet when muscle glycogen was very low.

In the hours between training sessions the subjects were required to consume calories that equaled their calculated total daily expenditures of approximately 4,000 kilocalories per day. Since many of these calories in the high-carbohydrate diet came from such complex carbohydrates as pasta, bread, and potatoes, the volume of food required was usually more than the runners wished to eat.

When subjects eat only as much food as they desire, *ad libitum*, they often underestimate their caloric needs and fail to consume enough carbohydrate to compensate for that used during training or competition. This discrepancy between glycogen use and carbohydrate intake may explain, in part, why some runners become chronically fatigued and need 48 hours or longer to completely restore muscle glycogen (41). Runners who train exhaustively on successive days must consume a diet rich in carbohydrates to reduce the heavy, tired feeling associated with a deficit in muscle glycogen.

Although athletes need supplemental carbohydrates during intense training periods, untrained individuals who consume excessive carbohydrates under normal conditions may elevate their plasma triglyceride levels, which has been associated with a high risk of heart disease (36, 39). In the endurance runner, supplemental carbohydrates restore muscle and liver glycogen rather than form blood fats.

Marathoners have quite low blood triglycerides, averaging less than 50 milligrams per 100 milliliters of blood, compared to nonmarathoners of similar ages, whose blood triglycerides average 80 to 120 milligrams per 100 milliliters of blood (22, 16). This is true even though the marathoners' diets are composed of 70 percent carbohydrate.

The type of carbohydrate, simple or complex, also has a bearing on the formation of blood cholesterol and other fat-related molecules (glycerides). When subjects eat simple sugars such as glucose or sucrose, serum cholesterol and glyceride concentrations increase more than they do when subjects eat the same number of calories in the form of starch (32). Since the simple sugars are absorbed rather quickly, their ingestion results in hyperglycemia, a sudden rise in blood glucose, which overloads the cells' energy-producing systems (Embden-Meyerhof pathways), favoring the formation of blood fats and cholesterol. Complex carbohydrates like starch produce smaller rises in blood glucose and cholesterol.

Since these observations were confined to relatively inactive subjects, it is speculative to suggest that the same patterns will occur among trained distance runners. Nevertheless, endurance-trained athletes generally demonstrate a smaller rise in blood glucose and a lower insulin response even to a feeding of sucrose (Figure 3-3). Endurance athletes divert the majority of carbohydrate foods to glycogen storage with little disturbance in their blood lipid (fat and cholesterol) profiles.

In light of the differences in simple and complex carbohydrates, we might anticipate differences in the rate and quantity of glycogen formation following diets rich in either glucose or starch. Tests of this theory, however, are inconclusive. We studied six men who were fed diets principally composed of either simple sugars or starches (70 percent of calories) for two days following exhaustive exercise (16). No significant difference in muscle glycogen formation was found between the two diets, although there was a trend toward greater glycogen storage when the men consumed starch. Recent studies, on the other hand, have shown that simple carbohydrates facilitate glycogen storage to a greater extent than complex carbohydrates (44). In light of these conflicting reports, the

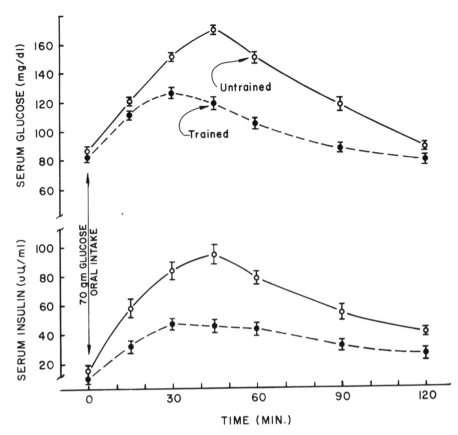

Figure 3-3. Oral glucose tolerance curves in trained distance runners and untrained subjects. Each subject was given 70 grams of glucose at the beginning (0 minutes). Serum glucose and insulin responses demonstrate that the trained runners can manage blood glucose better than the untrained subjects.

preferential use of either simple or complex carbohydrates for muscle glycogen replacement is unclear.

DIET BEFORE COMPETITION

In the preceding discussion we have established that different diets can markedly influence muscle glycogen stores and that endurance performance depends in part on the glycogen content at the onset of exercise. Based on muscle biopsy studies in the mid-1960s, a plan was formed to help runners store the maximum amount of glycogen possible, a process known as glycogen loading (5).

The plan proposed that runners prepare for endurance competition by completing an exhaustive training run seven days before the event. For the following three days, runners should eat fat and protein almost exclusively to deprive the muscles of carbohydrate and drive up glycogen synthase. The athlete should then eat a rich carbohydrate diet for the remaining days. The intensity and volume of training during the six-day period should be markedly reduced to prevent additional consumption of muscle glycogen and to maximize liver and muscle glycogen reserves.

While this regimen has been shown to elevate muscle glycogen to twice the normal level, it is somewhat impractical for the runners. During the three days of low carbohydrate intake, runners generally find it difficult to train, are often unable to perform mental tasks, are irritable, and show the usual signs of low blood sugar. In addition, exhaustive "depletion" runs performed seven days before the competition are of little training value and may impair glycogen storage rather than enhance it. These runs also expose the runners to possible injury or overtraining when they are already susceptible to breakdown.

Considering these limitations, we have proposed that the "depletion run" and low carbohydrate aspects of this regimen be eliminated, and that the runner simply reduce the training intensity and eat a normal mixed diet containing 55 percent of its calories from carbohydrates, until the final three days before the competition. In the 48 to 72 hours before the race, training should be reduced to a daily warm-up of one to three easy miles, and the runner should consume a rich carbohydrate diet. Following this plan, glycogen is elevated to 200 millimoles per kilogram of muscle, a level equal to that attained with the earlier regimen (16, 45).

Diet also plays an important role in preparing the liver for the demands of distance running. Studies have shown that liver glycogen stores will decrease rapidly when an individual is deprived of carbohydrates for only 24 hours, even when at rest. As a result of strenuous exercise lasting 60 minutes, liver glycogen was found to decrease from 244 to 111 millimoles per kilogram of muscle, a 55 percent reduction (33). In combination with a low carbohydrate diet, hard training may empty the liver glycogen stores. A single carbohydrate meal, however, will quickly restore liver glycogen to normal (33). Clearly, a rich carbohydrate diet in the days preceding competition will insure a large liver glycogen reserve and minimize the risk of hypoglycemia during distance races.

Since water is stored in the body at a rate of roughly 2.6 grams of water for each gram of glycogen, the increase or decrease in tissue glycogen generally produces a change in body weight of from one to three pounds. One of the most practical ways to monitor your muscle-liver glycogen stores is to note your early morning weight, recorded immediately after rising and emptying the bladder and before eating breakfast. Any sudden drop in weight may reflect a failure to replace glycogen, or a deficit in body water, or both.

The precompetition meal should be taken three to four hours before the race and should contain few fats and proteins since they digest slowly and do not provide fuels that are readily used during the event. A light carbohydrate meal of cereal, toast, and juice should be eaten since it digests quickly and will leave a minimum of residue in the stomach.

To this point, it would appear that carbohydrates can do no harm; they replace muscle and liver glycogen, maintain blood glucose, and provide the primary fuel for endurance performance. The one time that the runner should not consume carbohydrates is during the final 60 to 90 minutes before a long hard run. As early as 1939, studies showed that such feedings temporarily elevate blood glucose and insulin (6, 8). Since insulin transports glucose out of the blood and into the body tissues,

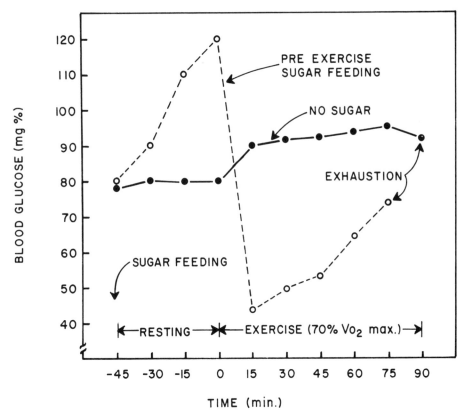

Figure 3-4. Effects of feedings of 70 grams of glucose, taken 45 minutes before the onset of exercise, on blood glucose during 90 minutes of activity.

elevated blood insulin at the beginning of exercise results in a rapid up-take of glucose by the muscles with a sudden drop in the sugar content of the blood.

Figure 3-4 illustrates that blood glucose declines rapidly within the first 15 minutes of exercise when sugar is consumed 45 minutes before exercise (14, 29). Elevated blood glucose and insulin levels at the onset of exercise also tend to suppress the liver's normal release of glucose, making it difficult for the body to quickly readjust the glucose after it has fallen to the low levels seen at 15 to 45 minutes of exercise. Although the subjects seldom experience obvious symptoms of low blood sugar, they use greater amounts of muscle glycogen and become exhausted ear-lier as a result of the preexercise sugar feeding (14). The key here is to ingest a light carbohydrate meal roughly two hours before exercise so that blood insulin and glucose have adequate time to return to normal levels.

Since the muscle and liver glycogen stores are limited, encouraging the muscles to use fat in the form of free fatty acids (FFA) as an al-ternative fuel could reduce the threat of exhaustion. Unfortunately, eat-ing fat does not stimulate the muscles to burn fat. Fatty foods only tend to elevate plasma triglycerides, complex fat molecules that must be brok-en down to free fatty acids before they can be used to produce energy.

Aside from endurance training, the only known stimulus to increase free fatty acids use is to elevate the concentration in blood. Laboratory studies have demonstrated that when the blood levels of free fatty acids are elevated following the injection of heparin, a anticoagulant that pro-hibits the clotting of blood, exercising muscles tend to use more fat and spare their glycogen reserves (14). The amount of glycogen used during 30 minutes of treadmill running was reduced by 40 percent when the blood free fatty acids were first elevated using the anticoagulant drug.

Dietary attempts to elevate plasma free fatty acids have been rela-tively unsuccessful (34). Some foods that contain caffeine, a stimulant to the nervous system, promote fat use and improve performance in pro-longed, exhaustive exercise when consumed an hour before exercise (15, 35). Caffeine ingestion of four to five milligrams per kilogram of body weight lessens the subjective feelings of effort during the exercise, which is similar to the effect of amphetamines. Twenty percent of the individ-uals tested experienced a negative reaction to caffeine, with no improve-ments in performance.

Despite the potential performance advantages offered by drinking tea or coffee, the ethical use of these items is questionable since they offer an unnatural advantage. Though international governing bodies like the International Olympic Committee have attempted to ban the use of such stimulants, policing their use is difficult and impractical.

FEEDINGS DURING DISTANCE RUNNING

Studies conducted early in this century noted the occurrence of low blood glucose during exhaustive long-distance running and cycling. Although it seems reasonable to assume that such a decrease in blood glucose might contribute to the sensations of fatigue, recent studies have suggested that hypoglycemia may not be directly to blame (26). Although 142 minutes of exhaustive exercise dropped blood glucose from normal levels of 5.0 millimoles per liter of blood to 2.5 millimoles in 30 to 40 percent of the subjects, the intake of glucose during exercise did not consistently delay exhaustion or alter the subjective sensations of exertion.

In contrast, several recent studies have noted improvements in performance when the subjects were given carbohydrate feedings during exercise lasting one to four hours (15, 23, 31). Although none of these studies noticed any differences in performance during the early phase of the exercise when carbohydrates were given, the subjects were able to perform better over the final stage of the experiments. We recently observed that repeated carbohydrate feedings during four hours of cycling reduced muscle glycogen depletion and improved the ability to sprint at the end of the activity. Carbohydrate feedings during exercise prevent a premature exhaustion of muscle glycogen. Elevating blood glucose via carbohydrate feedings enables the muscles to obtain more of their energy from the available glucose, lowering the demand placed on muscle glycogen. The runner can, therefore, go longer before the muscle glycogen stores become exhausted.

One may wonder why carbohydrate feedings **during exercise** do not produce the same hypoglycemic effects observed with the **preexercise feedings.** As can be seen in Figure 3-5, sugar feedings given during exercise result in smaller rises in both blood glucose and insulin, lessening the threat of an overreaction and a sudden drop in blood glucose. The cause for this finer control on blood glucose during exercise may be related to the fact that the muscle fibers become more permeable, allowing glucose to enter the muscle with the aid of less insulin. As a result, less insulin is released from the pancreas and the rise in blood glucose is smaller.

The only complication associated with sugar feedings during distance running is a delay in absorption. Before sugar solutions can be absorbed into the blood, they must pass through the stomach and into the small intestine. Since most carbohydrate solutions are held in the stomach for a short period, the first traces of any sugar solution do not appear in the blood for five to seven minutes after consumption (12). The delay is caused by the stomach's attempts to dilute the solution and offer the intestine fluids that can be rapidly absorbed. As we will discuss later

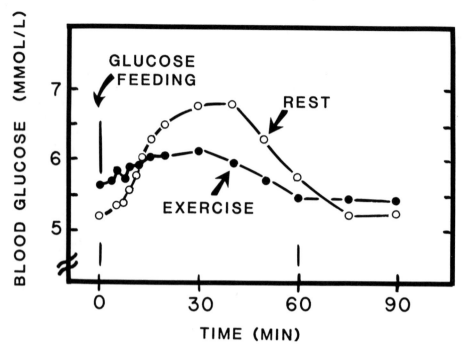

Figure 3-5. Changes in blood glucose and insulin following a sugar feeding of 70 grams under resting and exercise conditions. Note the smaller rise in both glucose and insulin when the subjects were running.

in this chapter, there are a number of factors to consider when selecting a carbohydrate drink during distance running.

EATING HABITS OF THE RUNNER[1]

Although we have learned a great deal from our research regarding the nutritional needs of runners before, during, and even after exercise, we know little about what they **actually** eat. To gain a little insight into their real practices, we had a group of runners record everything they ate and drank over a three-day period. Information was obtained in training periods and during the three days before a marathon. Our sample included athletes with a broad range of abilities, from Bill Rodgers, a 2

---

[1]This information originally appeared in *The Runner*, D. L. Costill and H. Higdon, May 1982, pp. 66–68.

hour:9 second marathoner, to others with personal records of 3 hours:45 seconds to 3 hours:50 seconds. Their daily mileages varied from a high of 19 to a low of three, and their training paces ranged from six minutes per mile to Tom Osler's 13 minutes per mile. In addition to Rodgers and Osler, other well-known participants were Martha Cooksey, Kiki Sweigert, Kenny Moore, and Ted Corbitt.

We analyzed each respondent's diet to determine the percentages of fats, proteins, and carbohydrates consumed. We also looked at whether the diets provided the Recommended Daily Allowance (RDA) of vitamins and minerals. Finally, we tried to match the number of calories consumed with calories used each day.

There was little difference between what elite and average runners ate. Diet could not be used as a single predictor of performance. Although specific items in the diets varied—from pork chops to pasta, from collard greens to candy bars—differences blurred over a period of days when food was analyzed for its percentages of fat, proteins, and carbohydrates, or amounts of vitamins and minerals. One interesting finding was how closely runners came to meeting the RDA, the standard considered necessary for good health.

Our runners ate diets containing 50 percent carbohydrates, 36 percent fats, and 14 percent proteins. In light of the need for a high carbohydrate diet when training for distance running, we might at first consider the carbohydrate intake of these runners to be low. These runners actually ate more then enough carbohydrate to meet the energy needed for training. Since their total calorie intake was nearly 50 percent higher than would be expected for individuals of similar size (145 pounds), their total carbohydrate intake was well above average (Table 3-2).

We also wanted to ascertain that their diets contained sufficient vitamins and minerals to guarantee good health and maximum performance. Some vitamins are essential in the production of energy and the maintenance of the body's normal operation. Without vitamins such as the vitamin B complex, one might have trouble converting carbohydrates into ATP or forming glycogen. These runners consumed adequate vitamins and minerals to at least equal the RDA, which contains a built-in cushion. Unless a runner's vitamin intake falls well below the RDA for an extended period, no effects on performance would be expected. Though diets rich in simple carbohydrates tend to be deficient in some of the B complex vitamins, only two runners appeared to consume too little vitamin B_{12}.

Although some experts have suggested that we need 1,000 milligrams of vitamin C per day, the RDA is only 60, well below that consumed by the runners in our survey. Most of the runners did not use vitamin supplements, contrary to some recent surveys about the habits of runners. Our participants also obtained more than adequate amounts

TABLE 3-2. A comparison of the 22 runners' diets with the RDA (Recommended Daily Allowance). Figures shown in parentheses represent estimates of the average values in the American diet, which may or may not be healthy. Even where the figure is low (as with folic acid and vitamin E), that does not necessarily suggest a deficiency since the RDA is somewhat arbitrary with a large safety factor.

DIET COMPOSITION	RUNNER'S AVERAGE	RDA
Calories (kcal/day)	3,012	(2,000)
Carbohydrate (gm)	375	(250)
Protein (gm)	112	(70)
Saturated fats (gm)	42	(26)
Unsaturated fats (gm)	64	(54)
Total fat (gm)	122	(66–100)
Cholesterol (mg)	377	(300)
Fiber (gm)	7	(3–6)
Vitamin A (IU)	10,814	5,000
Vitamin B_1 (mg)	1.9	1.3
Vitamin B_2 (mg)	2.5	1.6
Vitamin B_6 (mg)	2.2	2
Vitamin B_{12} (ug)	3.8	3
Folic acid (mg)	0.23	0.4
Niacin (mg)	27.3	16
Pantothenic acid (mg)	5.3	7.5
Vitamin C (mg)	205	55
Vitamin E (mg)	5.2	14
Iron (mg)	25	14
Potassium (gm)	4.3	2.5
Calcium (gm)	1.3	1.0
Magnesium (gm)	0.4	0.3
Phosphorus (gm)	2.0	1.0
Sodium (gm)	2.6	(6.0)

of minerals, including iron, as well as ample fiber, another item associated with good health.

In the last three days before a marathon, our subjects changed both their training and eating habits. Where previously they had averaged 8.5 miles per day, they reduced their daily mileage to 2.3. In an apparent attempt to load their muscles with glycogen, the runners increased their daily caloric intake from 3,012 kilocalories during training to a premarathon average of 3,730. Several ate more than 5,000 kilocalories, nearly twice their rate of caloric expenditure during that period.

Such overeating might hurt their performances. Since the marathoners had reduced their mileages, they were burning only about 2,526 kilocalories per day, while eating 3,730. The result was a daily surplus of 1,204 kilocalories that might have resulted in the storage of one extra pound of unnecessary and unproductive fat (3,600 kilocalories equals one pound of fat). From the standpoint of marathon performance, however, it is probably better to eat a bit too much food, principally carbohydrates, than to risk not being fully loaded with muscle and liver glycogen.

FLUID BALANCE

The ability to lose body heat during distance running depends, for the most part, on the formation and evaporation of sweat. The amount of sweat lost during exercise depends on one's running pace, body size, and the environmental heat stress. Running in warm weather may evoke sweat losses in excess of two quarts per hour (21). Despite efforts to drink fluids during a marathon, sweating and the loss of water in the air may reduce body water content by 13 to 14 percent.

Studies have shown that dehydrated runners are quite intolerant of exercise and heat stress (10). Distance runners are forced to slow their pace by 2 percent for each percentage of loss in body weight due to dehydration. Both heart rate and body temperature are elevated during exercise when the runner is dehydrated more than 2 percent of body weight.

The impact of dehydration on the cardiovascular system is quite predictable. Plasma volume is lost and the ability to provide adequate blood flow to the skin and muscle is reduced. Under such circumstances, it is common for subjects to collapse, showing the usual symptoms of heat exhaustion. It is difficult to understand how some athletes tolerate several hours of hard running in warm weather. In addition to the body water lost during long runs, many nutrients are known to escape (47). The following discussion will examine the effects of heavy sweating on body water and the mineral composition of body tissues.

Human sweat has been described as a "filtrate of plasma," since it contains many of the items present in the water portion of blood, including sodium chloride, potassium, magnesium, and calcium. However, even though sweat tastes salty, it actually contains far fewer minerals than other body fluids. Sweat is considered hypotonic, meaning it is a very dilute version of body fluids.

Sodium and chloride are the ions primarily responsible for maintaining the water content of the blood. Table 3-3 shows that the concentrations of sodium and chloride in sweat are roughly one third those found in plasma and five times those found in muscle. The ionic concentration of sweat may vary markedly between individuals and is strongly

TABLE 3-3. Electrolyte concentrations and osmolality in sweat, muscle, plasma.

| | ELECTROLYTES (mEq/LITER) | | | | OSMOLALITY (mOsm/LITER) |
	Na+	Cl−	K+	Mg++	
SWEAT	40–60	30–50	4–5	1.5–5	80–185
PLASMA	140	101	4	1.5	302
MUSCLE	9	6	162	31	302

Na^+ = sodium; Cl^- = chloride; K^+ = potassium; Mg^{++} = magnesium
osmolality—number of particles contained in a solution

influenced by the rate of sweating and the runner's state of heat acclimatization.

At the high rates of sweating reported during distance running, sweat contains relatively high levels of sodium and chloride, but little potassium, calcium, and magnesium. A sweat loss of nearly nine pounds, representing a 5.8 percent reduction in body weight, resulted in sodium, potassium, chloride, and magnesium losses of 155, 16, 137, and 13 milliequivalents, respectively (18). Based on estimates of the runner's body mineral contents, these losses would have lowered the body's sodium and chloride content by roughly 5 to 7 percent. At the same time, total body levels of potassium and magnesium, two ions principally confined to the inside of the cells, decreased by less than 1.2 percent.

The other major source of electrolyte loss is routine urine production. In addition to cleaning the blood of cellular waste products, the kidneys also control the body's water and electrolyte content. Under normal conditions, kidneys excrete about 1.7 ounces of water per hour. During exercise, however, blood flow to the kidneys decreases, and urine production drops to near zero. Consequently, electrolyte losses by this avenue are quite diminished during exercise.

There is another facet of the kidneys' management of electrolytes. If an individual eats 250 milliequivalents of sodium and chloride per day, normally the kidneys will excrete an equal amount of those electrolytes to keep their levels constant. Heavy sweating and dehydration, however, cause the release of aldosterone, a hormone from the adrenal gland that stimulates the kidneys to reabsorb sodium and chloride.

Since the body loses more water than electrolytes during heavy sweating, the concentration of these minerals in the body fluids rises. That means that instead of showing a drop in plasma electrolyte concentrations, there is actually an increase. Although this may seem confusing, the point is that during periods of heavy sweating, the need to replace body water is greater than the need to replace electrolytes.

There are obvious benefits from drinking fluids during prolonged exercise, especially during hot weather. Drinking will minimize dehydration, lessen the rise in internal body temperature, and reduce the stress placed on the circulatory system (42). Warm fluids near body temperature provide some protection against overheating, but cold fluids seem to enhance body cooling. It takes some of the deep body heat to warm a cold drink to the temperature of the gut.

The fluid composition of the drink has an effect on the rate that it empties from the stomach. Since little exchange of water occurs directly from the stomach, the fluids must pass into the intestine before entering the blood. In the intestine, absorption is rapid and unaffected by exercise, provided that the activity does not exceed 75 percent of the runner's Vo_2 max (13, 28). Many factors affect the rate at which the stomach will empty, including its volume, temperature, acidity, and osmolality (13).

Although large volumes of up to 600 milliliters empty faster from the stomach than small portions, runners generally find it uncomfortable to run with a nearly full stomach, as this interferes with breathing (13). Drinking three to six ounces at 10 to 15 minute intervals tends to minimize this effect. We have, however, observed dramatically different rates of stomach-emptying among individual runners. The suggestions offered here are based on averages and may not be appropriate for some individuals.

Cold drinks have been found to empty more rapidly from the stomach than warm fluids. Although fluids at refrigerator temperatures of 38 to 40 degrees Fahrenheit may reduce the temperature of the stomach from 99 to 35 or 40 degrees Fahrenheit, they do not appear to cause stomach cramps. Such stomach distress occurs more often when the volume of the drink is unusually large. Cold fluids also may upset the normal electrical activity of the heart, threatening the health of the runner. It is true that some electrocardiographic changes have been reported in a few individuals following the ingestion of ice-cold drinks (33 to 35 degrees Fahrenheit), but the medical significance of these changes has not been established. It seems that drinking cold fluids during distance running poses no threat to a normal heart.

Another factor known to regulate the rate at which the stomach empties is the drink's osmolality, the number of dissolved substances in the solution. Drink osmolalities above 200 mOsm per liter tend move out of the stomach more slowly than those below that level (13). The addition of electrolytes and other ingredients that raise the osmolality slows the rate of water replacement. Since dehydration is the primary concern during hot weather running, water seems to be the preferred fluid. Under less stressful conditions where overheating and large sweat losses are not as threatening, runners might use liquid feedings to supplement their carbohydrate supplies.

A number of "sports drinks" containing carbohydrates are currently on the market, grossing more than $100 million each year. Unfortunately, many of the claims used to sell these drinks are based on misinterpreted and often inaccurate information. Electrolytes, for example, have long been touted as important ingredients in sports drinks. But research shows that such claims are unfounded. A single meal adequately replaces the electrolytes lost during exercise. The body needs water to bring its concentration of the electrolytes back into balance. While the importance of minerals such as sodium, potassium, and magnesium should not be underestimated, blood and muscle biopsy studies have shown that heavy sweating has little or no effect on water and electrolyte concentrations in body fluids (18, 19, 20).

One might wonder if the intake of too much water could overdilute the blood electrolytes, leading to a body deficit. Apparently not. Even marathoners who lose six to nine pounds of sweat and drink nearly a half-gallon of water retain normal plasma sodium, chloride, and potassium concentrations. Marathoners and ultra-marathoners who ran 15 to 25 miles per day in warm weather and did not season their food, did not develop electrolyte deficiencies. Even when we fed test subjects only 30 percent as much potassium as they normally consumed and made them dehydrate by losing seven to eight pounds of sweat every day for eight days, body electrolytes remained unchanged (2, 37).

Some experts have suggested that during ultra-marathon running of 50 miles or more some individuals may experience unusually low blood sodium levels. A case study of two runners who collapsed after an ultra-marathon race in 1983 revealed that they had blood sodium values of 123 and 118 milliequivalents per liter of blood, remarkably lower than the normal values of 135 to 148. One of the runners experienced a grand mal seizure; the other man became disoriented and confused.

Although the cause of these aftereffects is unclear, the initial diagnosis tends to implicate the lack of body sodium. An examination of the runners' fluid intake (21 to 24 liters) and estimates of their sodium intake (224 to 145 milliequivalents) during the run suggested that they diluted their body sodium levels by consuming fluids that contained little sodium. Nevertheless, our studies during the marathon and exercise bouts lasting up to six hours suggests that electrolytes are not an essential ingredient for sports drinks.

There is evidence to support putting some carbohydrates in sports drinks, including several types of sugar (23, 31). Structurally, the simplest forms of sugar are the monosaccharides, glucose, and fructose. While even small amounts of glucose tend to slow the emptying of the stomach, small amounts of fructose can be used without inhibiting the stomach's action (24). Aside from this point, there is little difference whether the carbohydrate in the drink is glucose or fructose, since both take five to seven minutes before they first appear in the blood (12).

In our early studies, we suggested that the runner's drink should have less than 2.5 grams of sugar per 100 milliliters of water to speed its removal from the stomach (13). Unfortunately, this small amount of carbohydrate contributes little to the energy reserves. Even if you drank 200 milliliters of that drink every 15 minutes during a long run, you would only take in 20 grams of carbohydrate per hour. Our recent studies suggest that to improve performance with the aid of a carbohydrate drink, the runner must consume at least 50 grams of sugar per hour.

Most of the sports drinks on the market contain only about 0.6 grams of carbohydrate per ounce. A runner would have to drink a half-gallon of these drinks every hour to get enough carbohydrates to do any good. Since we know that most runners drink only nine to 15 ounces per hour during long runs, it would take a drink containing 3.8 grams of carbohydrate per ounce to be of any value. Such a rich mixture, however, may be delayed in the stomach, draw water from the stomach's lining, and cause an uncomfortable feeling of fullness.

Recent technological advances in the manufacture of carbohydrates have made it possible to combine many glucose molecules into one large molecule called a "glucose polymer." Using it, a drink does not have such a negative effect on the stomach and replaces both water and carbohydrates. The best mixture of carbohydrates for the runner's drink would be one containing small amounts of fructose and a sizeable quantity of the glucose polymer.

Finally, while no one will drink something that does not taste good, we all have different taste preferences. To confuse the issue even further, what tastes good before and after a long, hot run will not necessarily taste good during the race. Recently we conducted a series of taste tests before and after 60 minutes of running to determine what type of drinks runners preferred. Those studies demonstrated that most of the 50 subjects chose a drink with a relatively light flavor which did not have a strong aftertaste. In this regard, nearly all of the commercial sports drinks failed.

So what should the runner drink during the training and competition? Under the extreme stress of hot weather, water is the primary need and the preferred drink. It empties from the stomach with minimal delay, is easy to obtain, and reduces the dehydration associated with heavy sweating. Under cooler conditions, a carbohydrate drink will provide the lift needed for peak performance in events lasting an hour or longer.

It is important to realize that human thirst is a poor indicator of the body's water and electrolyte balance. No matter how efficiently the kidneys do their job, body fluid balance depends on a strong thirst sensation to stimulate fluid intake. Unfortunately, man's drive to replace body fluids is far less effective than that seen in other animals. Burros, for example, will replace a 40-pound body water loss in five to six minutes of continuous drinking, whereas humans who sweat away six to eight pounds are satisfied after drinking only a pint of fluid. If the runner's thirst is used as the only gauge of water need, it would take 12 to 24 hours to replace such a sweat loss. **During exercise and heavy sweating, you should always drink more than your thirst desires.**

SPECIAL DIETS AND SUPPLEMENTS

Athletes are always looking for an edge, something that will give them an advantage. Since the difference between winning and losing can often be measured in fractions of a second, no athlete wants to feel that he or she did not try everything possible to achieve a best performance. Manipulating the diet and taking extra quantities of various vitamins and minerals seem to be relatively harmless methods to make the body work its best. But do these efforts really help?

Vitamins are organic substances necessary for growth and cellular function. Though some vitamins can be produced in small quantities in the body and others stored in the body fat, most must be consumed in the diet (Table 3-4). Vitamins C and B complex, for example, are water soluble, cannot be stored, and must be constantly replenished by the diet. The fat-soluble vitamins (A, D, E, and K) are stored in the liver and fatty tissue of the body and can accumulate during a period of excess intake for use at times when they may not be readily available.

Unfortunately, there is no way to judge vitamin levels, unless a person is deficient in a vitamin. Only then do rather unpleasant symptoms appear. The characteristic sores and loss of vision associated with a deficiency in vitamin B_2 (riboflavin), for example, are rare in our society. Treatment with foods and tablets containing the essential vitamins generally eliminates the symptoms.

The earlier discussion regarding our survey of runners' diets demonstrated that, on the average, the intake of vitamins was equal to or greater than the RDA. Individually, however, a number of the runners were eating diets containing less than the RDA for vitamins B_6, B_{12}, pantothenic acid, and folic acid. When we consider that the levels needed of these vitamins vary in proportion to the number of calories consumed in the diet, things looked even worse. Some of the runners were taking in less than 50 percent of the recommended amount of these vitamins, based on the number of calories they were eating. One explanation for the low levels may be that some of the runners were vegetarians or ate diets low in such animal products as meats, cheese, milk, and eggs, which are the principal sources of B_6, B_{12}, and pantothenic acid.

Even though some runners consumed low levels of certain B vitamins, none of the runners exhibited any symptoms of vitamin B defi-

TABLE 3-4. Dietary sources, functions and daily requirements for selected vitamins for adults

VITAMIN	RECOMMENDED DAILY INTAKE (I.U.)			SOURCE	FUNCTION	SYMPTOMS OF DEFICIENCY
	NON-ATHLETE	STRENGTH ATHLETE	ENDURANCE ATHLETE			
A (I.U.)	5,000	10,000	10,000	Liver, Egg Yolk, Milk	Prevents Eye and Skin Disorders	Night Blindness
B_1 (mg)	1.4	4.6	6–10	Meat, Grains, Milk	Energy Metabolism	Beriberi
B_2 (mg)	1.6	3.0	4.0	Milk, Fish, Meat, Green Vegetables	Energy Metabolism	Mouth & Lip Lesions, Loss of Vision
B_6 (mg)	2.0	2.0	2.0	Bananas, Spinach, Greens	Protein & Glycogen Metabolism	Anemia and Convulsions
Niacin (mg)	18	25	35	Peanut butter, Greens, Fish	Fatty Acid Metabolism	Low Energy Production
B_{12} (ug)	5	10	10	Animal Foods	Energy Metabolism, nervous system function	Anemia, Muscular Weakness
Folic Acid (mg)	0.4	0.4	0.4	Greens, Mushrooms, Liver	Blood Cell Production	Anemia
C (mg)	60	100–200	100–200	Citrus Fruits, Tomatoes	Growth	Scurvy
D (I.U.)	400	400	400	Sunlight, Fish, Eggs	Absorption of Calcium	Rickets
E (I.U.)	20	40	60	Vegetable Oils, Greens	Antioxidant (?)	Unknown

ciencies, such as anemia or unusual fatigue. Despite such assurances, some of the runners were taking vitamin supplements, containing two to five times the amounts recommended by the RDA.

Over the past 40 years a variety of attempts have been made to resolve the question of whether vitamins taken in doses greater than the RDA will enhance performance and produce better health. To state that the research findings showed no benefits of vitamin supplementation would be inaccurate and somewhat misleading. There have been a number of studies that found increased endurance with enormous doses of vitamins C, E, and B complex, but there are far more studies demonstrating that vitamins in excess of the RDA will not improve performance in either strength or endurance activities. Experts generally agree that popping vitamins will not make up for a lack of talent or training or give one an edge over the competition.

As a matter of fact, too much of a good thing can be harmful. Extremely large doses of vitamins A and D may produce some undesirable effects. Large overdoses of vitamin A, for example, may cause a loss of appetite, loss of hair, enlargement of the liver and spleen, swelling over the long bones, and general irritability—scarcely ideal conditions for a good distance runner. We have never seen these symptoms, however, even in athletes taking two to three times the RDA for these vitamins.

All in all, it appears that the RDA values for the various vitamins are about optimal for normal body operations, though possibly on the conservative side. Certainly, there is no convincing evidence to prove that vitamin pills taken to supplement a balanced diet will improve endurance or running performance. Overdoses of vitamins may be of some value, if for some reason you wish to increase the vitamin content of your urine, since that is where most of the excess ends up. Perhaps that is why it is said that athletes have the most expensive urine in the world.

Minerals are the second most widely used diet supplements by athletes. Since perspiration tastes salty, many runners fear a large loss of body salts during periods of heavy sweating. Actually, as we have pointed out, sweat is quite dilute when compared to other body fluids (Table 3-3). There is, however, a wide individual variation in the quantity of electrolytes lost in sweat. Although fewer electrolytes are lost in the sweat of highly trained and heat-acclimatized runners than in untrained individuals, the mineral content of the diet can have an effect on the electrolyte concentration of sweat. A low-salt diet results in a low-salt sweat. The body adjusts the electrolyte content of sweat to keep pace with dietary intake. It seems that even without mineral supplements, the body can get all it needs from the natural minerals in food.

Iron is an essential component of hemoglobin, the oxygen-carrying component of blood, and of myoglobin, the oxygen-transporting pigment of muscle. Since iron deficiency anemia is known to impair endurance performance, it is important to distinguish between true anemia and the plasma volume dilution associated with repeated days of training in warm weather. Training tends to increase the volume of plasma more than the number of red blood cells, producing a drop in hemoglobin concentration with no apparent effect on oxygen transport or endurance.

Several studies have reported that between 36 and 82 percent of female runners are anemic or iron deficient (11, 43). In light of this high frequency of iron deficiency in females, it seems logical to suggest that they include iron-rich foods in their diets. Iron supplementation should be directed by a physician, since prolonged administration of iron can cause an iron overload, a potentially serious condition (7).

During the question and answer periods that often follow my lectures to distance runners, I am frequently asked, "How can a runner diet, lose weight, and train hard at the same time?" The answer is, "You can't." To lose fat the body must be forced to rely more heavily on its fat reserves for energy, while taking in little fuel. This results in a "caloric deficit" and a gradual reduction in the body's fat weight. Though a diet-exercise regimen accelerates the rate of weight loss, it fails to allow for adequate replacement of muscle and liver glycogen stores. As a result, a runner feels heavy, is easily fatigued, and is able to train only at a relatively slow pace and with reduced mileage.

Attempts to lose weight should be scheduled for periods when runners do not intend to prepare for competition. During those periods they can afford to put in the long, slow miles that stimulate the burning of calories, mostly fat. Though exercise aids in losing weight, the only way known to insure the removal of body fat is partial starvation. Too bad it isn't as easy or as enjoyable to get rid of body fat as it is to put it on!

THE WHOLE THING

The preceding discussion has made it clear that proper nutrition can play an important role in distance running performance. The key to success is the availability of carbohydrates for muscle energy, though fat serves as an alternative fuel source and contributes to the energy pool during the long, slower events. Muscle glycogen stores depend on a rich carbohydrate diet, though a complement of all the basic food groups, vitamins, and minerals are essential for peak performance. Repeated days of intense training can result in a slow recovery of muscle glycogen, leading to a chronic state of fatigue. Periods of reduced training and diets supplemented with carbohydrate foods promote good training and the adaptations needed for improvement.

During distance events lasting for several hours, it is important to consume fluids to replace the body water lost in sweat and heavy breathing. Although a variety of minerals are lost in sweat, there is little need to replace them during exercise, since their balance in the body is easily maintained through proper nutrition and the regulation of the kidneys. Inclusion of carbohydrate in the runner's drink appears to maintain blood glucose levels during long events, reduce the risk of muscle glycogen depletion, and improve performance. Unfortunately, the addition of most forms of carbohydrate to the drink tends to slow the stomach's emptying, delaying the delivery of water and carbohydrates to the body. In hot weather, where dehydration and overheating are the major concerns, cold water is the recommended fluid to take while running. The consumption of 3.5 to seven ounces of water every couple of miles during a long, hot run will reduce dehydration, with the least accumulation of fluid in the stomach.

Finally, runners who consume balanced diets have little need for vitamin and mineral supplements. Though there is some evidence to show that female runners may develop an iron deficiency, it is inaccurate to generalize that all runners should supplement their diets with this mineral. While some runners may take less than the RDA for specific vitamins, symptoms of vitamin deficiencies have not been reported.

BIBLIOGRAPHY

1. Anres, R., G. Cader and K. L. Zierler. The quantitatively minor role of carbohydrate in oxidative metabolism by skeletal muscle in intact man in the basal state. Measurements of oxygen and glucose uptake and carbon dioxide and lactate production in the forearm. *J. Clin. Invest*, 35:671–682, 1956.
2. Armstrong, L. E., D. L. Costill, W. J. Fink, M. Hargreaves, I. Nishibata, D. Bassett and D. S. King. Effects of dietary sodium intake on body and muscle potassium content in unacclimatized men during successive days of work in the heat. *Europ. J. Appl. Physiol.*, In Press:
3. Astrand, P. O. Diet and athletic performance. *Fed. Proc.*, 26:1772–1777, 1967.
4. Bergstrom, J. and E. Hultman. The effect of exercise on muscle glycogen and electrolytes in normals. *Scand. J. Clin. Lab. Invest.*, 18:16–20, 1966.
5. Bergstrom, J., L. Hermansen, E. Hultman and et al. Diet, muscle glycogen and physical performance. *Acta Physiol. Scand.*, 71:140–150, 1967.
6. Boje, O. Arbeitshypoglykamie nach Glukoseeingabe. *Skand. Arch Physiol.*, 308–312, 1940.
7. Bunch, T. W. Blood test abnormalities in runners. *Mayo Clin. Proc.*, 55:113–117, 1980.
8. Christensen, E. H. and O. Hansen. Zur Methodik der Respiratorischen Quotient-Bestimmungen in Ruhe und bei Arbeit. *Skand. Arch. Physiol.*, 81:137–143, 1939.
9. Christensen, E. H. and O. Hansen III. Arbeitsfahigkeit und Ernahrung. *Skand. Arch. Physiol.*, 81:160–171, 1939.
10. Claremont, A., D. Costill, W. Fink and P. Van Hadel. Heat tolerance following diuretic induced dehydration. *Med. Sci. Sports*, 8:239–243, 1976.
11. Clement, D. B. and R. C. Asmundson. Nutritional intake and hematologic parameters in endurance runners. *Phys. Sportsmed.*, 10:37–43, 1982.
12. Costill, D. L., A. Bennett, G. Branam and D. Eddy. Glucose ingestion at rest and

during prolonged exercise. *Jour. of Appl. Physiol.*, 34:764–769, 1973.

13. Costill, D. L. and B. Saltin. Factors limiting gastric emptying during rest and exercise. *J. Appl. Physiol.*, 37:679–683, 1974.

14. Costill, D. L., E. Coyle, G. Dalsky, W. Evans, W. Fink and D. Hoopes. Effects of elevated plasma FFA and insulin on muscle glycogen usage during exercise. *J. Appl. Physiol.*, 43:695–699, 1977.

15. Costill, D. L., G. P. Dalsky and W. J. Fink. Effects of caffeine ingestion on metabolism and exercise performance. *Med. Sci. Sports*, 10:155–158, 1978.

16. Costill, D. L., M. Sherman, W. Fink, C. Maresh, M. Witten and J. Miller. The role of dietary carbohydrates in muscle glycogen resynthesis after strenuous running. *Amer. Jour. of Clin. Nutr.*, 34, 1831–1836, 1981.

17. Costill, D. L., R. Bowers, G. Branam and et al. Muscle glycogen utilization during prolonged exercise on successive days. *J. Appl. Physiol.*, 31:834–838, 1971.

18. Costill, D. L., R. Cote and W. Fink. Muscle water and electrolytes following varied levels of dehydration in man. *J. Appl. Physiol.*, 40:6–11, 1976.

19. Costill, D. L., R. Cote and W. Fink. Dietary potassium and heavy exercise: Effects on muscle water and electrolytes. *Am. J. Clin. Nutr.*, 36:266–275, 1982.

20. Costill, D. L., R. Cote, W. Fink and P. Van Handel. Muscle water and electrolyte distribution during prolonged exercise. *Int. J. Sports Med.*, 2:130–134, 1981.

21. Costill, D. L., W. F. Kammer and A. Fisher. Fluid ingestion during distance running. *Arch. Environ. Health*, 21:520–525, 1970.

22. Costill, D. L., W. J. Fink, J. L. Ivy, L. H. Getchell and F. A. Witzmann. Lipid Metabolism in skeletal muscle of endurance-trained males and females. *Diabetes*, 28:818–822, 1979.

23. Coyle, E. F., J. M. Hagberg, B. F. Hurley, W. H. Martin, A. A. Ehsani and J. O. Holloszy. Carbohydrate feedings during prolonged strenuous exercise can delay fatigue. *J. Appl. Physiol.*, 55:230–235, 1983.

24. Crane, R. K. The physiology of the intestinal absorption of sugars. *Physiological Effects of Food Carbohydrates*, 2–19, 1975.

25. Felig, P. The glucose-alanine cycle. *Metabolism*, 22:179–207, 1973.

26. Felig, P., A. Cherif, A. Minagawa and J. Wahren. Hypoglycemia during prolonged exercise in normal men. *N. Engl. J. Med.*, 306:895–900, 1982.

27. Fink, W. J., D. L. Costill and P. J. Van Handel. Leg muscle metabolism during exercise in the heat and cold. *Europ. J. Appl. Physiol.*, 34:183–190, 1975.

28. Fordtran, J. S. and B. Saltin. Gastric emptying and intestinal absorption during prolonged severe exercise. *J. Appl. Physiol.*, 23:331–335, 1967.

29. Foster, C. C., D. L. Costill and W. F. Fink. Effects of preexercise feedings on endurance performance. *Med. Sci. In Sports*, 11:1–5, 1979.

30. Gollnick, P. D. Metabolism of substrates: Energy substrate metabolism during exercise and as modified by training. *Fed. Proc.*, 44:353–357, 1985.

31. Hargreaves, M., D. L. Costill, A. Coggan, W. J. Fink and I. Nishibata. Effect of carbohydrate feedings on muscle glycogen utilization and exercise performance. *Med. Sci. Sports Exer.*, 16:219–222, 1984.

32. Hodges, R. E. and W. A. Krehl. The role of carbohydrates in lipid metabolism. *Amer. J. Cli. Nutr.*, 17:334–346, 1965.

33. Hultman, E. and L. H. Nilsson. Liver glycogen in man: Effect of different diets and muscular exercise. *Muscle Metabolism During Exercise*, B. Pernow and B. Saltin, ed. New York: Plenum Press, 143–151, 1971.

34. Ivy, J. L., D. L. Costill, W. J. Fink and E. Maglischo. Contributions of medium and long chain triglyceride intake to energy metabolism during prolonged exercise. *Int. J. Sports Med.*, 1:15–20, 1980.

35. Ivy, J. L., D. L. Costill, W. J. Fink and R. W. Lower. Influence of caffeine and carbohydrate feedings on endurance performance. *Med. Sci. In Sports*, 11:6–11, 1979.

36. Katz, L. N., J. Stamler and R. Pick. *Nutrition and Atherosclerosis.* 1958.
37. King, D. S., D. L. Costill, W. J. Fink, M. Hargreaves and R. A. Fielding. Muscle metabolism during exercise in the heat in unacclimatized and acclimatized man. *J. Appl. Physiol.,*
38. Levine, S. A., B. Gordon and C. L. Drick. Some changes in the chemical constituents of the blood following a marathon race. *JAMA,* 82:1778–1779, 1924.
39. Nestle, P. J. and P. J. Barter. Triglyceride clearance during diets rich in carbohydrates and fats. *Am. J. Clin. Nutr.,* 26:241–245, 1973.
40. Piehl, K. Time course for refilling of glycogen stores in human muscle fibers following exercise-induced glycogen depletion. *Acta Physiol. Scand.,* 90:297–302, 1974.
41. Piehl, K. Time course for refilling of glycogen stores in human muscle fibers following exercise-induced glycogen depletion. *Acta Physiol. Scand.,* 90:297–302, 1974.
42. Pitts, R. F. Physiology of the Kidney and Body Fluids. *Year Book,* 1965.
43. Plowman, S. A. and P. C. McSwegin. The effects of iron supplementation on female cross country runners. *J. Sports Med. Phys. Fitness,* 21:407–416, 1981.
44. Roberts, K. M., E. G. Noble, D. B. Hayden and A. W. Taylor. The effect of simple and complex carbohydrate diets on skeletal muscle glycogen and lipoprotein lipase of marathon runners. *Clinical Physiol.,* 5:41, 1985.
45. Sherman, W. M., D. L. Costill, W. J. Fink and J. M. Miller. Effects of exercise-diet manipulation on muscle glycogen and its subsequent utilization during performance. *Int. J. Sports Med.,* 2:1–15, 1981.
46. Sherman, W. M., D. L. Costill, W. J. Fink, L. E. Armstrong and T. M. M. F. C. Hagerman. The marathon: Recovery from acute biochemical alterations. *Biochem. Exer.,* 13:312–317, 1983.
47. Vellar, O. D. Studies on sweat losses of nutrients. I. Iron content of whole body sweat and its association with other sweat constituents, serum iron levels, heatological indices, body surface area and sweat rate. *Scand. J. Clin. Lab. Invest.,* 1:157–167, 1968.
48. Wahren, J. Quantitative aspects of blood flow and oxygen uptake in the forearm during rhythmic exercise. *Acta. Physiol. Scand.,* 67:92, 1966.
49. Wahren, J., P. Felig, G. Ahlborg and et al. Glucose metabolism during exercise in man. *J. Clin. Invest.,* 50:2715–2725, 1971.

CHAPTER 4

Training: The Price for Success

In its simplest form, endurance training serves as a constructive type of stress. Regular physical activity causes the body to become more tolerant of the demands of exercise so that it can run farther and faster. During each training run the leg muscles demand that energy be rapidly replenished, often at 200 times the resting rate. Day by day such training stress triggers the muscles and circulation to grow stronger and more capable of generating energy.

Assuming that one training program will work effectively for every runner is as logical as assuming that all runners are gifted with the same natural talents. Researchers who have evaluated different training programs are aware of the wide individual variations in endurance gains. Some runners will show very large gains in their aerobic capacities and endurance performances, whereas others may gain little from the same efforts. There are, however, some basic physiological adaptations that occur in all runners, though the magnitude of these changes may differ markedly.

MUSCULAR ADAPTATIONS

The repeated muscle contractions demanded during distance running require the breakdown and rebuilding of adenosine triphosphate (ATP), which is produced and stored within the muscle fibers (see Chapter 1). Production of ATP during long, relatively slow distance runs depends almost exclusively on the availability of oxygen and the aerobic breakdown of carbohydrates and fats. Endurance training enhances the mechanisms that control the rate of aerobic energy production. The factors responsible for better muscle endurance as a result of distance training include: (1) improved blood flow and oxygen delivery to the muscle, (2) improved oxidative or aerobic systems within the muscle fibers to produce ATP, (3) greater storage of glycogen and fat within the fibers, and (4) better removal of the by-products of energy production.

The gas exchange between the blood and the muscle fiber occurs in the small vessels or capillaries that surround each muscle cell. Training increases the number of capillaries bordering the fibers, sometimes by up to 40 percent (2, 10). The photographs in Figure 4-1 reveal a remarkable increase in the number of capillaries in a runner after several months of endurance training. Such an increase in the number of capillaries provides for greater exchange of gases, heat, and fuels between the blood and the interior of the working muscle fiber. This maintains an advantageous environment for energy production and repeated muscle contractions.

Once oxygen is delivered to the cell membrane, it is held and transported within the fiber by myoglobin, a compound similar to hemoglobin. Myoglobin's main function is to deliver oxygen from the cell membrane to the mitochondria. Myoglobin content in skeletal muscle increases significantly following endurance training (53). This increase in myoglobin, however, occurs only within the muscles involved in the training and does not take place in less active fibers.

Aerobic energy production (ATP) is the exclusive responsibility of the mitochondria. Muscle biopsy studies have shown that there are two major changes associated with mitochondrial energy production following endurance training: an increase in the number and the size of the mitochondria (35, 40, 45). Research has shown a progressive weekly increase of approximately 5 percent in the number of muscle mitochondria over a 27-week period of endurance training (46). At the same time, the average size of the mitochondria increased from 11.5 to 15.5 microns^2 × 10^{-2}, a 35 percent increase. These steady but gradual changes in mitochondria suggest that the structural improvements associated with endurance training may take months and perhaps years to fully develop.

Within each mitochondrion, the breakdown of fuels and ultimate production of ATP depend on the action created by special protein mol-

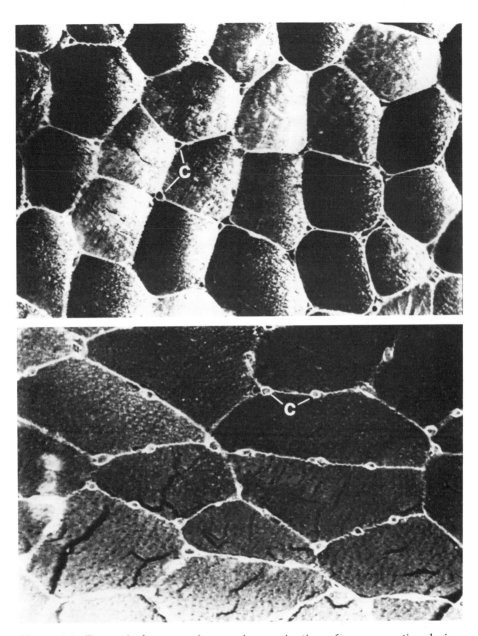

Figure 4-1. Frame A shows a microscopic examination of a cross-sectional view of muscle fibers and capillaries (c) from an untrained man. Note the few number of capillaries located between the fibers. Frame B shows a second sample of muscle taken from the same subject after several months of training. There was a marked increase in the number of capillaries surrounding each fiber. (Photographs courtesy of L. Hermansen)

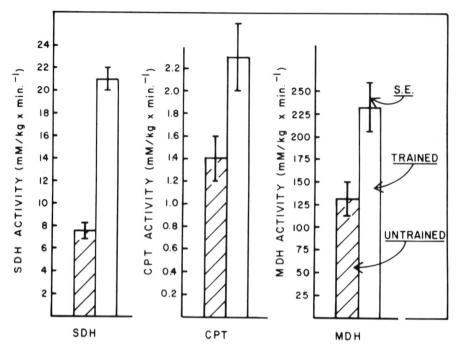

Figure 4-2. Changes in selected aerobic enzymes with three months of endurance running. The enzymes shown here are SDH (succinate dehydrogenase), CPT (carnitine palmityl transferase), and MDH (malate dehydrogenase).

ecules called enzymes. Distance running training increases the amount of these enzymes dramatically (27, 36, 42, 43). Figure 4-2 provides some examples of increases in selected muscle enzymes after three months of endurance training (18).

Special adjustments in the action of these enzymes make it possible for the endurance-trained muscle to burn fat better, lessening the demands on the limited muscle glycogen reserves. Improvements in the delivery of oxygen and its use within the muscle fiber result in a larger capacity to produce energy and a shift toward a greater reliance on fat for ATP production.

In Chapter 2 we mentioned the selective use of muscle fibers during distance running. Measurements of glycogen depletion from different muscle fibers indicates that during long training runs and competition slow twitch fibers are used more than the fast twitch. Only after the slow twitch fibers begin to fatigue or the running speed is increased do the fast twitch fibers become active.

Long, slow distance running will place most of the stress on the slow twitch fibers, with few adaptations occurring in the fast twitch. Incorporating more quality or speed into the training program taxes both fiber types, increasing their aerobic capacities (6, 36). Likewise, when extremely long runs are incorporated into the training program, both fiber types show improvements in aerobic energy production. Fast, anaerobic running, on the other hand, produces little improvement in muscles' aerobic capacity, though it may improve the endurance of the fast twitch fibers to a small degree (15).

Although aerobic capacity in leg muscles is vastly improved with training, the anaerobic capacity of both slow twitch and fast twitch fibers in runners is often below that found in untrained or strength-trained individuals. Several of the enzymes important in glycolysis, which is the anaerobic breakdown of glycogen, are reduced or unchanged after aerobic training (20, 41). This may explain, in part, why distance runners find it difficult to sprint and produce little lactate when they attempt anaerobic running. In fact, distance runners' muscles seem better suited to using lactate than they are to producing it.

These muscular adaptations make it clear that the gains during endurance training are specific to the speed and distance employed by the runner. While endurance training improves the aerobic capacity of the muscles, it reduces their ability to perform anaerobic or strength type activities. Strength training, on the other hand, produces no improvements in aerobic capacity, but it improves muscle power and anaerobic energy production. Football players and other anaerobically-oriented athletes have remarkable strength and anaerobic tolerance, but they score no better than sedentary individuals in tests of aerobic capacity (75).

Despite the extensive reliance on the slow twitch fibers during distance running, these fibers do not appear to grow any larger than the fast twitch fibers during training (30, 69). There is, however, considerable variability in the size of these muscle fibers among different runners. Some individuals have unusually large slow twitch fibers, while other runners may have larger fast twitch fibers (30). This point may be only of academic importance, since a runner's muscle size seems to have little relationship with performance. Muscle fiber size may be more critical in events that demand greater power and strength, such as sprint running and weightlifting (22, 17).

Most recent studies have shown that the percentage of slow twitch and fast twitch fibers does not change with distance running. Although few studies have been done on children or on runners over many years of training, current evidence indicates that these fiber types are not convertible. Fiber type is determined by the type and size of the neuron responsible for innervating each muscle fiber. Conversion would require a structural modification of the size and function of the motor nerve cells.

The only artificial methods known to change fiber type are: (1) surgically changing the nerve input to the muscle fiber, giving a fast twitch

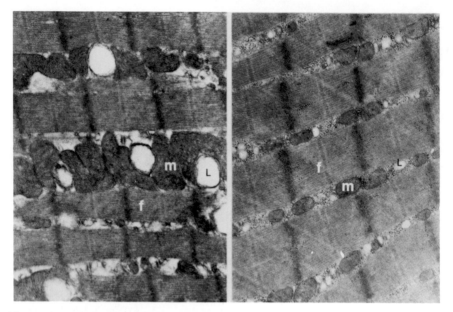

Electron micrographs looking inside the leg muscle fibers of a highly trained runner (left) and an untrained man (right). Note the larger number and size of the mitochondria (m) in the trained muscle. The trained fiber also has more stored fat (L) than the untrained muscle. Both factors provide an endurance advantage for the trained muscle.

fiber a slow twitch nerve, or (2) sending false signals to the muscle fibers through chronic electrical stimulation.

Endurance training can, however, cause subtle changes in the fast twitch fiber subtypes. Years of training seem to convert fast twitch *b* fibers to fast twitch *a* fibers (69). Neither the cause nor the effect of this change is known. Studies have suggested that the fast twitch *b* fibers are used less often than the fast twitch *a* fibers and consequently have lower aerobic capacities. Long-distance running may force the fast twitch *b* fibers into action, forcing them to take on the characteristics of the fast twitch *a* fibers. This conversion may simply reflect the greater use of the fast twitch fibers during long, exhaustive training runs.

Despite the variety of changes that occur in the leg muscles during training for distance running, the adaptations in elite runners differs little from those seen in less talented individuals. All individuals who train with the same volume and intensity will show similar adaptations in muscle, regardless of their innate talents. This does not mean that less gifted individuals can achieve the performance level of those who were born with greater talents. Champions are born with the "right stuff" but must suffer the stresses of training to achieve their full potential. Those of us made of more mortal matter are limited to greater degrees by our genetic endowments than by our abilities to adapt to training.

OXYGEN TRANSPORT

Shortness of breath, or the inability to ventilate the lungs, is perhaps the first signal of fatigue during exercise in untrained individuals. In these individuals, the muscles of the chest wall and diaphragm responsible for moving air in and out of the lungs are often as untrained as the leg muscles. Even during relatively slow running these muscles tire easily, making it difficult for the poorly conditioned runner to breathe. Endurance training improves the aerobic capacity and strength of these muscles, lessening respiratory distress.

Early studies showed few changes in lung function as a result of endurance training (65). They observed only an increase in the rate of gas diffusion from the alveoli to the arterial blood passing through the lungs. Training increases the rate of blood flow through the lungs, delivering more blood to receive oxygen and expel carbon dioxide. Consequently, the oxygen gradient (difference) between the alveoli and the blood remains high, promoting a faster exchange of gases.

Upon leaving the lungs, arterial blood is nearly saturated with oxygen. Only during very intense, exhaustive running does the blood leave the lungs with less than a maximum load of oxygen. Endurance training improves the ability of the respiratory muscles to move air in and out of the lungs, increases blood flow through the lungs, and enhances the rate at which oxygen can diffuse into the blood. As a result of these improvements, the runner is able to run faster and produce more energy without lowering the oxygen content of the blood.

The amount of oxygen carried by the blood is, in part, determined by the number of red cells and hemoglobin content of the blood. Several investigators have shown that a runner's Vo_2 max is closely related to his or her red blood cell volume (5, 37, 68). Though training increases Vo_2 max, there is little agreement regarding the effect of training on red cell volume or total hemoglobin content (5, 37, 68). Nevertheless, experts generally agree that years of training will increase the number of red blood cells without changing the amount of hemoglobin in each cell.

Physical activity also significantly increases the volume of plasma, the watery part of the blood (12, 65, 73). Three weeks of bed rest will lower plasma volume by about 15 percent; one week of activity is sufficient to return it to normal (12). Endurance training will elevate plasma volume an additional 10 to 15 percent (12).

Without some increase in red cell volume, a rise in plasma volume will result in a marked hemodilution, more plasma than red cells. This may account for the low hematocrits and hemoglobin values often observed in runners during periods of intense training (19). Some authorities have suggested that red cells may be damaged or destroyed during intense physical exercise, lowering the oxygen-carrying capacity of the blood. Regardless of any fluctuations in red cell and plasma volumes, experts generally concede that total blood volume increases with training. Whether these changes are of significant enough magnitude to affect oxygen delivery to the muscles remains debatable.

Recently, some attention has been given to the use of blood reinfusion or blood doping to improve running performance (32). In theory, the addition of red blood cells to circulation might be expected to increase the oxygen-carrying capacity of blood, thereby improving the runner's Vo_2 max. Swedish investigators observed that Vo_2 max decreased by 13 to 18 percent when 400 to 800 milliliters of blood were withdrawn from well-trained men (26). Four weeks later, after their bodies had replaced the missing red cells, the blood was reinfused, thereby elevating the amount of red cells and hemoglobin well above normal. This procedure was found to improve physical performance capacity by 23 percent and Vo_2 max by 9 percent. Although there have been some conflicting reports regarding the effects of blood reinfusion on endurance performance, physiologists generally agree that this procedure does increase oxygen transport and improve stamina (11, 59, 74).

In addition to improvements in the blood's capacity to carry oxygen, the major cardiovascular adaptation to training is an increased cardiac output during **maximal** exercise (12, 73). Cardiac output is the volume of blood pumped from the left ventricle per minute. It is calculated by multiplying the heart rate by the stroke volume, which is the amount of blood ejected from the heart with each beat. Although cardiac output during **submaximal** running is unaffected by training, there is a striking reduction in a runner's heart rate when he or she is running at a set pace. A slower exercise heart rate can only occur if the stroke volume increases. The following example illustrates how cardiac output can be the same during submaximal running both before and after training, because heart rate is lower.

Cardiac Output = (stroke volume) × (heart rate)

(untrained)   10,000 ml/min = (80 ml/beat) × (**125 beats/min**)

(trained)   10,000 ml/min = (100 ml/beat) × (**100 beats/min**)

The cause for this increase in the heart's stroke volume during both submaximal and maximal exercise is often attributed to an enlargement or hypertrophy of the heart with endurance training (28). The increase in heart size often seen in endurance athletes is the result of an enlarged ventricular cavity, but there is little increase in the thickening of the ventricular wall. This means that the volume of blood that fills the ventricles and is pumped out of the heart is also larger. It should be noted, however, that heart volume does not always increase following physical training. Nevertheless, the ventricles may be stronger and able to empty their contents more fully as a consequence of endurance training. These changes in ventricular structure and function are responsible for the lower resting and submaximal heart rates observed among distance runners.

Maximal heart rate, on the other hand, may show little change with training. With the same maximal heart rate and an enlarged stroke volume, the total amount of blood pumped by the heart or maximal cardiac output during exhaustive exercise is strikingly greater in the trained runner.

It has been suggested that maximal stroke volume is the most distinguishing difference between champion endurance athletes and well-trained individuals (64). As mentioned, the increased stroke volume following training is, in part, achieved by an increase in heart volume (65). The late Steve Prefontaine, holder of numerous American distance running records, had a heart volume of 1,205 milliliters, approximately 30 to 40 percent larger than the average-sized heart of a man of equal age, height, and weight.

Training for distance running results in a combination of respiratory, circulatory, and muscular adaptations directed toward a greater capacity to produce energy and sustain muscular effort for long periods. The accumulated effect of all these physiological changes is an increase in Vo_2 max. Though the magnitude of the increase in Vo_2 max varies considerably, an improvement of 5 to 20 percent can be anticipated for individuals older than 16 years who initially train for eight to 12 weeks (54). As shown in Figure 4-3, the amount of improvement in Vo_2 max is determined partly by the amount of training performed by the runner. In the example, the untrained runner has a Vo_2 max of 40 milliliters of oxygen per minute for each kilogram of body weight (ml/kg × min). Training for several months at 25 miles per week results in a 12 ml/kg × min increase; when the training was doubled to 50 miles per week there was an additional rise of six to seven ml/kg × min. The first reaction to such findings is to conclude that Vo_2 max will continue to improve simply by increasing the training mileage. Unfortunately, the secrets of training are not so simple or straightforward.

TRAINING DISTANCE: MILEAGE

As noted in Figure 4-3, improvements in aerobic capacity are, in part, determined by the length of each training run and the total work performed over several weeks. Over the past 15 to 20 years runners have

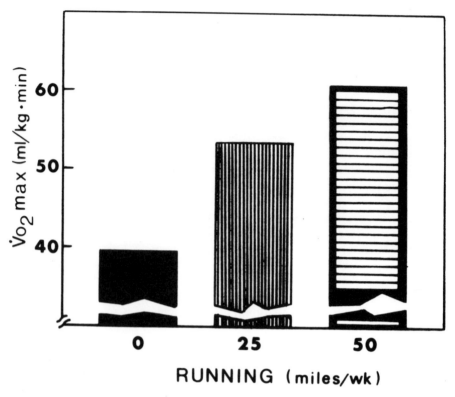

Figure 4-3. Maximal oxygen uptake for a 40-year-old man in the untrained state and after several months of training at 25 and 50 miles per week.

learned to judge their readiness for competition on the basis of their weekly mileages. Conversations among distance runners inevitably turn to "How many miles per week have you been running?" While most runners think that the more miles you run, the better your chances of success, it is easy to overtrain and perform poorly. It is important to remember that **the purpose of training is to stress the body, so that when you rest it will grow stronger and more tolerant of the demands of distance running.** Unfortunately, most runners forget that you can train too hard, or allow too little rest, which overstresses the body and allows no opportunity for growth.

Some years ago at our laboratory we studied two marathon runners following a six-month layoff when they were at different stages in their reconditioning. Muscle biopsies and treadmill tests for Vo$_2$ max were made as they gradually increased their weekly mileages. As one might have predicted, the muscles showed dramatic improvements in aerobic capacity with as little as 25 miles of running per week. Figure 4-4 shows

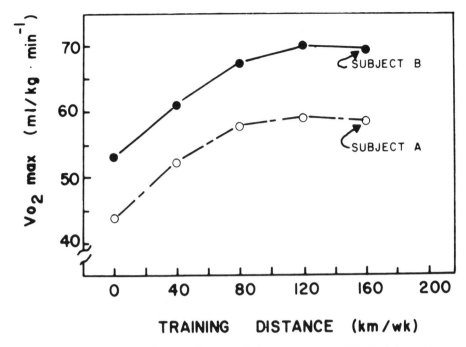

Figure 4-4. Changes in VO_2 max for two distance runners while training at various distances. Note that training 40 to 80 kilometers per week resulted in significant improvements in VO_2 max, whereas greater training distances produced no greater increases.

that the runners' VO_2 max values increased when they increased their weekly mileages to 50 and then 75 miles per week. Beyond that level of training, however, our laboratory tests found no additional gains in endurance. During a one-month period they even trained at 225 miles per week, with no improvement in endurance.

There is a point of optimal distance that will cause the body to adapt to its full aerobic capacity. Based on the results of these two runners and other laboratory observations, we have concluded that the mileage needed for the maximum training benefits varies between 60 and 90 miles per week. There is a point of diminishing returns, a point at which you can increase weekly mileage but see little or no improvement in performance.

If you are currently training at 25 to 40 miles per week, there are physiological advantages to be gained from additional mileage, but there are also pitfalls to avoid. **Don't increase your mileage too fast!** The body can tolerate slightly greater amounts of stress, but too much too fast will lead to a breakdown in adaptation rather than gains. Most runners can tolerate a 5 to 10 percent increase in their weekly mileages without becoming chronically fatigued. If, for example, you are already doing 50 miles per week, you can increase the mileage by three to five miles without overdoing it.

In light of the previous discussions regarding the use and replacement of muscle and liver glycogen, the training regimen should allow for adequate recovery. Most runners attempt to train hard every day, with the idea that the more they do, the better they will be. Running the same distance at the same pace each day does not allow the runner's body to recover sufficiently and offers little opportunity to inject any quality or speed into the training program.

The rate at which the body adapts to the training stimulus is relatively slow. The benefits gained from a given workout may not be realized for several weeks, since the body grows slowly. The training regimen should be planned over a three- or four-week period, rather than day-to-day or week-by-week. Be gradual in your training progression.

Although you have to stress the body hard to raise your exercise tolerance to a new and better level of fitness, once you have gained the benefits of increased mileage, you can reduce your training without losing anything. In fact, after training for a few weeks at 60-plus miles you can probably perform better by decreasing your total weekly mileage to 40 or 50 miles. Our studies have shown that you can perform at your best only during two- to six-week periods of reduced training. During that period, however, you still need to have one long training run every week or two. Whereas this might mean a 20-mile run for the marathoner, a 10-mile run should satisfy the specific needs of a 10-kilometer runner. These long runs appear to develop and maintain the muscles' energy systems, specifically the abilities to use fat and spare the use of muscle glycogen.

A survey of today's runners reveals that 60 percent run 45 to 52 miles per week, while nearly 40 percent run more than 100 miles per week (52). On the average, elite U.S. distance runners train at 100 to 150 miles per week (20). This contrasts with some elite runners of earlier periods. Alfred Shrubb, who in 1904 ran 50 minutes:55 seconds for the 10-mile, and 9 minutes:17.8 seconds for the two-mile, covered only 35 miles of moderate running per week (66). Walter George, world record holder for the mile (4 minutes:12.8 seconds) in 1882, reported that he ran fewer than 10 miles per week, most of it at a relatively slow pace (66). Training was more intense for the runners at the 1962 Western Hemisphere Marathon, where those who finished among the leaders trained year-round, twice per day, and ran more than 100 miles per week (52).

Both experience and scientific evidence suggests that optimal training distance for maximal endurance development is between 60 and 90 miles per week. Runners who are less tolerant of heavy training may achieve greater benefits from training at less than 60 miles per week, where they are less likely to become overstressed.

TRAINING INTENSITY: PACE

Although the volume of running during training, rather than the speed, is the most important determinant for developing aerobic endurance, distance racing success also depends to a large degree on the quality, or speed, of training. The major disadvantage of concentrating on "volume" in a training program is that long, slow distance training is considerably slower than racing pace. Such training fails to develop the neurological patterns of muscle fiber recruitment that will be needed during races which require a faster pace. Since the selective use of muscle fibers differs according to running speed, runners who only train at speeds slower than race pace will not train all of the muscle fibers needed for competition. Runners who use only long, slow running in training show marked improvements in performance when they race frequently. This suggests that the faster speeds of competition supplement the runners' aerobic endurance with patterns of movement that make their running more efficient.

AEROBIC INTERVAL TRAINING

High-intensity training may include either intermittent running, known as intervals, or continuous running at near racing pace. Although interval training has been used for many years, most runners consider it highly anaerobic. While some interval training can be performed at speeds that produce large lactate accumulations, it is also possible to use this training format to develop the aerobic system. Repeated runs at a faster pace over shorter distances with brief rest intervals will achieve the same benefits as long continuous runs. This form of "**aerobic interval**" training has become the framework for aerobic swimming conditioning. It involves repeated short swims at slightly slower than race pace with very brief rest intervals of five to 15 seconds.

Table 4-1 offers an example of some **aerobic intervals** for runners who are preparing to compete in a 10-kilometer race. Since volume is the key to successful aerobic training, the runner must perform a large number of these repeated runs. In this example, 20 repetitions of 400 meters results in a total of 8,000 meters or roughly five miles. The pace is five to six seconds per minute slower than that maintained during a 10-kilometer race, but it is generally faster than a speed that could be sustained easily during a straight five-mile run. The hard part of this interval set is that the prescribed rest between repetitions is relatively brief, 10 to 15

TABLE 4-1. Example of aerobic intervals for runners training to run a 10-kilometer race.

BEST 10 KM MIN:SEC	INTERVAL SET			
	REPS	DISTANCE (METERS)	REST (SEC)	PACE (MIN:SEC)
46:00	20	400	10–15	2:00
43:00	20	400	10–15	1:52
40:00	20	400	10–15	1:45
37:00	20	400	10–15	1:37
34:00	20	400	10–15	1:30

seconds. These short rest intervals keep the circulatory system working at a relatively high level, yet give the runner a brief escape from the muscular stress of the faster running.

Figure 4-5 illustrates a runner's heart rate and oxygen uptake while running a set of five 800-meter aerobic intervals. There is little recovery of either heart rate or oxygen uptake during the 15-second rest intervals, with energy levels at 73 percent of the runner's Vo_2 max. Little or no

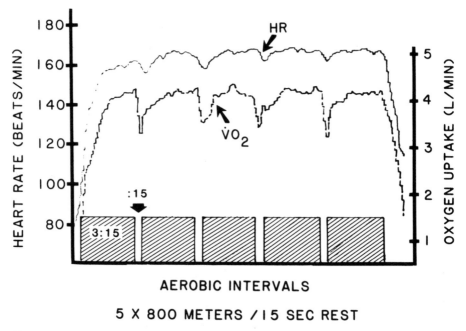

AEROBIC INTERVALS

5 X 800 METERS / 15 SEC REST

Figure 4-5. Heart rate and oxygen uptake (Vo_2) during a series of **aerobic interval** runs with 15-second rests between each run.

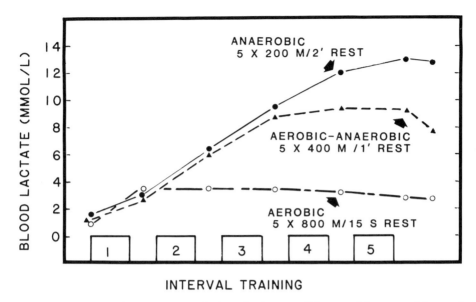

Figure 4-6. Blood lactate accumulation during **aerobic, aerobic-anaerobic,** and **anaerobic interval** training. Note that despite the very short rest intervals of 15 seconds provided during the aerobic intervals, very little lactate accumulated. The longer rest intervals of two minutes and faster running speeds of the anaerobic intervals, on the other hand, resulted in a large lactate accumulation.

lactate accumulated in the blood of this runner (see Figure 4-6), suggesting that she was able to perform the interval set without demanding energy from the anaerobic metabolism. One advantage of this form of training is that the runner can systematically increase the training load and plot his or her improvement.

It can be argued that a straight run of five miles at a similar pace will give the same aerobic benefits, but some runners find this form of training lacking in stimulation. When it comes to the aerobic aspects of training, personal preference can be the deciding factor. Whether you prefer one hard run of five or six miles or a series of repeated, short runs with brief rest intervals, the aerobic benefits will be the same.

AEROBIC-ANAEROBIC INTERVAL TRAINING

To train the leg muscles to produce the force required for racing and to coordinate the various muscles involved in running fast, a portion of the runner's training should be performed at or near racing pace. By far the most effective way to accomplish this goal is to perform interval sets at speeds approximating race pace, referred to as "**aerobic-anaerobic intervals.**" These race-pace-oriented intervals have also been termed "anaerobic threshold intervals," when the running intensity of the repetitions produces a small amount of lactate of less than four millimoles per liter, as in marathon race-pace training. Faster preparation for the mile, five-kilometer, or 10-kilometer may produce a large blood lactate accumulation of more than five to six millimoles per liter.

Figure 4-7 illustrates the heart rate and oxygen uptake values during aerobic-anaerobic interval sets run at marathon pace and at 10-kilometer pace. The lactate accumulation in blood during these intervals is shown in Figure 4-6. Unlike the purely "aerobic intervals," these repeated race-pace runs require greater energy production rates of between 80 and 95 percent Vo_2 max, resulting in some lactate accumulation and heart rates above 160 beats per minute.

Table 4-2 illustrates sets of 400-meter repeated runs at the average speed of the runners' best 10-kilometer performances. Note that the total distance covered (4,000 meters) is less than that covered during the 400-meter "aerobic" repeats in Table 4-1, but the rest intervals are greater to allow for recovery from these faster runs. Though the rest intervals shown

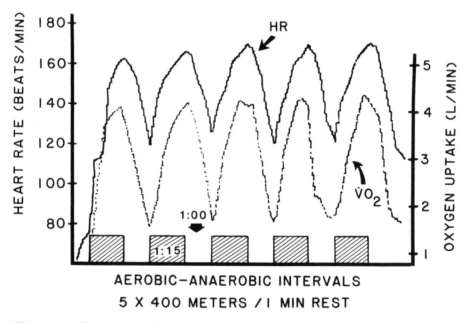

Figure 4-7. Oxygen uptake and heart rate and during **aerobic-anaerobic intervals** run at marathon and 10-kilometer paces. This runner's best performances for those events were 3 hours:21 minutes and 40 minutes:18 seconds, respectively.

TABLE 4-2 Example of aerobic-anaerobic intervals for runners training to run a 10-kilometer race.

BEST 10 KM MIN:SEC	INTERVAL SET			
	REPS	DISTANCE (METERS)	REST (SEC)	PACE (MIN:SEC)
46:00	10	400	60–90	1:51
43:00	10	400	60–90	1:44
40:00	10	400	60–90	1:37
37:00	10	400	60–90	1:29
34:00	10	400	60–90	1:16

in this table are two minutes, experience and conditioning will help runners judge how much rest is needed.

Since the objective of the "aerobic-anaerobic intervals" is to develop speed and to learn the feel for proper pace, only enough rest to enable the runner to hold the desired pace for all the runs should be allowed. If fatigue during the latter runs forces a reduction in pace, then either the rest interval is too brief or the pace is too fast. The preselected pace for these interval runs should not be faster than what is realistic for the runner's anticipated pace during the race. The key to success in aerobic-anaerobic interval training is to manipulate the rest intervals, so that eventually the repeated runs are performed at racing speed with rests of only 30 to 45 seconds.

This form of interval training will also produce maximal gains in aerobic endurance, but it is too stressful to perform more than two or three times per week. Since this form of training produces some lactate accumulation (Figure 4-6) and a rapid breakdown of muscle glycogen, day-to-day recovery will be slower than during continuous and aerobic interval training. When coaches design sets of aerobic-anaerobic intervals, the running pace should be constant at racing speed, regardless of the distance covered during each run.

ANAEROBIC INTERVAL TRAINING

Speed training is by far the most stressful form of muscular exercise. The energy for sprint running is derived, in large part, from the anaerobic breakdown of muscle glycogen, which places great stress on the muscle fiber membranes and connective tissue. While these stresses improved strength and speed, there is also a greater risk of muscle injury due to the high tension of **anaerobic interval training.** Warming up and mild stretching before these interval runs are a must. It is also wise to perform the first of the runs a bit slower than the average time for the set.

The primary objective of these anaerobic intervals is to improve the runner's leg strength and to develop the ability to remove lactate from the muscles, thereby enhancing the runner's tolerance for faster than race-pace running. In light of the stress on the muscle during anaerobic interval training, there should be fewer repetitions and longer rests than there are in other forms of interval training. This training is aimed at developing strength and not aerobic endurance, so the total distance covered is not as important. Since much of the energy produced during these interval runs will be produced anaerobically, there is a build-up of acid within the muscle, leading to early exhaustion if the pace is too fast.

Figure 4-8 illustrates the physiological responses to a set of ten 200-meter anaerobic intervals. Despite rests of two minutes between the runs, blood lactate, heart rate, and oxygen uptake were nearly at maximum during the final repetitions.

Although the example shown in Table 4-3 may help to gauge the proper pace for a set of anaerobic intervals, the final decision on running

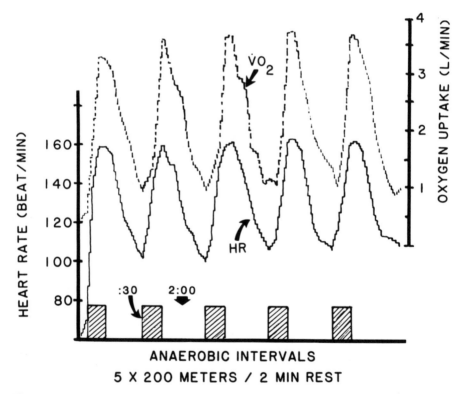

Figure 4-8. Oxygen uptake and heart rate during a set of **anaerobic,** sprint intervals.

TABLE 4-3. Example of an anaerobic interval series for runners training to run a 10-kilometer race.

BEST 10 KM MIN:SEC	INTERVAL SET			
	REPS	DISTANCE (METERS)	REST (MIN)	PACE (SEC)
46:00	10	200	2	46
43:00	10	200	2	43
40:00	10	200	2	40
37:00	10	200	2	38
34:00	10	200	2	36

pace becomes a matter of experience and conditioning. Like other forms of strength training, this muscle overloading should not be repeated on successive days, and no more than one or two such training sessions should be performed in any seven-day training plan.

TRAINING PLAN

Though we have discussed some of the building blocks of the training program, their integration into a regimen to promote peak performance is unclear. How many days per week and how many times per day should one train? Most attempts to evaluate the impact of training frequency on endurance capacity have been limited to studies using previously sedentary subjects (7, 55, 56).

Studies have shown significant improvements in Vo_2 max with two and four exercise bouts per week, but after seven to 13 weeks, there were no differences between the two- and four-day per week training groups (7, 56). After 20 weeks of training, however, the subjects who trained four days per week showed significantly greater gains in Vo_2 max (56).

It is difficult to apply these data to serious runners, whose training frequency and volume are substantially greater than those of the subjects used in the experimental studies. Judging from current training methods, the greatest gains in aerobic capacity are achieved when runners train three to five days per week (33).

The factors which determine the number of training sessions per week are: (1) the runner's state of training, (2) individual tolerance to training, and (3) the pace and distance of each training session. Even among highly trained runners, there are some who may respond better to training four days per week, while others may thrive on six or seven days per week with two daily training sessions. Individual differences in training tolerance are determined by each runner's recovery rate, which is the amount of rest needed between training sessions to allow for improvement.

During the early stages of conditioning, in periods following months or years of relative inactivity, the body is ill-prepared to meet the demands of hard exercise. The oxygen transport system is weak, muscle fuel supplies are low, and the ability to produce energy is poor. It takes little exercise to stimulate new growth and improve endurance.

Unfortunately, most athletes believe that if they train hard and long, they will get into condition faster than they will with a less stressful program. The body tissues have an optimal rate of adaptation to training. When the training stress is either too small or too great, the rate of adaptation is lower and the conditioning is slower than desired.

Since it is impossible to prescribe the "optimal" training regimen for every beginning runner, it is prudent to design a training program that is a bit conservative and easily tolerated by the runner. The aim of this initial phase of conditioning is to stimulate a progressive increase in Vo_2 max. Table 4-4 offers a training plan for the first four weeks of training, beginning in the "untrained" state. Though this regimen illustrates the need for a progressive increase in volume, the running pace is of less importance. As a rule, all of these sessions should be performed at conversational paces, which are speeds that do not cause the runner to feel short of breath.

This gradual progression in training distance should continue for the first eight weeks, reaching a maximum of four to six miles of continuous running per training session. Regardless of the frequency of training (two, four, or five days per week), the major improvements in Vo_2 max are attained within the first eight weeks of training (33, 34). This period is essential in establishing an "aerobic base" to prepare the runner for more intense training efforts.

TABLE 4-4. A four-week training plan for the beginning runner, after a long period of inactivity. The "m" denotes miles covered in each training session, and the "*" indicates that each run may be performed as intermittent running and walking to keep the session exclusively aerobic.

| | DAYS OF TRAINING | | | | | | |
	DAY 1	DAY 2	DAY 3	DAY 4	DAY 5	DAY 6	DAY 7
Week 1	1 m*	1 m*	Rest	1.5 m*	1.5 m*	Rest	Rest
Week 2	1.5 m*	1 m	Rest	1.5 m	1.5 m	Rest	Rest
Week 3	2 m	1.5 m	Rest	2 m	1.5 m	Rest	2 m
Week 4	2 m	Rest	2.5 m	2 m	Rest	2.5 m	2 m

TABLE 4-5. A **sample** training plan for 10-kilometer competition. Abbreviations Ae (aerobic), Ae-An (aerobic-anaerobic), and An (anaerobic) denote the training emphasis for that day. Refer to Tables 4-1, 4-2, and 4-3 for an explanation of the pace and rest used with the sample interval set shown below the Ae-An and An sessions.

	DAY 1	DAY 2	DAY 3	DAY 4	DAY 5	DAY 6	DAY 7
Week 1	Ae 6 m	Ae-An 10 × 800	Ae 6 m	Rest	Ae-An 20 × 400	Ae 6 m	Rest
Week 2	Ae 8 m	Ae-An 5 × 1,500	Ae 6 m	Rest	Ae 7 m	Ae-An 6 × 1,200	Rest
Week 3	Ae 9 m	Ae-An 15 × 600	Rest	An 10 × 200	Ae 7 m	Ae-An 6 × 800	Rest
Week 4	Ae 6 m	Ae-An 10 × 400	Rest	Ae 6 m	Ae-An 3 × 1,500	Ae 5 m	Rest
Week 5	Ae 8 m	Ae-An 5 × 1,200	Ae 6 m	An 5 × 400	Ae-An 15 × 600	Ae 7 m	Rest
Week 6	Ae 10 m	Ae-An 40 × 200	Ae 7 m	An 7 × 300	Ae-An 6 × 1,000	Ae 7 m	Rest
Week 7	Ae 8 m	Ae-An 8 × 800	Ae 6 m	Rest	Ae 6 m	Ae-An 4 × 1,500	Rest
Week 8	Ae 10 m	An 6 × 400	Ae-An 2 × 4,000	Ae 6 m	An 10 × 200	Ae-An 5 × 1,200	Rest

*"m" denotes miles, whereas the interval sets are described as the number of repetitions and the distance in meters (10 reps × 400 meters).

10-KILOMETER TRAINING

The second stage of training, the preparation for competition, emphasizes the quality or pace of training, with small increments in training distance. At this point, both the training distance and speed of running are determined by the runner's planned racing distance. If the runner is preparing for a marathon, the total daily mileage should **gradually** be **increased** to eight or 10 miles with one extra long, aerobic run of 15 to 20 miles every week or two. Training for 10,000 meters, on the other hand, requires more of the aerobic-anaerobic type of training, with a maximum training distance of six or eight miles per session. The longest weekly run should not exceed 10 to 12 miles, at a strictly aerobic pace.

Table 4-5 illustrates an eight-week training plan, showing the mixture of aerobic, aerobic-anaerobic, and anaerobic training for 10-kilometer racing. To improve both aerobic capacity and leg power, the weekly training sessions provide a gradual increase in mileage and training pace. Since the aerobic-anaerobic and anaerobic training sessions tend to impose more stress on the energy reserves, allowances must be made for aerobic training on days following these sessions. This progression also allows for weekly variations in stress. As shown in Figure 4-9, this train-

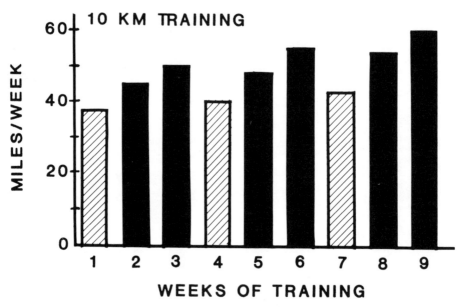

Figure 4-9. A training plan, demonstrating light, moderate, and hard weeks of training within every three-week cycle. Each cycle imposes the greatest training stress during the third week, followed by a light week to allow for recovery and growth.

ing plan recommends a three-week cycle, with progressive increments in mileage. Note that the longest mileage weeks of training are followed by a week of reduced effort.

In addition to the interval training sessions shown in Table 4-5, each workout should start with one to two miles of easy, aerobic running. Although the scientific documentation on the value of warm-up is unclear, a slow entry into the intense portion of the workout will lessen the risk of injury and permit some physiological adjustment to the energy demands of hard exercise.

The value of warming-down is debatable. Many coaches and runners recommend one to two miles of easy running at the end of the training session. Recovery from a highly anaerobic training bout will be faster if the runner continues to do some easy aerobic running. The rate of lactate removal from the blood is faster with an "active recovery" than it is when the subject stops exercise (39). There is, however, evidence that some of the muscle glycogen used during intense exercise is replaced from lactate after the exercise (14, 39). As shown in Figure 4-10, continued muscular activity after an intense sprint bout produces an additional breakdown of muscle glycogen, whereas complete inactivity results in 50 to 75 percent recovery. This would lead us to conclude that during repeated days

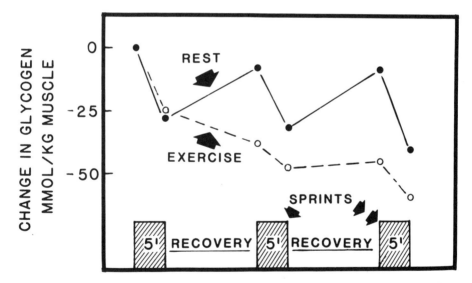

Figure 4-10. Effects of active (exercise) and inactive (rest) recovery following five minutes of sprint exercise. Note that muscle glycogen decreases with each sprint bout, then continues to decline when the runners perform light activity during the recovery. Complete rest after the sprint bouts, on the other hand, results in a marked recovery of muscle glycogen (14).

of intense training, it may be better to avoid warming-down, in order to reduce the day-to-day loss of muscle glycogen. The implications of these findings, however, deserve further study.

MARATHON TRAINING

Several major adjustments must be made in the preceding training plan to accommodate the specific adaptations needed for marathon running. There are, however, more similarities than differences in the 10-kilometer and marathon training programs. This may explain why many of the best marathoners have years of training and competitive experience as 10-kilometer runners. The marathon requires more emphasis on aerobic endurance than on leg speed and power, but it is still a race against time. Consequently, the difference between surviving the distance and performing one's best will be determined by the runner's efficiency and specific leg strength. As we have pointed out in the preceding chapters, specificity is a key consideration in all forms of training. Training only at speeds slower than one's racing pace will not fully pre-

TABLE 4-6. A sample training plan for marathon competition. Abbreviations Ae (aerobic) and Ae-An (aerobic-anaerobic) denote the training emphasis for each day. Refer to Tables 4-1 and 4-2 for an explanation of the pace and rest used with the sample interval sets shown below the Ae-An sessions.

	DAY 1	DAY 2	DAY 3	DAY 4	DAY 5	DAY 6	DAY 7
Week 1	Ae 8 m	Ae 6 × 1 m	Ae-An 10 × 800	Ae 4 m	Ae 8 m	Ae-An 20 × 400	Rest
Week 2	Ae 10 m	Ae 3 × 2 m	Ae-An 15 × 600	Ae 5 m	Ae-An 8 × 1 m	Ae 8 m	Rest
Week 3	Ae 12 m	Ae-An 8 × 1 m	Ae 2 × 4 m	Ae 6 m	Ae-An 20 × 400	Ae 9 m	Rest
Week 4	Ae 9 m	Ae 6 × 1.5 m	Ae-An 10 × 800	Ae 5 m	Ae 9 m	Ae-An 15 × 600	Rest
Week 5	Ae 11 m	Ae 4 × 2 m	Ae-An 8 × 1 m	Ae 6 m	Ae-An 20 × 400	Ae 9 m	Rest
Week 6	Ae 14 m	Ae-An 30 × 300	Ae 2 × 5 m	Ae 7 m	Ae-An 9 × 1,000	Ae 10 m	Rest

"m" denotes miles, whereas the interval sets are described as the number of repetitions and distance in meters (10 reps × 400 meters)

pare the energy, circulatory, and neurological systems for the demands of competition.

Table 4-6 provides a **sample** six-week training plan for the marathoner comparable to the regimen proposed for the 10-kilometer shown in Table 4-5. As shown in Table 4-6, the amount of intense (aerobic-anaerobic) training remains relatively constant from week to week, but the total volume and longest weekly training runs increase within each three-week cycle. The aerobic interval sets shown in this table are performed with short rest intervals and at speeds slower than racing pace (see Table 4-1). The aerobic-anaerobic (Ae-An) intervals, on the other hand, are run at the desired racing pace, but with substantially longer rest intervals (see Table 4-2). Again, the aerobic-anaerobic intervals should be preceded by a one- to two-mile easy warm-up run. This plan is designed to provide progressive, yet specific training for the marathon. Since the physiological adaptations to training are relatively slow, it seems that this phase of training will require eight to 12 weeks for optimal benefits.

The illustrations presented in the preceding tables are examples and should be modified to suit individual abilities, racing distances, and responses to each form of training. The distance and number of repetitions illustrated in the various forms of interval training can be increased or decreased to provide variety and to modify the volume of training. Although the examples provide some basis for 10-kilometer and marathon running, the same plans can be modified to help the runner prepare for most racing distances. Previously, the traditional approach to training distance runners has focused only on the importance of increasing the runner's weekly mileage. There is now sound evidence to show that the quality of training is equally as important as the quantity.

STRENGTH TRAINING FOR DISTANCE RUNNING

Although distance running improves muscular endurance, it may produce a decline in leg strength. As noted in Chapter 1, distance runners lack the ability to sprint and jump. Though there is no clear evidence to explain the loss in leg power, some investigators have demonstrated that endurance training produces changes in the nerves and muscles (23). It has been shown that endurance training reduces the maximal tension in isolated muscle fibers (31). Since running speed depends on specific leg strength, such decrements in muscle power tend to negate the full benefits of training for peak performance. As a result, many runners incorporate some form of muscular overload into their training programs to compensate for any loss in leg strength with distance training.

Although there are numerous anecdotal reports describing the benefits of strength training for distance running, there is no scientific evidence to support this practice. Those runners who engage in strength training most frequently use free weights, isokinetic resistance exercise, hand-held weights, ankle weights, and weighted vests. These methods differ only in the way that they impose additional overloads to the muscle.

Free weightlifting and isokinetic strength training, for example, tend to isolate specific leg and arm actions in an effort to strengthen the muscles used during distance running. The major fault with these approaches is that any strength gained while working against a given piece of strength equipment is not transferred to the task of running. The runner may be able to lift a heavier weight or exert greater force, but there is no assurance that he or she will be able to run faster or easier. The problem is specificity. Unless the strength training is done while the runner is running, it is not likely to be beneficial.

Based on this principle, some runners elect to add resistance to the muscles by wearing weights to the trunk, arms, or legs. The addition of a pound of weight to the ankle, for example, is equivalent to adding four pounds to the trunk. In theory, these methods would seem to offer a more specific approach to improve strength and speed, but the benefits are undocumented. The major disadvantage of these methods is that adding weights to the body tends to change one's running style. Because it costs a runner more to carry the added weight, he or she will be forced to run slower while working at the same relative effort (percent Vo_2 max). Being forced to run slower by the addition of weight works in opposition to the principle of specificity: to race fast you must, within reason, train fast. Strength gained during slow running will not insure strength gains for racing. Running with weights provides no greater training stimulus for the oxygen transport system than running without the use of added weight. If you want to train at a higher percentage of your Vo_2 max, then you need only run faster.

Thus, the most specific method for strength training is to overload the muscles while running at increased speeds for short distances. The strength needed for long distance running is not the same as that demanded by power events like weightlifting. Nevertheless, the training principles are much the same. The load on the muscles must be near maximum for very brief periods. Anaerobic interval training (Table 4-3) is designed to promote strength gains that are directly transferable to improvements in leg speed. Since leg speed and strength are of diminishing importance during races of greater and greater distance, the emphasis on anaerobic intervals should be virtually eliminated from training regimens for races greater than 10 to 12 miles. Since this form of training is highly taxing, it should be used no more than three days per week. Even within a given training session, the amount of anaerobic (sprint) training should make up only about 10 percent of the total daily mileage.

TRAINING FOR THE HEAT

The ability to compete well in hot weather depends, in part, on prior training. Prolonged and repeated training runs in the heat gradually improve the runner's ability to eliminate excess body heat, reducing the risk of heat exhaustion and heat stroke. This process, termed "heat acclimatization," results in a number of adjustments in the distribution of blood flow and sweating. Though the amount of sweat produced during exercise in the heat does not always change with heat acclimatization, the distribution of sweating over the skin often increases in those areas that have the greatest exposure and are most effective in dissipating body heat (8, 73).

Heat acclimatization is generally characterized by reductions in heart rate and rectal temperature during exercise in the heat (25, 73). These physiological adjustments improve rapidly with successive days of training in the heat, being fully improved within eight to 12 days (3, 47, 60). Heat acclimatization depends on the running speed, the duration of heat exposure, and the environmental conditions during each exercise session (8).

Laboratory studies have frequently required runners to exercise at a low intensity of about 50 percent Vo_2 max for 80 to 100 minutes in a chamber heated to between 90 and 120 degrees Fahrenheit to induce a full heat adjustment (3, 47, 60, 61). Unfortunately, there is no information to show the rate and degree of acclimatization during short training runs of 30 to 60 minutes at higher intensities of 70 to 80 percent Vo_2 max. Nevertheless, the physiological responses of trained runners suggest that they are quite tolerant of hot weather running, as long as at least part of their training is performed in the heat. As with all other forms of training, the adjustments to the heat are specific to the conditions. Heat acclimatization can only be achieved by exercising in the heat, not by enjoying passive activities such as sunbathing.

Figure 4-11 illustrates the adjustments in a runner's heart rate and rectal temperature during 90 minutes of exercise at 60 percent Vo_2 max in heat of 102 degrees Fahrenheit before and after eight days of heat acclimatization (16). Although some investigators have reported decreases in oxygen uptake during exercise in the heat, we have observed only minor changes in the rate of energy and heat production as a consequence of acclimatization (3, 16, 47, 72).

Improved heat tolerance is associated with an earlier onset of sweating at the beginning of exercise (50). As a result, skin temperatures are lower, and the difference between the temperatures of body and skin is

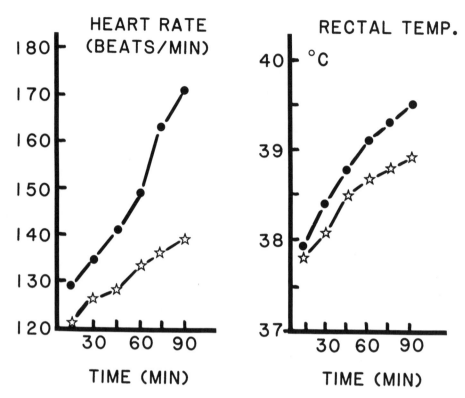

Figure 4-11. Heart rate and rectal temperature during 90 minutes of exercise in the heat (102 degrees Fahrenheit) before and after eight days of heat acclimatization. Note the lower recording after training in the heat.

greater. Thus, less blood flow to the skin is required to transfer excess body heat. Although some investigators have found an increase in blood volume with heat acclimatization, this change is somewhat temporary. It is probably related to the body's efforts to retain sodium, which causes the body to retain more water.

What does all this mean to distance runners, and how can they train to gain the greatest degree of heat acclimatization? Although runners must be exposed to the heat to fully adjust, they gain partial heat tolerance by training in a cooler environment. In addition, when the runners become acclimatized to a given level of heat stress, they will also be able to perform better in cooler weather. If the runner must compete in hot weather, then at least part of the training should be conducted in the warmest part of the day. Early morning and evening training runs will not fully prepare a distance runner to tolerate the heat of midday.

One possible side effect of running in the heat is the stress it places on muscle glycogen stores. Running at a given speed in the heat will

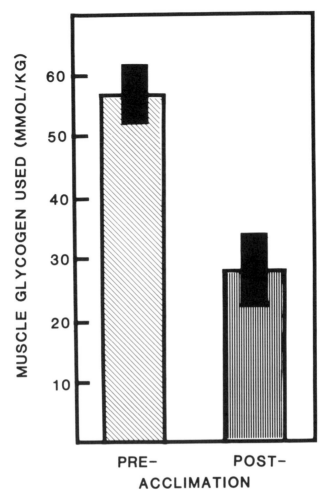

Figure 4-12. Amount of muscle glycogen used during six hours of exercise in heat of 102 degrees Fahrenheit before and after eight days of heat acclimatization. Note the smaller amount of glycogen used after heat acclimatization.

require a greater use of muscle glycogen than the same run in cooler air (29). As a result, repeated days of training in the heat may cause a rapid depletion of muscle glycogen and the symptoms of chronic fatigue. Heat acclimatization reduces this rate of glycogen use by as much as 50 to 60 percent, thereby reducing the risk of exhaustion due to a depletion of the muscle's energy reserves (see Figure 4-12).

Runners must guard against injuries such as heat stroke and heat exhaustion. Heat acclimatization cannot be accelerated by avoiding water during training. You cannot adapt to dehydration! Taking fluids will minimize the hazards of heat injury and enable you to train better.

TRAINING IN THE COLD

Some runners believe that the heat produced by exercise provides the necessary warmth for cold weather running. Since most runners lack the fatty insulation needed to retain body heat, this may not be the case. We have, on a number of occasions, observed rectal temperatures below resting levels in distance runners after long runs of 10 to 25 miles in temperatures ranging from 20 to 30 degrees Fahrenheit. Although the runners were warmly clothed, rectal temperatures decreased from resting values of 99.2 degrees Fahrenheit to less than 98 degrees Fahrenheit.

Numerous investigators have found no evidence of cold acclimatization in humans (44, 70, 71). Some cold adjustment has been observed among men during resting conditions, but evidence is lacking concerning running performance and cold exposure.

While there is limited research to describe the effects of cold weather running on the distance runner, one might theorize that under extremely cold conditions, the quantity of heat lost may exceed that produced by the muscles. The risk of becoming hypothermic is greatest in long races where fatigue may force the runners to decrease their pace, which lowers the rate of body heat production. Although the distance runner tends to perform better under cool conditions, extreme body heat loss can cause the runner to weaken and even collapse.

Despite low environmental temperatures, men have been found to sweat profusely, which causes substantial weight losses and surprisingly low skin temperatures (13). Accumulation of sweat in the clothing and on the skin provides a rapid mechanism for heat loss by conduction to the cold, wetted microenvironment surrounding the runner.

Other major threats posed by running in subfreezing air are those associated with frostbite and irritations to the respiratory tract. The wind chill imposed by running increases the risk of freezing injuries. Though such injuries to the skin may occur at temperatures barely below freezing, irritations and tissue damage to the respiratory tract seldom occur when the temperature is above 10 degrees Fahrenheit. Experts generally agree that training and racing should not be attempted below 10 to 12 degrees Fahrenheit.

TRAINING FOR ALTITUDE

Much of the preceding discussion has described the human capacity to perform endurance exercise under relatively compatible climatic conditions. However, the atmosphere that provides the oxygen needed for aerobic energy production is not uniform. Running is markedly influenced by the reduced oxygen content of the air at high altitudes.

The exchange of oxygen between the air sacs of the lungs and the blood passing through the lungs depends on the difference in the number of oxygen molecules available in the lungs and in the air. When the runner moves from sea level to an elevation of 8,200 feet (Mexico City), the number of oxygen molecules in the lung will decrease nearly 30 percent. Under resting conditions there are few noticeable effects since the runner can simply increase his or her breathing to compensate for the lack of oxygen. With the increased demands of distance running, however, respiration becomes more limiting, and the ability to consume oxygen is reduced.

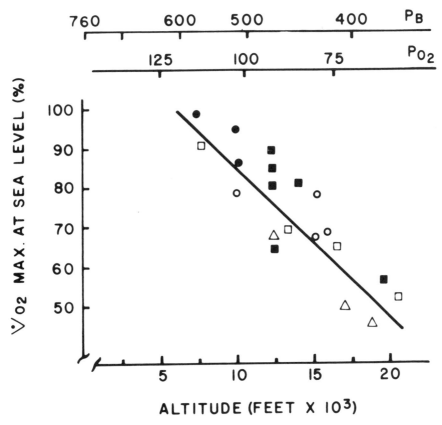

Figure 4-13. The influence of altitude (barometric pressure, P_B, and oxygen tension, P_{O2}) on maximal oxygen uptake, which decreased roughly 3.2 percent for each 1,000 feet increase in altitude above 5,000 feet.

As illustrated in Figure 4-13, Vo_2 max decreases roughly 3.2 percent for each 1,000-foot increase in altitude above 5,000 feet. Below 5,000 feet it is difficult to detect any decrement in performance or Vo_2 max. Early studies demonstrated that the average time for a three-mile run at Mexico City was 8.5 pecent slower than at sea level (58). In the mile run, performance decreased 3.6 percent. This means that a sea level time of 13 minutes for three miles would correspond to a 14 minute:7 second performance at an altitude of 7,500 feet.

In addition to the fewer number of oxygen molecules in the air, high altitude offers several other conditions which differ from sea level. Gas molecules in the air are further apart, so they offer less resistance as they move in and out of the lungs. Consequently, the runner's maximal breathing capacity is greater at altitude than at sea level (4, 21). At the same time, there is less air at altitude to resist movement of the body. This is most noticeable in the sprint events, since air resistance changes with the wind velocity raised to the third power (57). Another consideration is the relatively cooler, drier air at altitude. Although this facilitates heat exchange, it also promotes respiratory water loss. As a result, many athletes lose weight abruptly through dehydration during the first few days at altitude, compounding their already reduced capacities for oxygen transport. Finally, solar radiation is more intense at altitude, which may cause sunburn and radiant heat gains during long runs.

The adaptations which result from endurance training at altitude are confined to: (1) an increase in breathing, (2) an increase in blood hemoglobin concentration, and (3) some small changes in muscle energy systems such as increased oxidative enzymes, myoglobin content, and capillarization. During the first few days at high altitudes runners will be less able to tolerate lactate production, limiting their abilities to perform repeated bouts of maximal anaerobic exercise (38, 62).

Physiological adaptations to altitude are related to the duration of exposure. Since the rate of adaptation is not uniform for all physiological systems, full acclimatization to altitude may require several months.

Training at altitude does not seem to improve the distance runner's performance at sea level. Studies have shown that there is no difference in the effects of hard endurance training at 7,500 feet and equivalently severe sea level training on Vo_2 max values or two-mile performance times among runners who were already well-conditioned (1). Training at altitude only improves performance at altitude. After 20 weeks of training at altitude the runners showed marked improvements in their performance at altitude.

There is no evidence to support the concept that breathing gases low in oxygen content while exercising for one to two hours per day will induce even a partial adaptation to altitude (51). It has, however, been demonstrated that this procedure may enhance the maximal exercise breathing capacity. Since most athletes cannot afford the time or expense involved in long stays at altitude, it is pertinent to consider the benefits for acclimatization of intermittent visits to altitude. Investigators have observed that alternating periods of training seven to 14 days at 7,500 feet with periods of five to 11 days at sea level was adequate for altitude acclimatization (24). Sea level stays of up to 11 days did not interfere with the usual adjustments to altitude as long as training was maintained.

Runners who wish to prepare for competition at moderate altitude must realize: (1) full adaptation may require several months, (2) work capacity must be reduced during the initial days at altitude, (3) the rate of acclimatization is unaffected by brief periods at sea level, (4) short exposure to gases containing reduced levels of oxygen will not stimulate adaptation to altitude, and (5) sea level performance is not improved by altitude training in runners who are already well-trained.

ALL THINGS CONSIDERED

Without a doubt, the most outstanding aspect of training is the ability of the body to adapt and become more tolerant of the physiological demands of repeated days and weeks of exercise. Improvements in blood circulation, oxygen delivery, energy production, and waste product removal make it possible for someone who could not run a single mile in 10 minutes before training to race a marathon several minutes per mile faster. Though nearly all forms of regular aerobic exercise will improve one's endurance, the mode, frequency, and duration of training determine the degree of improvement in running performance.

Designing a training program for the distance runner is an art. The individual variations in human physiology, anatomy, and psychology make it impossible to design a single regimen that will meet the abilities and needs of all runners. Nevertheless, there are a number of factors to help in planning a training program that will help the runner reach his or her potential. These factors include the following:

1. Specificity of Training. The physiological adaptations to training are closely related to the speed, distance, and mode of exercise performed during repeated days of exercise. Since there is little crossover from one type of exercise to another, the best way to prepare for distance competition is to run at speeds that develop the energy systems needed for racing. Non-specific exercises like cycling and swimming do little to prepare the individual for running.

2. Balance Work and Rest. The purpose of training is to stimulate the runner's anatomy and physiology to grow stronger during periods of rest and repair. Without adequate rest, the benefits of training cannot be fully realized.

3. Hard Days and Easy Days. In addition to a need for complete rest, there must be some variation in the level of stress imposed during each training session. One or two days of hard training should be followed by a day or two of lighter intensity.

4. Progression. The body grows slowly and responds best to a gradual increase in training stress. Mileage and speed should be increased gradually over a period of several weeks and months. Although the progression of stress is always upward, weeks of hard training should always be followed by periods of markedly reduced effort.

5. Mileage. Although the number of calories burned during training seems to directly influence the degree of aerobic improvement, there is little value in running more than 60 to 100 miles per week. Mileage greater than that produces little, if any, improvement in the runner's performance or physiology. Lesser mileage allows greater opportunity for quality training.

6. Hot and Cold Training. Although circulation and sweating adjust to exercise in the heat, there is little adaptation to cold weather running. Though heat acclimatization can be achieved after four to 12 days of training in a warm environment, the risk of heat injury is still the greatest single health threat to the runner.

7. Altitude Training. Acclimatization to high altitude may take several months. Though running performances at altitude will improve with acclimatization, altitude training does not appear to improve a runner's performances at sea level.

BIBLIOGRAPHY

1. Adams, W. C., E. M. Bernauer, D. B. Dill and J. B. Bomar. Effects of equivalent sea-level and altitude training on VO$_2$ and running performance. *J. Appl. Physiol.*, 39:262–266, 1975.
2. Andersen, P. and J. Henrickson. Capillary supply of the quadriceps femoris muscle of man: Adaptive response to exercise. *J. Physiol.*, 270:677–690, 1977.
3. Armstrong, L. E., D. L. Costill, W. F. Fink, D. Bassett, M. Hargreaves, I. Nishibata and D. S. King. Effects of dietary sodium on body and muscle potassium content during heat acclimation. *Europ. J. Appl. Physiol. (In Press)*.
4. Astrand, P. -O. *Experimental studies of physical working capacity in relation to age and sex.* Copenhagen: Munksgaard, 1952.
5. Astrand, P. -O. and K. Rodahl. *Textbook of Work Physiology*, 563. New York: McGraw-Hill, 1970.
6. Baldwin, K., G. Glinerfuss, R. Terjung, P. Mole and J. Holloszy. Respiratory capacity

of white, red, and intermediate muscle: Adaptive response to exercise. *Am. J. Physiol.*, 222:373–378, 1972.

7. Bartels, R. L. Interval training and cardiorespiratory conditioning. (abstract). *A.A.H.P.E.R. Convention Proceedings*, 1968.

8. Bass, D. E. Thermoregulatory and circulatory adjustments during acclimatization to heat in man. *Temperature: Its Measurement and Control in Science and Industry*, 3:Part 3. New York: Reinhold Book Corp., 1963.

9. Bevegard, B. S. and J. T. Shepherd. Regulation of the circulation during exercise in man. *Physiol. Rev.*, 47:178, 1967.

10. Brodal, P., F. Inger and L. Hermansen. Capillary supply of skeletal muscle fibers in untrained and endurance-trained men. *Am. J. Physiol.*, 232:H705–H712, 1977.

11. Buick, F. J., N. Gledhill, A. B. Froese and E. C. Spriet. Double blind study of blood boosting in highly trained runners. *Med. Sci. Sports*, 10:49, 1978.

12. Buskirk, E. R. and R. Moore. Exercise and body fluids. *Science and Medicine of Exercise and Sport*, ed. W. R. Johnson. New York: Harper and Brothers. 1960.

13. Costill, D. L. What research tells the coach about distance running. *Am. Assoc. Health, Phys. Ed., Recreation*, 45–46, 1968.

14. Costill, D. L. and B. Saltin. Muscle glycogen and electrolytes following exercise and thermal dehydration. *Metabolic Adaptations to Prolonged Physical Exercise*, 352–360. Basel, Switzerland: Birkhauser Verlag, 1975.

15. Costill, D. L., E. F. Coyle, W. F. Fink, G. R. Lesmes and F. A. Witzmann. Adaptations in skeletal muscle following strength training. *J. Appl. Physiol.*, 46:96–99, 1979.

16. Costill, D. L., H. Kuipers, M. J. Burrell, W. J. Fink, J. Kirwan and J. Kovaleski. Effects of heat acclimation on leg blood flow and muscle metabolism. *(In preparation)*.

17. Costill, D. L., J. Daniels, W. Evans, W. Fink, G. Krahenbuhl and B. Saltin. Skeletal muscle enzymes and fiber composition in male and female track athletes. *J. Appl. Physiol.*, 40:149–154, 1976.

18. Costill, D. L., P. Cleary, W. Fink, C. Foster, J. L. Ivy and F. Witzmann. Training adaptations in skeletal muscle of juvenile diabetics. *Diabetes*, 28:818–822, 1979.

19. Costill, D. L., R. Cote, T. Miller and S. Wynder. Water and electrolyte replacement during repeated days of work in the heat. *Aviat. Space Environ. Med.*, 46:795–800, 1975.

20. Costill, D. L., W. Fink and M. Pollock. Muscle fiber composition and enzyme activities of elite distance runners. *Med. Sci. Sports*, 8:96–100, 1976.

21. Cotes, J. E. Ventilatory capacity at altitude and its relation to mask design. *Proc. Roy. Soc.*, B 143:32–37, 1954.

22. Coyle, E. F., S. Bell, D. L. Costill and W. J. Fink. Skeletal muscle fiber composition of world class shot-putters. *Res. Quart.*, 49:278–284, 1978.

23. Crockett, J. L., V. R. Edgerton, S. R. Max and R. J. Barnard. The neuromuscular junction in response to endurance training. *Exp. Neurol.*, 51:207–215, 1976.

24. Daniels, J. and N. Oldridge. The effects of alternate exposure to altitude and sea level on world-class middle-distance runners. *Med. Sci. Sports*, 2:107–112, 1970.

25. Eichma, L. W. and others. Thermal regulation during acclimatization to hot, dry environment. *Amer. J. Physiol.*, 163:585, 1950.

26. Ekblom, B., A. N. Goldbarg and B. Gullbring. Response to exercise after blood loss and reinfusion. *J. Appl. Physiol.*, 33:275–280, 1972.

27. Eriksson, B. O., P. D. Gollnick and B. Saltin. Muscle metabolism and enzyme activities after training in boys 11–13 years old. *Acta Physiol. Scand.*, 87:231–239, 1972.

28. Falsetti, H. L. Invasive and noninvasive evaluation of exercise in humans. *Med. Sci. Sports*, 9:262–267, 1977.

29. Fink, W., D. L. Costill and P. Van Handel. Leg muscle metabolism during exercise in the heat and cold. *Europ. J. Appl. Physiol.*, 34:183–190, 1975.

30. Fink, W. J., D. L. Costill and M. L. Pollock. Submaximal and maximal working capacity of elite distance runners. *Ann. N.Y. Acad. Sci.*, 301:323–327, 1977.

31. Fitts, R. H. and J. O. Holloszy. Contractile properties of rat soleus muscle: Effects of training and fatigue. *Am. J. Physiol.*, 233:C86–C91, 1977.

32. Flippin, R. Did they or didn't they? *The Runner*, 7:72, 1985.

33. Fox, E., R. Bartels, C. Billings, R. O'Brien, R. Bason and D. Mathews. Frequency and duration of interval training programs and changes in aerobic power. *J. Appl. Physiol.*, 38:481–484, 1975.

34. Fox, E. L., R. L. Bartels, C. E. Billings, D. K. Matthews, R. Bason and W. M. Webb. Intensity and distance of interval training programs and changes in aerobic power. *Med. Sci. Sports*, 5:18–22, 1973.

35. Gollnick, P. D. and D. W. King. Energy release in the muscle cell. *Med. Sci. Sports*, 1:23–31, 1969.

36. Gollnick, P. D., R. B. Armstrong, B. Saltin, C. W. Saubert, W. L. Sembrowich and R. E. Shephard. Effect of training on enzyme activities and fiber composition of human skeletal muscle. *J. Appl. Physiol.*, 34:107–111, 1973.

37. Grimby, G. and B. Saltin. A physiological analysis of still active middle-aged and old athletes. *Acta Med. Scand.*, 179:513–520, 1966.

38. Hansen, J. E., G. P. Stelter and J. A. Vogel. Arterial, pyruvate, lactate, pH, and Pco_2 during work at sea level and high altitude. *J. Appl. Physiol.*, 23:523–526, 1967.

39. Hermansen, L. and O. Vagge. Lactate disappearance and glycogen synthesis in human muscle after maximal exercise. *Am. J. Physiol.*, 233:E422–E429, 1977.

40. Hoeppeler, H., P. Luthi, H. Clasassen, E. R. Weibel and H. Howald. The ultrastructure of the normal human skeletal muscle. A morphometric analysis on untrained men, women, and well-trained orienteers. *Pflugers Arch.*, 344:217–232, 1973.

41. Holloszy, J. O. Biochemical adaptations in muscle. *J. Biol. Chem.*, 242:2278–2282, 1967.

42. Holloszy, J. O., L. B. Oscai, P. A. Mole and I. J. Don. Biochemical adaptations to endurance exercise in skeletal muscle. *Muscle Metabolism During Exercise*, 51–56. New York: Plenum Press, 1971.

43. Holloszy, J. O., L. B. Oscai, I. J. Don and P. A. Mole. Mitochondrial citric acid cycle and related enzymes: Adaptive responses to exercise. *Biochem. Biophys. Res. Comm.*, 40:1368–1373, 1970.

44. Horvath, S. M., Acclimatization to extreme cold. *Amer. J. Physiol.*, 150:99–108, 1947.

45. Howald, H., Ultrastructural adaptation of skeletal muscle to prolonged physical exercise. *Metabolic Adaptations to Prolonged Physical Exercise*, 372–383. Basel, Switzerland: Birkhauser, Verlag, 1975.

46. Kiessling, K. H., K. Piehl and C. G. Lundquist. Effect of physical training on ultrastructural features in human skeletal muscle. *Muscle Metabolism During Exercise*, 97–101. New York: Plenum Press, 1971.

47. King, D. S., D. L., Costill, W. J. Fink, M. Hargreaves and R. A. Fielding. Muscle metabolism during exercise in the heat in unacclimatized and acclimatized man. *J. Appl. Physiol. (In Press)*.

48. Kjellberg, S. R., U. Rudhe and T. Sjostrand. Increase of the amount of hemoglobin and blood volume in connection with physical training. *Acta Physiol. Scand.*, 19:146–154, 1949.

49. Kjellberg, S. R., U. Ruhde and T. Sjostrand. The amount of hemoglobin and the blood volume in relation to the pulse rate and cardiac volume during rest. *Acta Physiol. Scand.*, 19:136–145, 1949.

50. Leithead, C. S. and A. R. Lind. *Heat Stress and Heat Disorders*. Philadelphia: F. A. Davis Company, 1964.

51. Loeppky, J. A. and W. A. Bynum. Effects of periodic exposure to hypobaria and exercise on physical work capacity. *J. Sports Med. and Phys. Fitness*, 10:238–247.

52. Lumian, N. C. and V. F. Krumdick. Physiological, psychological aspects of marathon training for distance runners. *Athletic Journal*, 45:68, 1965.

53. Pattengale, P. and J. Holloszy. Augmentation of skeletal muscle myoglobin by a pro-

gram of treadmill running. *Am. J. Physiol.*, 213:783–785, 1967.

54. Pollock, M. The quantification of endurance training programs. *Exercise and Sports Sciences Reviews*, 1:155–188, 1973.
55. Polloci, M. L., J. Broida, Z. Kendrick, J. H. S. Miller, R. Janeway and A. C. Linnerud. Effects of training two days per week at different intensities on middle-aged men. *Med. Sci. Sports*, 4:192–197, 1972.
56. Pollock, M. L., T. K. Cureton and L. Greninger. Effects of frequency of training on working capacity, cardiovascular function, and body composition of adult men. *Med. Sci. Sports*, 1:70–74, 1969.
57. Pugh, L. G. C. Oxygen uptake in track and treadmill running with observations on the effect of air resistance. *J. Physiol.*, 207:825–835, 1970.
58. Pugh, L. G. C. Athletes at altitude. *J. Physiol.*, 192:619–747, 1967.
59. Robertson, R., R. Gilcher, K. Metz, H. Bahnson, T. Allison, G. Skrinar, A. Abbott and R. Becker. Effect of red cell reinfusion on physical working capacity and perceived exertion at normal and reduced oxygen pressure. *Med. Sci. Sports*, 10:49, 1978.
60. Robinson, S. Training, acclimatization and heat tolerance. *Proceedings of the International Symposium on Physical Activity and Cardiovascular Health*, October 11–13, 1966.
61. Robinson, S., Circulatory adjustment of men in hot environments. *Temperature: Its Measurement and Control in Science and Industry*, 3:Part 3, 1963.
62. Roughton, F. J. W. Transport of oxygen and carbon dioxide. *Handbook of Physiology*, 1:767. Washington, D.C., American Physiological Society, 1964.
63. Rowell, L. B. Factors affecting the prediction of the maximal oxygen intake from measurements made during submaximal work. *Dissertation*, University of Minnesota, 1962.
64. Saltin, B. Physiological effects of physical conditioning. *Med. Sci. Sports*, 1:50–56, 1969.
65. Saltin, B., G. Blomqvist, J. H. Mitchell, R. L. Johnson, K. Wildenthal and C. B. Chapman. Response to exercise after bedrest and after training. *Circulation*, Suppl. 7:1968.
66. Shrubb, A. A. Long distance running. *Training for Athletes*, 46–53. London: Health and Strength, Ltd., 1904.
67. Sjostrand, T. The total quantity of hemoglobin in man and its relation to age, sex, body weight, height. *Acta Physiol. Scand.*, 18:325–333, 1949.
68. Sjostrand, T. Functional capacity and exercise tolerance in patients with impaired cardiovascular function. *Clinical Cardiopulmonary Physiology*, 1960.
69. Staron, R. S., R. S. Hikida, F. C. Hagerman, G. A. Dudley and T. F. Murray. Human skeletal muscle fiber type adaptability to various workloads. *J. Histochem. Cytochem.*, 32:146–152, 1984.
70. Stein, H. J. Physiological reactions to cold and their effects on the retention of acclimatization to heat. *J. Appl. Physiol.*, 1:575–585, 1949.
71. Stein, H. J. Hormonal alterations in men exposed to heat and the retention of acclimatization to heat. *J. Clin. Endocrinol.*, 9:529–547, 1949.
72. Strydom, N. B. Acclimatization to humid heat and the role of physical conditioning. *J. Appl. Physiol.*, 21:636–642, 1966.
73. Taylor, H. L., E. Buskirk and A. Henschel. Maximal oxygen intake as an objective measure of cardiorespiratory performance. *J. Appl. Physiol.*, 8:73–81, 1955.
74. Williams, M. H., A. R. Goodwin, R. Perkins and J. Bocrie. Effect of blood reinjection upon endurance capacity and heart rate. *Med. Sci. Sports*, 5:181–186, 1973.

CHAPTER 5

Peaking for Performance

Endurance training alone does not insure the best possible performance. Despite a high level of physical conditioning, many athletes fail to achieve their full potential as a result of poor management. Such factors as improper nutrition, overtraining, and poor pacing during a race can negate many of the qualities gained through months of preparation. In this chapter we will discuss factors that must be monitored and properly managed for runners to do their best.

AVOIDING OVERTRAINING

One of the fine arts of coaching lies in the ability to design a training regimen that provides the level of stress needed for optimal physiological improvements without exceeding the runner's tolerance. Although most coaches employ a set of intuitive standards to judge the volume and intensity of each training session, few are able to assess the relative impact of the workout on the runner. By the time most coaches realize that they have overstressed an athlete, it is too late. The damage done by repeated days of excessive training can only be repaired by days and, in some cases, weeks of reduced training or complete rest.

It seems that the runners most susceptible to overtraining or staleness are those who are the most highly motivated, attempting to perform their best during every training run or competition. Sudden increases in mileage or running intensity or both may overload the systems of adaptations.

Though the symptoms of overtraining may vary from one runner to another, the most common are a feeling of heaviness and an inability to perform well during training and competition. Physical symptoms may include one or more of the following: (1) body weight loss with decreased appetite; (2) muscle tenderness; (3) head colds or allergic reactions or both; (4) occasional nausea; or (5) elevated resting heart rate or blood pressure or both.

Psychologically, runners who are overtrained may exhibit symptoms of depression, irritability, and anxiety. The most common complaint among these runners is that they have trouble falling asleep or that they awaken frequently during the night for no apparent reason. Overtraining results in abnormal psychological, physiological and performance responses.

The underlying causes of overtraining or staleness are often a combination of emotional and physical factors. Hans Selye (44) has noted that a breakdown in one's tolerance of stress can occur as often from a sudden increase in anxiety as from an increase in physical distress. The emotional demands of competition, the desire to win, fear of failure, unrealistically high goals, and the expectations of coaches and fellow runners can be sources of intolerable emotional stress. Sources of physical stress include not only exercise and training, but also environmental temperature, altitude, and improper nutrition.

Day-to-day variations in the sensations of fatigue should not be confused with overtraining. It is not uncommon for a runner's legs to feel heavy after several days of hard training or after a stressful race. Unlike the feelings of being stale, the short-lived sensations of heaviness are usually relieved with a day or two of easy training and a carbohydrate-rich diet. Overtraining is accompanied by a loss in competitive desire and a loss in enthusiasm for training.

There are few warning signs of overtraining. Most of the symptoms are subjective and identifiable only after the runners have overextended themselves. We have observed that runners who suddenly begin to perform very well during training may be on the verge of disaster. They feel so good during workouts that they tend to extend themselves beyond their day-to-day tolerances, resulting in performance breakdowns.

A number of investigators have used various physiological measurements to diagnose overtraining. Unfortunately, none has proven totally effective. It is often difficult to differentiate whether the measurements are abnormal and related to overtraining or simply the normal physiological responses to heavy training.

Measurements of blood enzyme levels have been used to diagnose overtraining with only limited success. Such enzymes as CPK (creatine phosphokinase), LDH (lactate dehydrogenase), and SGOT (serum glutamic oxaloacetic transaminase) are important in muscle energy production but are generally confined to the inside of the cells. The presence of these enzymes in blood suggests some damage to or structural change in the muscle membranes (20, 33). Following periods of heavy training, these enzymes have been reported to increase two to 10 times the normal levels (20, 28, 33, 36, 37, 38). Recent studies tend to support the idea that these changes in blood enzymes may reflect varied degrees of muscle tissue breakdown (17, 19, 26). Examination of tissue from the leg muscles of marathon runners has revealed that there is remarkable damage to the muscle fibers after training and marathon competition (19, 26). The onset and time course of these muscle changes seemed to parallel the degree of muscle soreness experienced by the runners.

The electronmicrograph presented in Figure 5-1 shows a sample of the damage done to some muscle fibers as a result of marathon running (19, 26). In this case the cell membrane or sarcolemma has been totally ruptured, with its contents floating freely between the other normal fibers. Though not all of the damage done to the muscle cells is as severe as that shown in Figure 5-1, there are other examples of disruptions within the fibers.

Figures 5-2a and 5-2b illustrate some changes in the contractile filaments or Z-lines, which are the points of contact and support for the contractile proteins. They provide structural support for the transmission of force when the muscle fibers are activated to shorten. Figure 5-2a shows the normal ultrastructure of the muscle fiber before the marathon race, with the Z-lines intact. Figure 5-2b shows Z-lines after the marathon, pulled apart from the force of eccentric contractions or the stretching of tightened muscle fibers.

Although the effects of muscle damage on running performance are not fully understood, experts generally agree that they may be, in part, responsible for the localized muscle pain, tenderness, and swelling associated with muscle soreness. There is, however, no evidence that this condition is linked to the symptoms of overtraining. We suspect that blood enzyme levels rise and muscle fibers are damaged frequently during eccentric exercise and are independent of the state of overtraining. In addition to being difficult and expensive to measure, blood enzyme levels do not appear to be a valid indicator of overtraining.

White blood cells or eosinophils serve as a defense against foreign materials that enter the body or conditions that threaten the normal function of body tissues. Since the white blood cell count tends to rise during exhaustive exercise, some investigators have suggested that it may provide a warning signal for impending staleness. However, again it is not clear whether this change is a sign of overstress or simply a normal reaction to intense training.

Early studies have reported abnormal resting electrocardiographic

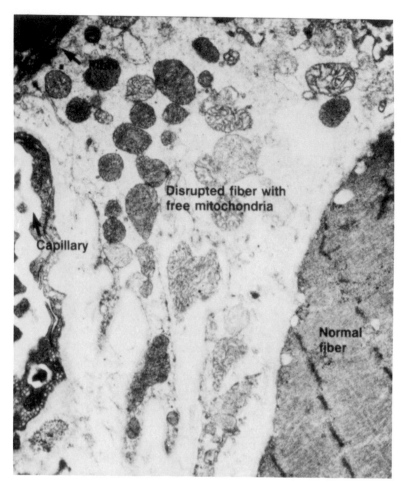

Figure 5-1. An electronmicrograph of a muscle sample taken immediately after a marathon, showing the disruption of the cell membrane in one muscle fiber (19).

(EKG) tracings among swimmers who showed signs of overtraining (6, 7). Typically, those swimmers who showed sudden decrements in performance often exhibited T-wave inversions. Since such EKG changes are associated with abnormal repolarization of the heart ventricles, it was suggested that these changes among training athletes may reveal signs of overtraining. On the other hand, a number of the swimmers who clearly exhibited symptoms of overtraining had normal EKG tracings.

It has been suggested that unusually high resting blood lactate concentrations may be a sign of overstress (33). Another group of swimmers had high resting lactate concentrations when they were swimming poorly and had normal concentrations when they were swimming well. Since a number of external factors such as diet and prior activity might elevate an athlete's resting blood lactate, additional observations are needed to confirm the value of this measurement as a valid index of overtraining.

Despite various attempts to objectively diagnose overtraining, no single physiological measurement has proven 100 percent effective. Since performance is the most dramatic indicator of overtraining, we have monitored runners' physiological reactions during standard, submaximal six-minute mile runs. When they show symptoms of overtraining, their heart rates and oxygen consumption during the runs are significantly higher.

Some years ago we observed a college cross-country runner who had an oxygen uptake of 49 milliliters of oxygen per minute for each kilogram of body weight (ml/kg $\times$ min) and heart rate of 142 beats per minute while running a six-minute mile. During the same period of this test, his best performance for the 10-kilometer was 30 minutes:53 seconds, which ranked him as the third best runner on the team. Later in the season his 10-kilometer performance deteriorated to 32 minutes:10 seconds, placing him eighth on the team. At that time it cost him significantly more to run the six-minute mile test, 56 ml/kg $\times$ min, with a heart rate of 168 beats per minute (Figure 5-3). Interestingly, his maximal oxygen uptake of 70 ml/kg $\times$ minute was not changed, despite the diminished performance. While the first six-minute mile required him to work at 70 percent of his Vo_2 max, the same run required 80 percent of his Vo_2 max when he exhibited symptoms of overtraining. In terms of aerobic fitness, overtrained runners do not lose their conditioning, but they may demonstrate a deterioration in running form. Though the causes for this loss in running skill are not fully understood, overtraining may cause some local muscular fatigue through selective glycogen depletion, forcing runners to alter their mechanics to achieve the same pace.

Although it is impractical for most coaches and runners to consider measuring oxygen uptake during such a six-minute mile test, current technology makes it relatively easy to record heart rate. Figure 5-4 shows a system we currently use to test the Ball State University runners. Chest leads pick up the electrical impulses from the heart and transmit them to a recording memory system on the runner's wrist. As the runner performs an evenly paced mile run, the recording system stores heart rates every five seconds. The data presented in Figure 5-5 illustrate a runner's heart rates during the six-minute mile test at the beginning of training, after training, and during a period when he demonstrated symptoms of being overtrained.

Although we use a six-minute mile test with the college runners, a similar test might be performed at eight or nine minutes per mile for less skilled runners. The advantage of this test is that it provides an objective

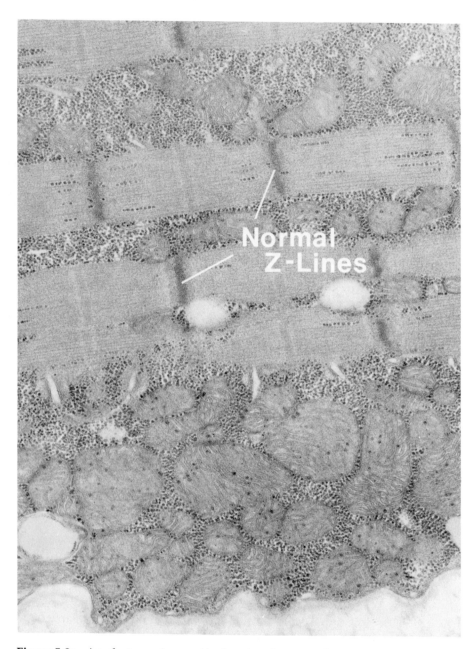

Figure 5-2a. An electronmicrograph showing the normal arrangement of the actomyosin filaments and Z-line configuration in the muscle of a runner before a marathon race (19).

Figure 5-2b. An example of Z-line streaming caused by the eccentric contractions of running. This sample of muscle was taken immediately after a marathon race (19).

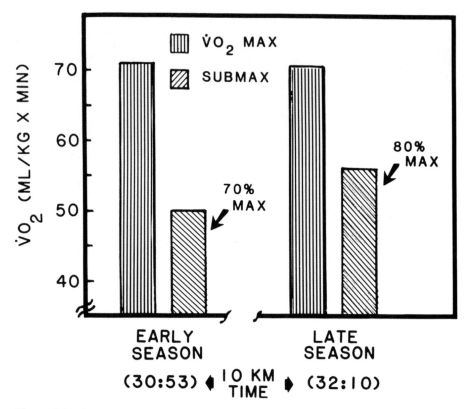

Figure 5-3. Oxygen uptake during maximal (Vo₂ max) and submaximal (six-minute mile) running during two periods of the season for a college cross-country runner. Note that there was no change in the runner's Vo₂ max, despite a marked decrement in his time for the 10-kilometer. At the same time, the amount of energy needed to run at the submaximal speed was notably greater when he was overtrained.

measurement of the runner's physiological response during a given amount of work. Blood lactate measurements taken after this test correlate very closely with the runner's heart rate. Since heart rates are relatively simple to record and provide immediate information for the runner and coach, such a test serves as an objective method to monitor the runner's conditioning and may provide a warning signal of overtraining.

Though the causes for a deterioration in performance are not clear, it appears that the intensity or speed of training is a more potent stressor than training mileage (37). Relief from overtraining only comes with a marked reduction in training pace or complete rest. Although most coaches suggest a few days of slow, easy training runs, we are inclined to feel that runners recover their running form faster when they rest completely

Figure 5-4. Ball State runners wired to record their heart rates during a standard submaximal run. The chest strap picks up and transmits the electrical impulses from the heart to the memory device worn on the wrist. After the run the recordings can be played back for interpretation.

for three to five days or engage in some other form of low-intensity exercise like walking. In some cases, counseling may be needed to help the runner cope with job, school, or social pressures. At other times the problem may simply be a matter of poor nutrition, insufficient sleep, or both. If the runner shows continued signs of fatigue and substandard performances despite rest and counseling, medical help should be sought.

As noted by Ernie Maglischo (33), "Prevention is always preferable to curing an overtrained state." The best way to minimize the risk of overstressing is to follow cyclic training procedures by alternating easy, moderate, and hard periods of training. Chapter 4 discussed the value and incorporation of rest in the training scheme. Although tolerance limits vary from one runner to another, even the strongest runners have periods when they are susceptible to overtraining. As a rule, one or two days of intense training should be followed by an equal number of easy, aerobic training days. Likewise, a week or two of hard training should be followed by a week of reduced mileage with little or no emphasis on anaerobic running. Special attention must be given to the runner's carbohydrate intake to minimize the risk of chronic muscle glycogen depletion. As noted in Chapter 3, repeated days of hard training will result

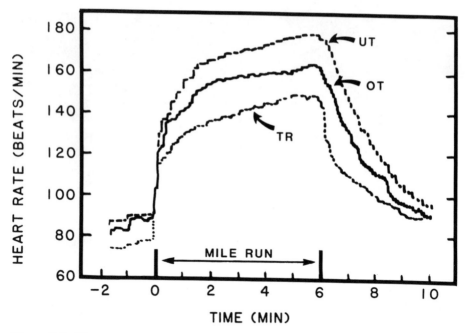

Figure 5-5. Heart rate responses during a standard, six-minute mile, submaximal run before training (UT), after eight weeks of training (T), and during the period when the runner exhibited symptoms of being overtrained (OT).

in a gradual reduction in muscle glycogen. Unless the runner consumes extra quantities of carbohydrate-rich foods during these periods, muscle and liver glycogen reserves may be depleted, leaving the most heavily recruited muscle fibers incapable of generating the energy needed for running.

MONITORING TRAINING STRESS

Preventing overtraining is a matter of anticipating other stresses and taking care to eliminate them before they take their toll on the runner's performance. What may be stimulating and enjoyable to one runner may add excessive stress to another. This fact makes it nearly impossible to eliminate the problem of overtraining in sports. Only with careful monitoring of the runners' attitudes and performances can we hope to minimize the risk of a breakdown in the system of adaptation. Coaches must consider the pace, distance, and accumulated stresses of their training plans.

In an effort to evaluate objectively the physical stress imposed by a given workout, we have developed a system that assesses training stress and written a program that offers the runner a quick, accurate method to monitor the demands of a given workout.[1]

First, this program considers the runner's physiological ability (Vo_2 max) and his or her current state of training. As mentioned in Chapter 1, Vo_2 max can be predicted from running performance in the mile, two-mile, or 10-kilometer (16). The relative intensity of the training run can be calculated as the percentage of Vo_2 max used during the run. The oxygen uptake during the training run must be calculated from the equation:

$$Vo_2 = (329/P) - 5.24$$

where P = running pace in minutes per mile

(example: at 6 minute/mile the Vo_2 = 49.6 ml/kg × minute)

$$\% Vo_2 \text{ max} = (Vo_2/Vo_2 \text{ max}) \times 100$$

Vo_2 max is calculated as described in Chapter 1.

In order to rate the pace or intensity of a given run, the percent Vo_2 max is divided by 70 percent, a level of effort known to be neither hard nor easy for the runner. If, for example, the runner trained at 70 percent Vo_2 max, then the training intensity (IR) would be rated as 1.0 (70/70 = 1.0). On the other hand, a training pace requiring 85 percent Vo_2 max would be given a rating of 1.21, a stressful pace.

To rate the distance of a given workout, the mileage is divided by five miles, a distance known to be neither hard nor easy for the runner. If the runner has been averaging five miles per day for the last few weeks, then he or she would be given a distance rating (DR) of 1.0 (5 miles/5 miles) for a five-mile run. If the runner did a training run of seven miles, then the distance rating would jump to 1.40, a marked increase in training stress.

The distance rating and the intensity rating help to estimate the demands of training. Although these two factors may offer different levels of stress, we average the two ratios in an effort to obtain one overall rating (TI) for the workout. Finally, the overall rating is multiplied by 100 in order to eliminate decimals.

$$TI = 100((DR + IR)/2)$$

The advantage of this approach is that it provides a single index of

---

[1]Copies of this program are available for Apple and IBM compatible systems from Peak Performance, Inc., P.O. Box 60681, Palo Alto, CA., 94306.

the physiological demands placed on the runner, a rating that can be used to plan subsequent training sessions. Workouts that receive an overall rating above 105 are usually quite stressful, indicating a need for lighter training on the following day. A workout rated at 100 or less is tolerated well by the runner and can be repeated for several days.

As noted earlier, progressive improvements in conditioning can only be achieved by a systematic increase in mileage and speed. Such an approach, however, necessitates that the training program be closely monitored to ensure this progression and to reduce the risk of overtraining the runner.

TAPERING: FINAL PREPARATION

Since peak performance requires a sharpening of both physical and psychological tolerance to the stress of running, the runner should be permitted some relief from the chronic demands of training. During periods of frequent competition, most runners take several days of light training and rely on carbohydrate-rich diets to boost their performances. In light of our previous discussions about training, overtraining, and carbohydrate loading, one might question whether these brief periods of tapering are adequate to promote optimal performance. Experience in other sports, such as swimming, suggests that the taper period may need to cover two or more weeks for best results.

Periods of intense training reduce muscular strength, lessening the performance capacity of athletes (12, 46). To compete at their peak, many athletes reduce their training for five to 21 days before a major competition. Although this regimen is widely practiced in a variety of sports, most runners would fear the loss of their conditioning and top running forms if they reduced training for such a long period before a major competition. A number of studies make it clear, however, that this fear is totally unwarranted (5, 23, 25, 29).

Maximal oxygen uptake can be maintained at the training level with a two-thirds reduction in training frequency (5, 25). It appears that a greater amount of work is needed to increase Vo_2 max than to maintain it at the training level. Whereas Vo_2 max and the ability to perform exercise are measurably improved within one week of training (22, 24), the rate of decline in physical performance with reduced training is much slower.

Swimmers who reduced their training from an average of 10,000 to 3,200 yards per day over a 15-day period showed no loss in Vo_2 max or endurance performance (1, 12). Measurements of blood lactate after a standard 200-yard swim were actually lower after the taper period than before. More importantly, the swimmers showed an average improvement in performance of 3.5 to 3.7 percent as a result of the reduced training.

But what does this mean to the distance runner? The swimmers' higher training volume of 10,000 yards per day corresponds to running about 22.5 miles per day, and swimming 3,200 yards per day, as at the end of the taper period, corresponds to running about seven miles per day. Since few runners are training with such long mileages, it is more accurate to think in terms of decreasing training by a given percentage. During the taper period the runner should run only about 30 percent of the normal daily mileage. A runner who averages six miles per day during normal training, for example, should only run two miles per day during the taper period.

If the runner were to improve 3.5 percent with the taper, then a 40-minute 10-kilometer runner would be expected to run the same distances in 38 minutes: 48 seconds. We anticipate that a 60 to 70 percent reduction in training during the two weeks before a major race would dramatically improve a runner's performance.

The most notable change during the taper period is a marked increase in muscular strength. As a consequence of reduced training, the swimmers demonstrated an increase in arm strength and power of 17.7 to 24.6 percent. This is a reasonable explanation for at least part of the improvement in performance seen with tapering. Similar benefits could be of significant aid to the runner's performance, since it is the responsiveness of the muscles that makes for "easy speed."

One characteristic side effect of a prolonged two- or three-week taper is that the athletes often feel fatigued and unable to extend themselves during the days of reduced training. This is, of course, the opposite of what we would expect, but it may simply reflect a change in the athletes' psychological state and a subconscious inability to stress themselves. It is interesting to note that on the day of the race, the runners find the exercise to be nearly effortless. Their biggest problems are controlling the pace, since they tend to run too fast.

Table 5-1 offers a two-week tapering plan. Although this taper schedule assumes that the runner has been training an average of eight miles per day, six days per week, a similar plan can be calculated for runners who have been doing more or less by using a similar percentage decrease in the daily training mileages.

During the taper period, keep the fast running to a minimum and eliminate all painful, highly anaerobic workouts. This does not mean that the training excludes all race-pace running. On the contrary, it is important to inject a few paced runs in each workout, but the rest and distance of these runs should be controlled to allow the runner to perform each one without feeling overly tired. The runner should be able to recover quickly from each workout during the taper period. We can

TABLE 5-1. A sample tapering program in preparation for a 10,000-meter race. The runner used in this example had been averaging eight miles of running per day, six days per week for six to eight weeks prior to this taper. The percentage values (%DEC) show the amount of change in training as compared to the runner's average daily mileage.

Day	Mileage	%DEC
Avg. Training	8 miles/day	—
1	5 mile (Ae); 4 × 800 m/2 min rest	−12%
2	4 mile (Ae); 4 × 400 m/1 min rest	−38%
3	5 mile (Ae)	−38%
4	4 mile (Ae)	−50%
5	3 mile (Ae); 2 × 1 mile/4 min rest	−38%
6	REST (No Running)	
7	2 mile (Ae); 3 × 1.5 mile/5 min rest	−19%
8	4 mile (Ae)	−50%
9	2 mile (Ae); 2 × 1200 m/3 min rest	−56%
10	3 mile (Ae)	−62%
11	REST (No Running)	
12	2 mile (Ae); 2 × 800 m/3 min rest	−62%
13	2 to 3 mile Warm-up only (Ae)	
14	***10,000 meter race***	

not exclude the possibility that part of the improvement in performance following the taper is psychological and the result of removing the psychological stress of hard training.

Attempts to achieve a peak performance at a specific time add another dimension to the art of coaching the distance runner. Tapering the exercise intensity during the two weeks before a marathon should produce a positive effect on performance, since it allows time for healing and recovery of the body's energy stores. Although most runners feel an urge to perform one long run a week or two before the competition, there is little justification for such action. The training gains from a 15- to 20-mile run are usually not realized for three to four weeks. The risk of injury far outweighs the conditioning effect or the psychological boost of an overdistance run within the last two weeks before the race.

Runners ask how the frequency and length of tapering or reduced training periods will affect their conditioning. Swimming coaches have reported no loss in performance or general conditioning when their swimmers trained at 50 percent of their normal yardages for up to seven weeks. In some cases, world records have been set by swimmers who have been on reduced training regimens for nearly two months. Once the athlete has trained vigorously for a period of several months, much less training is needed to maintain the trained state.

This system of tapering for peak performance, however, may only prove useful two or three times per year. Inevitably, the peak performance will be lost and can only be revived again after a period of basic, noncompetitive training and relief from the psychological stress of competition.

STRATEGIES OF RACING

The tactics of competition are more a matter of artistry than science. Nevertheless, there are several points that may aid the runner in designing a competitive "battle plan."

First, the runner should remember that the primary source of energy during the early stage of a race will be the glycogen stored in the muscles. If the pace is unusually fast in the first few minutes, the quantity of glycogen used will be markedly greater and the muscles' stores will be seriously depleted. At the same time, the by-products of rapid glycogen breakdown may result in a large production of lactic acid, which increases the acidity of the muscle fibers. It is wise to run a bit slower than the desired racing pace during the first few minutes of the race, and to gradually accelerate to racing pace after the third to fifth minutes of running. Although this plan may be impractical in races shorter than 10 kilometers, it can spare a sizeable amount of glycogen in the longer events. Proper pacing can minimize the threat of glycogen depletion and lessen the chance of premature exhaustion.

There seems to be little agreement among runners about the proper way to pace a race. Most runners have preconceived ideas or past successes with a variety of pacing patterns. Peter Karpovich (30) suggests that the maximum speed that can be maintained during a race depends on the muscles' capacity to generate energy and the runner's efficient use of that energy. Since the energy requirements increase dramatically with even slight acceleration, most physiologists advocate an even or steady pace during distance running.

Sid Robinson (41) studied the effects of variable pace on the oxygen requirements and blood lactates of four well-conditioned subjects during exhaustive treadmill runs. The subjects were tested at three pace patterns: constant, slow to fast, and fast to slow. The runners became exhausted in 3.37 minutes while running 1,245 meters at a constant speed of 13.9 miles per hour (4.19 minutes per mile). However, when they ran the first 2.37 minutes at 13.5 miles per hour and the last minute at 14.9 miles per hour, the subjects were able to cover the same distance in the same total time with a lower oxygen requirement and less blood lactate accumulation. When the runners ran the first 2.37 minutes at 14.9 miles per hour and the last minute at 13.5 miles per hour, they consumed more oxygen and had more blood lactate than when they ran at the constant speed of 13.9 miles per hour. The reader should note that these results may be specific to races of relatively short duration.

A study of heart rate responses to various pace patterns during the running of a mile revealed that the slow-fast pattern required less overall energy than the other pace patterns (26). However, the fast-slow pace pattern was identified as the pattern that produced the fastest one-mile times.

Adams (1) conducted another study on the energy required to run a 4 minute: 37 second mile, which was simulated on a treadmill. A steady paced run consisted of a constant time of 69.25 seconds for each 440 yards throughout the trial. The fast-slow-fast run involved consecutive 440 yard times of 64, 73, 73, and 67 seconds. The slow-fast pace required the subjects to run each 440-yard segment of the mile run in 71, 71, 67.5, and 67.5 seconds. The researchers concluded that when the pace varied, a significantly higher oxygen debt was incurred and that the steady-pace plan was the most efficient means of utilizing energy reserves. The best physiological plan for accomplishing the fastest time in middle distance running was the steady-pace strategy.

Additional support for steady pace effort has been offered by physiologists at Ohio State University (35), who studied the mechanical efficiency of exercise with the following distribution of effort: steady, light-heavy, and heavy-light. Their findings indicated that steady pace was significantly more efficient with regard to oxygen uptake. Another study, on the other hand, found no evidence of detrimental effects from varying the pace during a 1,320-yard run (47). Clearly, experts do not agree on the optimal pace for distance running. The steady-pace plan, however, appears to hold the greatest scientific support.

In selecting the best running speed for any given distance race, the coach should remember that running pace is limited by the runner's capacity to consume oxygen and to tolerate fatigue. A series of investigations concerning the energy expenditure during various distance races has demonstrated a close relationship between the distance of the race and the percentage of Vo_2 max used by the runner (11). Runners competing in the two-mile, for example, were found to consume oxygen at a level equal to their maximal capacity, whereas runners competing in six-mile and marathon races used 88 to 94 percent and 68 to 75 percent of their maximal oxygen uptakes, respectively. This fractional use of the aerobic capacity is responsible for a runner's sensations of effort and ultimately dictates his or her running pace.

Although little attention has been given to the biomechanical aspects of distance running, this topic has been discussed in some detail elsewhere (see: Slocum, D. B. and W. Bowerman. The Biomechanics of Running. *Clinical Ortheopedics* 23: 39–45, 1962). There is evidence to support the tactic of running in the aerodynamic shadow of one's competition, since the energy needed to overcome the resistance of air increases exponentially with running velocity or headwind resistance. To gain full advantage of this technique, it is best to permit two or three runners "break the way" and to stay within a meter of this leading group.

During the latter stage of a race, care should be taken to reserve one's finishing sprint until the final 150 to 200 meters. Although it may seem tactically wise to increase the pace to break free of a competitor, runners should feel as though they still have some energy in reserve. Such timing is supported by knowledge about muscle stores of creatine phosphate (CP) and adenosine triphosphate (ATP). These high energy compounds permit the explosive energy needed for an all-out sprint. During the final dash, creatine phosphate decreases rapidly, followed by a fall in muscle adenosine triphosphate. The trick is to begin the final sprint as early as possible without running out of energy short of the finish. If the runner's pace has been relatively steady, then the muscle energy stores should be sufficient to sustain a sprint lasting roughly 20 to 30 seconds.

RECOVERY FROM COMPETITION

Though recovery from some races is no more distressful than the aftermath of a typical training run, most runners have experienced the painful hours and days that follow an all-out effort like a marathon. Despite variations in the degree of discomfort after competition and very long runs, there are a number of specific physiological and anatomical changes that can be blamed for the painful side effects.

In 1977, exercise physiologists studied the biochemical changes in the blood of six runners during a marathon race and for three days afterward (34). Probably the most interesting finding of this study was the persistently elevated epinephrine levels in the days following the race. This hormone is normally secreted by the adrenal glands in response to both physical and emotional stress, and it exhibits a strong influence on energy production and the excitability of the nervous system. Like other hormones, such as glucagon, norepinephrine, and cortisol, the amount of epinephrine is dramatically increased during the marathon (18, 34). While these other hormones returned to normal levels within 24 hours after the race, epinephrine remained elevated for 24 to 48 hours after the competition (Figure 5-6). Though this persistence of an elevated epinephrine level seems to have little effect on the body's use of fuels during the recovery period, it may be responsible for the heightened psychological state that is known to persist for 24 to 48 hours after the mara-

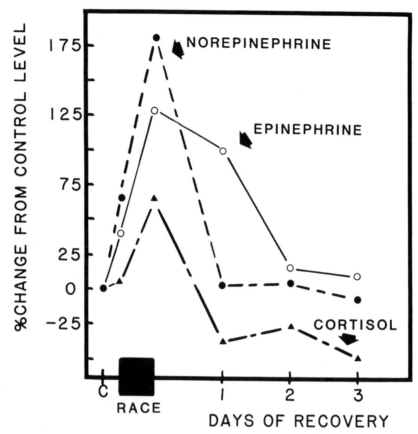

Figure 5-6. Percentage changes in blood norepinephrine, epinephrine, and cortisol during and after a marathon race in six runners. The control (C) values were determined 10 days before the race. Note the rise in all hormones before and during the race, and their subsequent decline on the days after the competition. Only epinephrine remained elevated in the days after the race. (ref. 21).

thon. Marathoners commonly have great difficulty sleeping for one or two nights after the marathon, which may reflect the effect of epinephrine on the central nervous system.

During the race, muscle glycogen is used as a primary fuel. Fortunately, not every cell runs out of glycogen at the same moment, and there are always some cells that have not been extensively used. Fatigue comes in stages with the selective exhaustion of some muscle cells. The fibers that were easily recruited by the nervous system in the early part of the race no longer respond to signals from the nerves. Trying to maintain the pace, the runner concentrates harder in an attempt to activate the muscle fibers that were somewhat dormant in the first stages of the run. The smooth, comfortable pace that allowed the runner to enjoy the scenery in the early stage of the race is gradually replaced by a strained effort that occupies the runner's entire concentration. The observable changes that occur in the runner's form over the final miles of a marathon can be attributed to an emptying of the muscle cells' glycogen. Unfortunately, recovery of the energy reserves necessary to resume normal running does not come quickly.

Some years ago, our Human Performance Laboratory at Ball State University in Muncie, Indiana, joined exercise physiologists at Ohio University in Athens to study recovery from the marathon (3, 45, 46). The specific goal of this study was to determine the rate of recovery of muscle glycogen for one week following the competition. Ten marathoners allowed us to take muscle biopsies from their calves before and immediately after the Athens, Ohio Marathon. In addition, samples of muscle were taken one, three, five, and seven days following the marathon. Portions of the muscle specimens were analyzed for glycogen content, and a small part of each biopsy was examined under an electron microscope to determine if the marathon had caused any structural damage to the muscle.

Four of the 10 men placed in the top 13 places (1st, 2nd, 4th, and 13th) out of a field of 350. Although all the runners were exhausted by the race, two of the slower runners, whose times were 3 hours:8 minutes:1 second and 3 hours:16 minutes:50 seconds, respectively, were the most devastated by their efforts. Both men appeared to be in shock for two hours after the race and experienced severe muscle pain for the next six to seven days. Though all of the runners started the race with very large amounts of muscle glycogen of 196 millimoles per kilogram of muscle, at the finish they all had less than 25 millimoles per kilogram of muscle. The two most exhausted runners had less than eight millimoles per kilogram of muscle.

Our research has taught us that the fastest way to recover the used muscle glycogen is to eat extremely large quantities of carbohydrates like bread and pasta, much as you might do prior to a marathon. The day following the marathon our subjects ate 400 grams of carbohydrate, nearly three times the normal daily carbohydrate intake. Despite this large carbohydrate intake, the runners' muscle glycogen levels averaged only 79 millimoles per kilogram of muscle 24 hours after the race, far below their starting level. During the week following the race, the men ate roughly 450 grams of carbohydrate each day.

Since some authorities have suggested that moderate exercise in the week after a marathon might accelerate recovery, we divided the 10 runners into two groups. One group rested completely during the recovery week, while the other five men ran on a treadmill for 20 to 45 minutes per day at an easy pace. Over that period of time the muscle glycogen restoration was the same in both groups, reaching a high value of 131 millimoles per kilogram of muscle on the fifth day. Although this muscle glycogen value is well below the prerace value, it is a level we often see in trained runners. In addition to the glycogen values similarities, the groups displayed no differences in the subjective sensations of muscle soreness or general fatigue. These facts suggest that light exercise following a marathon does not expedite recovery.

We have considered a number of possible explanations for the somewhat incomplete recovery of muscle glycogen after the marathon. At first we thought it might be a disadvantage to take in so much carbohydrate during the first 24 hours after the race. We reasoned that overloading the system with carbohydrate in such a brief time period might suppress the enzyme activity of glycogen synthase within the cell that is responsible for the reformation of glycogen. However, more recent unpublished studies in our lab suggest that the muscle damage and subsequent inflammatory reactions that occur during distance running may diminish the rate of muscle glycogen formation. We have observed that when rat muscle fibers are mechanically damaged after exhaustive exercise, they store 40 percent less glycogen than undamaged muscles. But at the time of the Athens Marathon study we had yet to confirm that marathon running caused any damage to the muscle.

Another team of specialists at Ohio University, headed by Robert Hikida, examined small pieces of the muscles under an electronmicroscope. As noted earlier in this chapter, the findings were quite surprising. In nearly all samples studied, including those taken before the race, there was evidence of ruptured fibers and inflammation within the muscle (Figure 5-1, 5-2a, and 5-2b). Many of the substances normally confined to the inside of the cells were found outside the fibers in the fluids that bathe the muscle cells. Even red and white blood cells were found outside the blood vessels. Occasionally the observers noted derangements in the contractile filaments (Figure 5-2a and 5-2b). Because the abnormalities were found in the premarathon samples and persisted for a week after the race, it seems that these changes were caused by the intensity of both the training and the racing. It even appears that the inflammatory reaction that accompanies such running may be a major cause for the post-exercise symptoms of muscle soreness.

Why does this trauma occur during an event like the marathon? Does it also happen during other endurance events like cycling and swimming? Recent studies by Harm Kuipers at the University of Limburg in Holland revealed that cyclists and swimmers do not experience the muscle fiber damage and soreness observed in runners. There must be something special about running that other forms of exercise do not contain.

That "something" is probably due to the eccentric contractions that occur during running. Concentric contractions normally shorten the muscle in the process of developing force, while eccentric contractions involve lengthening the muscle at the same time it is attempting to shorten. Bending the elbow and shortening the biceps muscle, for example, involves concentric contractions, but following this movement with a slow extension of the elbow will develop additional tension as the biceps muscle is stretched through an eccentric contraction. In running, the concentric forces generated by the leg muscles are used to drive the body forward, while the eccentric contractions of the thigh muscles prevent the knee and hip from yielding to the pull of gravity when the heel strikes the ground.

In downhill running, the tension developed in the leg muscles to resist gravity is enormous. The muscles are attempting to shorten but are literally pulled apart. Consequently, the fiber membranes and connective tissues are physically stretched beyond their limits. The next obvious questions are: Is this muscle damage permanent? Does it ultimately impair performance? There is no evidence that these disruptions in the muscle cell membranes and microcirculation cause any permanent damage. Studies with both humans and small animals have shown that the muscle is easily capable of repairing itself (8, 9). It has even been demonstrated that the muscle can be reconstructed after it has been excised, minced, and replaced in the original muscle compartment. Within about 30 days, a competent whole muscle, complete with tendon and nerve connections, will be regenerated (39). The muscle makes a few modifications during such regeneration, becoming more fibrous with added connective tissue to make it more tolerant of future eccentric stresses. It also seems that the more a person performs eccentric exercise, the less soreness and muscle trauma they experience.

One of the aftereffects of a long exhaustive run is the loss of muscle strength and power, which may persist for several days (15, 46). A recent study compared the effects of complete rest and mild exercise on the rate of strength recovery during seven days after a marathon (46). Both the rest-recovery and exercise-recovery groups regained some of their loss of muscle function during the first three days of recovery. Though both groups continued to regain leg strength, five days after the marathon the men who had rested completely showed a greater recovery of both leg extension strength and work capacity (Figure 5-7). While the work capacity of the leg muscles may return to normal with adequate rest, muscle strength remained depressed even after seven days of rest. These and other findings raise doubts about the value of exercise during the days following an exhaustive event like the marathon.

Certainly there are other physiological and psychological aspects of recovery from long-distance running that have not been covered here. Current evidence, however, makes it clear that recovery from events like the marathon involve nutrition and healing injured tissues. Though some

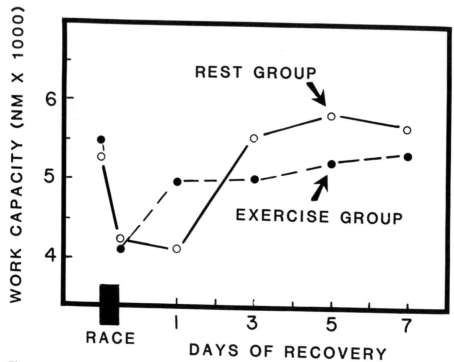

Figure 5-7. Changes in leg extension work capacity as a result of the marathon and during recovery. The rest group did no running for seven days after the marathon, whereas the exercise group ran 20 to 45 minutes per day at 50 to 60 percent Vo_2 max during the recovery week. Note the difference between the rate of recovery of the two groups. (ref. 14)

aspects of recovery may be accomplished within a few hours, others may require a month or more.

DETRAINING: USE IT OR LOSE IT

Most athletes agree that it is bad enough to suffer the pain of an injury, but it is even worse when the condition forces them to stop training or detrain. Aside from the psychological trauma of such inactivity, runners fear most that all they have gained through hard training will be lost after a few days or weeks without running. The discussion on tapering made it clear that a few days of rest or a reduction in training will enhance performance. Runners realize, however, that at some point a reduction in training or inactivity will produce a deterioration in performance.

Apparently, it takes much less daily exercise to sustain the aerobic benefits of endurance training than it does initially to increase the runner's Vo_2 max. Unfortunately, the fitness gained from miles and miles of running are quickly lost when the runner stops all training. With the cessation of training, improvements in Vo_2 max, maximal cardiac output, skeletal muscle capillarization, and the aerobic capacity of the leg muscles vanish at varied rates (10, 14, 27). If for some reason the endurance athlete is unable to train for just one week, the muscles' aerobic capacity may decline by 10 to 50 percent (13). This finding is supported by observations that the activities of the mitochondrial enzymes are markedly reduced with the cessation of exercise training (21, 27, 31). Some physiologists have shown that the enzymes may begin to decline within just 48 hours if muscles are not exercised. After an additional week of inactivity, the muscles' aerobic capacity remains depressed, though trained muscles still have far more endurance than untrained muscles.

Another important change that takes place with detraining is a decrease in the number of capillaries that surround each muscle fiber and deliver oxygen and nutrients to the muscle cells. Studies have shown that the number of capillaries around each muscle fiber decreases by 10 to 20 percent within five to 12 days after the last training session. As a result, the delivery of oxygen to these muscle cells and their ability to produce energy are dramatically impaired.

During the same period of detraining, significant changes take place in the central portion of the cardiovascular system. Specifically, the capacity of the heart to pump blood during maximal effort begins to decrease within the first five to 12 days of inactivity (6, 43). The combination of a lower maximal cardiac output and a smaller blood flow around the muscle fibers lessens the transport of oxygen to the runner's muscle fibers and slows the removal of waste materials from the working muscles.

One of these waste products is lactic acid, the result of muscular effort to produce energy without sufficient oxygen. A well-trained runner accumulates very little blood lactate during long runs. With the cessation of training and the subsequent weakening of the oxygen transport system, blood lactate levels are substantially higher during aerobic-anaerobic running. Figure 5-8 demonstrates the changes in blood lactate concentration for a runner who performed a six-minute mile when he was untrained, after five months of training, and at weekly intervals during a period of inactivity. Note that by the fourth week of detraining, blood lactate is well on its way to reaching the untrained level. We estimate that with six to eight weeks of detraining the runner will have lost all of the endurance advantage gained from the five months of training.

All physiological changes associated with the muscles' ability to produce energy do not decline at the same rate when the runner stops training. The real question is: "How quickly will performance be affected after

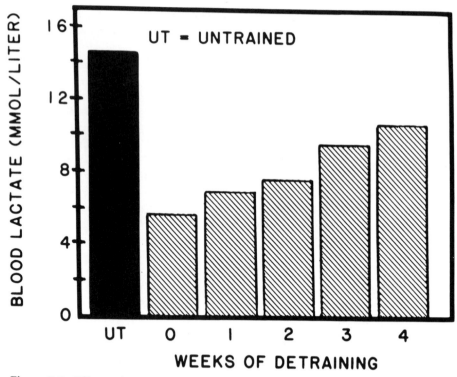

Figure 5-8. Effects of training and detraining on blood lactate concentration after a treadmill run at a set speed of six minutes per mile.

the runner stops training?" In general, there is no loss for five to seven days. As a matter of fact, running performance may even be improved after two to five days of inactivity. As noted earlier, such rest periods allow the muscles and nervous system to recover and rebuild from the stress of training and provide the runner with improved energy reserves and tolerance of endurance exercise.

Taking a few days of rest before a major competition to enhance one's muscle glycogen stores is a common practice among most runners. Prior training plays a key role in this process of muscle glycogen storage. Runners who are well-trained, rested, and properly fed have 50 to 100 percent more muscle glycogen than untrained individuals. With detraining, this fuel advantage is gradually lost, and by the fourth week of inactivity, muscle glycogen levels in an idle athlete may be no better than those in an untrained individual. Such a change would be noticed by the runner as an inability to do a long run or to train hard on two or more consecutive days, though he or she might be able to do one run and feel fine.

Although most runners train year-round, injuries often demand a few weeks or months of inactivity. Recently, some physiologists have suggested that a substitute form of exercise might delay the loss of muscle conditioning. Though it is true that riding a bike and swimming may continue to stimulate the heart and respiratory muscles, such activities are not specific to running. Consequently, those special changes that take place in and around the runner's muscles are lost, as if the runner were doing no exercise at all. Activities that simulate the action of running, however, may delay this loss of muscle conditioning. Performing a running action in shallow or deep water may provide sufficient stress to stimulate energy production in some of the muscles used in running, thereby maintaining these systems. Unfortunately, there is no activity that can serve as a perfect substitute for running.

Though it appears that the physiological gains from training are short-lived in detraining, the rate of retraining seems to be affected by the status of conditioning prior to the lapse. A classical study on detraining and retraining (42) demonstrated an average 26 percent decrease in Vo_2 max level in a group of runners after 20 days of complete bed rest. In the two subjects who were most active before the bed rest period, one to two months of retraining were needed to regain their aerobic capacities. The least active subjects in that study improved their Vo_2 max values rapidly after the period of bed rest, returning to the initial levels with only 10 to 15 days of training. As illustrated in Figure 5-9, the difference in the rate of retraining the Vo_2 max may be related to the initial fitness of the subjects. Those individuals with the highest level of fitness prior to complete bed rest appear to suffer the greatest decrements in Vo_2 max and the slowest recovery during retraining.

After a layoff of more than a couple of weeks, a runner should not expect an immediate return to his or her original state of fitness. Because of the weakened state, the runner who is trying to retrain is quite susceptible to overtraining. Consequently, care must be taken to initiate the training at a low intensity and to progress back to the pre-layoff level over a two- to four-week period.

The physiological gains of training are short-lived when regular activity ceases. Though moderate amounts of running can maintain performance levels for many weeks, total inactivity can mean a loss of all training benefits within a few months. Our laboratory tests have shown that even the most gifted distance runners are indistinguishable from the sedentary individual after six to 12 months of inactivity. To accommodate the stress of running competition, the body tissues must constantly be reminded of the physiological and biochemical demands of maximal effort. Without such reinforcement, the benefits of training are lost.

FINER POINTS

The preceding discussion provides a number of general and specific principles that are important for runners to achieve their best perfor-

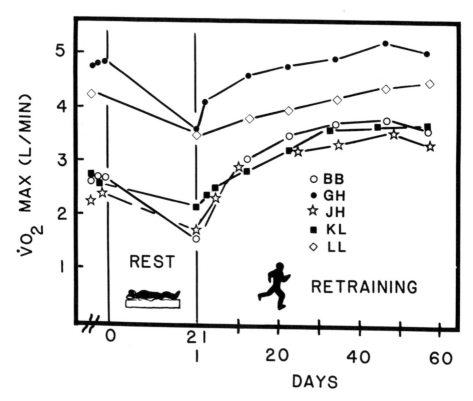

Figure 5-9. Maximal oxygen uptake in five men who were subjected to bed rest for 20 days and thereafter underwent a physical conditioning program for 55 days. Subjects GH and LL were physically active prior to the start of the study, whereas subjects BB, JH, and KL were sedentary. (42).

mances. Certainly, our limited knowledge of individual variations in response to training precludes the development of a single racing strategy that will work equally well for all runners. Nevertheless, previous research offers some guidelines that are essential if the runner hopes to attain a peak in performance.

1. Enough Is Enough. A gradual progression in training stress enhances the muscles' capacity to generate energy and remove the by-products of intense exercise. Improvements in fitness result from a balance between exercise and rest. Excessive training stress or inadequate recovery time or both cause a breakdown in adaptation and a loss in conditioning. The secret of a good training program is to be able to judge how much and what type of training will produce the greatest amount of improvement in conditioning. Once an athlete is overtrained, a period of reduced training or complete rest may be necessary to regain an optimal level of performance. Reductions in the training load are also essential for maximal speed and stamina. Tapering for one to two weeks before a major competition allows time for recovery from heavy training and a reprieve from the psychological demands of exhaustive exercise. Once trained, the runner can reduce his or her training for several weeks without a measurable loss in the quality of performance. While a few days of rest may actually improve a runner's performance, several weeks of complete inactivity will lead to a rapid loss in conditioning and a deterioration in performance. Detraining for more than six to eight weeks will lower the runner's endurance capacity to that of a sedentary individual. Retraining the runner after such a layoff requires a slow and easy start to prevent overstress.

2. Diet and Rest.   The keys to maximal glycogen loading are: (1) to reduce the intensity and duration of your training runs to minimize the daily burn-off of both muscle and liver glycogen stores and (2) to increase the percentage of carbohydrates in your diet. There is no reason to use a high-fat protein diet or a depletion run to stimulate extra glycogen storage. The endurance-trained muscle needs only a few days of rest and a rich carbohydrate diet to allow for maximal glycogen loading.

On the day of the race, the runner should eat a light carbohydrate meal three to four hours before the competition to allow for complete digestion. Substances that are hard to digest, like meat and fatty foods, should be excluded. The idea is to have as little as possible in the stomach when the race starts. In three to four hours even a stack of pancakes will generally be emptied into the intenstine, but meat can be found in the stomach 10 to 12 hours after a meal.

3. Warm-up.   Some experts suggest warming up for a distance race to increase muscle temperature, prevent muscle and tendon injuries, bring on "second wind" sooner, and rehearse the pace and relaxation which will be required during the actual competition. Measurements of rectal temperature before and after a 10,000-meter race in hot weather demonstrate that warming up may not be wise in the heat. Studies (40) have shown that warming up raises the internal body temperature by 1.5 degrees Fahrenheit above the resting level, causing runners to risk overheating during the race.

4. Pacing.   In light of the body's limited supply of fuel and its restricted capacity to generate energy, running efficiency and pace are critical to the overall performance. Although an evenly paced race strategy appears to be the best plan, the speed or rate of energy expenditure must be based on the runner's physiological limits and the environmental heat stress. Hot weather running takes a costly toll on performance and exposes the runner to the threat of heat injury. Unfortunately, many runners attempt to run at their fastest tolerable speeds, regardless of the environmental temperature.

Another common mistake in pacing comes when runners think they can run a bit faster during the early stages of the race to gain a few minutes' or seconds' advantage that might compensate for the fatigue-induced slowdown near the finish. My running partners, who hope to average eight minutes per mile for the marathon, invariably run the first 10 miles at 7 minutes: 45 seconds, thereby gaining a 2 minute: 30 second lead on their desired overall pace. Unfortunately, this slightly faster pace costs them a great deal more muscle glycogen, exhausting their fuel supplies at 18 to 22 miles. Consequently, the seconds gained in the early stage of the race are replaced by many minutes of slow running and walking. It is surprising that they cannot understand why they "hit the wall." It is simply a matter of poor pacing.

5. Post-Race Recovery. The rate of recovery from an exhaustive competition depends, to a large degree, on the amount of muscle trauma and glycogen depletion experienced during the race. It seems that a combination of rest and a carbohydrate-rich diet offer the best plan for recovery. If the runner experiences severe muscle soreness or tenderness under the pressure of palpation, there is little value in training until these symptoms have disappeared. Returning to training too soon will only delay recovery and increase the risk of overtraining. Despite both rest and carbohydrates, full recovery from an extremely exhaustive run may be relatively slow, precluding a quick return to further racing.

BIBLIOGRAPHY

1. Adams, W. C. The effects of selected pace variations on the O2 requirements of running a 4:37 mile. *Natl. College P.E. Assoc. for Men*, 1966.
2. Armstrong, L. E., W. M. Sherman and D. L. Costill. Muscle soreness following exhaustive long distance running. *Track Field Quart. Rev.*, 82:47–51, 1982.
3. Bowles, C. J. Telemetered heart rate responses to pace patterns in the one-mile run. *Doctoral Dissertation*, University of Oregon at Eugene, 1965.
4. Brynteson, P. and W. E. Sinning. The effects of training frequencies on the retention of cardiovascular fitness. *Med. Sci. Sports*, 5:29–33, 1973.
5. Carlile, F. and U. Carlile. *New Directions in Scientific Training*. Sidney, Australia: Pub. by authors, 1978.
6. Carlile, F. F. *Carlile on Swimming*. London: Pelham Press, 1966.
7. Carlson, B. M. Regeneration research in the Soviet Union. *Anat. Rec.*, 160:665, 1968.
8. Carlson, B. M. An investigation into a method for the stimulation of regeneration of skeletal muscle. *Anat. Rec.*, 157:225, 1967.
9. Chi, M. M.-Y., C. S. Hitz, E. F. Coyle, W. H. Martin, J. L. Ivy, P. M. Nemeth, J. O. Holloszy and O. H. Lowry. Effects of detraining on enzymes of energy metabolism in individuals human muscle fiber. *Am. J. Physiol.*, 224:C276–C287, 1983.
10. Costill, D. L. Practical problems in exercise physiology. *Res. Quart.*, 56:215–225, 1985.

11. Costill, D. L. Metabolic responses during distance running. *J. Appl. Physiol.*, 28:251–255, 1970.
12. Costill, D. L., D. S. King, R. Thomas and M. Hargreaves. Effects of reduced training on muscular power in swimmers. *Physician & Sportsmed.*, 13:94–101, 1985.
13. Costill, D. L., W. J. Fink, M. Hargreaves, D. S. King, R. Thomas and R. Fielding. Metabolic characteristics of skeletal muscle during detraining from competitive swimming. *Med. Sci. Sports Exer.*, 17:339–343, 1985.
14. Coyle, E. F., W. H. Martin and J. O. Holloszy. Cardiovascular and metabolic rates of detraining. *Med. Sci. Sports Exer.*, 15:158, 1983.
15. Forsburg, A., P. Tesch and J. Karlsson. Effect of prolonged exercise on muscle strength performance. *Biomechanics VI-A*, 6:62–67, 1979.
16. Foster, C., D. L. Costill, J. T. Daniels and W. J. Fink. Skeletal muscle enzyme activity, fiber composition and Vo₂ max in relation to distance running performance. *Europ. J. Appl. Physiol.*, 39:73–80, 1978.
17. Friden, J. Muscle soreness after exercise: Implications of morphological changes. *Int. J. Sports Med.*, 5:57–66, 1984.
18. Galbo, H., E. A. Richter, J. Hilsted, J. J. Holst, N. J. Christensen and J. Henricksson. Hormonal regulation during prolonged exercise. *The Marathon: Physiological, Medical, Epidemiological, and Psychological Studies*, 301:72–80, 1977.
19. Hagerman, F. C., R. S. Hikida, R. S. Staron, W. M. Sherman and D. L. Costill. Muscle damage in marathon runners. *Physician and Sportsmed.*, 12:39–48, 1984.
20. Hansen, K. N., J. Bjerre-Knudsen, U. Brodthagen, R. Jordal and P.-E. Paulev. Muscle cell leakage due to long distance training. *Eur. J. Appl. Physiol.*, 48:178–188, 1982.
21. Henriksson, J. and J. S. Reitman. Time course of changes in human skeletal muscle succinate dehydrogenase and cytochrome-oxidase activities and maximal oxygen uptake with physical activity and inactivity. *Acta. Physiol. Scand.*, 99:91–97, 1977.
22. Hickson, R. C., J. M. Hagbert, A. A. Ehsani and J. O. Holloszy. Time course of the increase in Vo₂ max in response to training. *Fed. Proc.*, 37:633, 1978.
23. Hickson, R. C., J. C. Kanakis, A. M. Moore and S. Rich. Effects of frequency of training, reduced training and retraining on aerobic power and left ventricular responses. *Med. Sci. Sports Exercise*, 13:93, 1981.
24. Hickson, R. C., H. A. Bomze and J. O. Holloszy. Linear increase in aerobic power induced by a strenous program of endurance exercise. *J. Appl. Physiol.*, 42:372–376, 1977.
25. Hickson, R. C. and M. A. Rosenkoetter. Reduced training frequencies and maintenance of increased aerobic power. *Med. Sci. Sports Exercise*, 13:13–16, 1981.
26. Hikida, R. S., R. S. Staron, F. C. Hagerman, W. M. Sherman and D. L. Costill. Muscle fiber necrosis associated with human marathon runners. *J. Neuro. Sci.*, 59:185–203, 1983.
27. Houston, M. E., H. Bentzen and H. Larsen. Interrelationships between skeletal muscle adaptations and performance as studied by detraining and retraining. *Acta Physiol. Scand.*, 105:163–170, 1979.
28. Hunter, J. B. and J. B. Critz. Effect of training on plasma enzyme levels in man. *J. Appl. Physiol.*, 31:20–23, 1971.
29. Kanakis, C. J., A. Coehlo and R. C. Hickson. Left ventricular responses to strenuous endurance training and reduced training frequencies. *J. Cardiac Rehab.*, 2:141–146, 1982.
30. Karpovich, P. V. *Physiology of Muscular Activity*, 1-278. Philadelphia: W. B. Saunders, 1965.
31. Klausen, K., L. B. Anderson and I. Pelle. Adaptive changes in work capacity, skeletal muscle capillarization, and enzyme levels during training and detraining. *Acta. Physiol. Scand*, 113:9–16, 1981.
32. Lamb, D. R. *Physiology of Exercise*. New York: Macmillan, 1978.
33. Maglischo, E. W. *Swimming Faster*, 368–375. Palo Alto: Mayfield Publishing Co., 1982.

34. Maron, M. B., S. M. Horvath and J. E. Wilkerson. Blood biochemical alterations during recovery from competitive marathon running. *Europ. J. Appl. Physiol.*, 38:231–238, 1977.
35. Mathews, D. L. Aerobic and anaerobic work efficiency. *Res. Quart.*, 34:393–397, 1963.
36. Maxwell, J. H. and C. M. Bloor. Effects of conditioning on exertional rhabdomyolysis and serum creatine kinase after severe exercise. *Enzyme*, 26:177–181, 1981.
37. Miller, R. E. and J. W. Mason. Changes in 17-hydroxycorticosteroid excretion related to increased muscular work. *Walter Reed Institute of Research*, 137–151, 1964.
38. Misner, J. E., B. H. Massey and B. T. Williams. The effect of physical training on the response of serum enzymes to exercise stress. *Med. Sci. Sports*, 5:86–88, 1973.
39. Reedy, M. *Physiology and Biochemistry of Muscle as a Food*, 73. Eds. E. J. Briskey, R. G. Cassens, B. B. Marsh. Madison: Univ. of Wisc. Press, 1970.
40. Robinson, S. Influence of fatigue on the efficiency of men during exhaustive runs. *J. Appl. Physiol.*, 12:197–201, 1958.
41. Robinson, S. Influence of fatigue on the efficiency of men during exhausting runs. *J. Appl. Physiol.*, 12:197–201, 1958.
42. Saltin, B., G. Blomquist, J. H. Mitchell, J. R. L. Johnson, K. Wildenthal and C. B. Chapman. Response to exercise after bedrest and after training. *Circulation*, (Suppl.) 7:1968.
43. Saltin, B. and L. B. Rowell. Functional adaptations to physical activity and inactivity. *Fed. Proc.*, 39:1506–1513, 1980.
44. Selye, H. *The Stress of Life*, 324. New York: McGraw-Hill, 1956.
45. Sherman, W. M., D. L. Costill, W. J. Fink, F. C. Hagerman, L. E. Armstrong and T. F. Murray. Effect of a 42.2-km footrace and subsequent rest or exercise on muscle glycogen and enzymes. *J. Appl. Physiol.*, 55:1219–1224, 1983.
46. Sherman, W. M., L. E. Armstrong, T. M. Murray, F. C. Hagerman, D. L. Costill, R. C. Staron and J. L. Ivy. Effect of a 42.2-km footrace and subsequent rest or exercise on muscular strength and work capacity. *J. Appl. Physiol.*, 57:1668–1673, 1984.
47. Sorani, R. The effect of three different pace plans on the cardiac cost of 1320-yard runs. *Dissertation*, Univ. of S. Calif., Los Angeles, 1967.

CHAPTER 6

Special Considerations

The preceding chapters have focused on the wide variations in individual responses to single and repeated bouts of exercise. While we explained that genetic traits largely determine one's running potential, we emphasized the contributions of training, diet, and proper race management to running performance (16, 46).

In running, as in life, one must contend with the impact of gender and age on performance. This chapter will focus on the physiological consequences of being male, female, old, and young. The amount of scientific information supporting this chapter is not vast and the conclusions are not firm, because most studies of distance running have been conducted on young males. In addition, the number of female runners is smaller and the history of their participation in distance running is shorter. The effects of aging have been difficult to track as well, since runners are rarely monitored for their entire lives.

Nevertheless, females and older athletes are rightfully commanding more attention and scrutiny. The data that are available on gender and aging offer some provocative and helpful insights.

A MATTER OF GENDER

Efforts to describe the unique characteristics of the female distance runner commonly focus on the differences between males and females.

The basic physiological and performance characteristics of the female runners are no different than those of men. As Fox and Mathews (33) have noted, ". . . the cellular mechanisms controlling most physiological and biochemical responses to exercise are the same for both sexes." There are, however, interesting variations between the sexes in the magnitude of those physiological responses.

Figure 6-1 illustrates the difference between the average running speeds measured in minutes per mile for the American record holders at distances from one mile to the marathon. On the average, the females ran 15 percent slower than their male counterparts, a difference of about 41 seconds per mile. These comparisons may be a bit distorted, since several of the distances (9.3, 15.5, and 18.6 miles) are not heavily contested.

Nevertheless, even at 6.2 miles (10 kilometers) and 26.2 miles (the marathon), two of the most frequently raced distances, the difference between the records averaged 13.0 percent or 35.8 seconds per mile. When the 10-kilometer records for 15- to 35-year-old runners are averaged, the difference between men and women is 14.8 percent or 41.3 seconds per mile.

Although it has been suggested that the performance differences be-

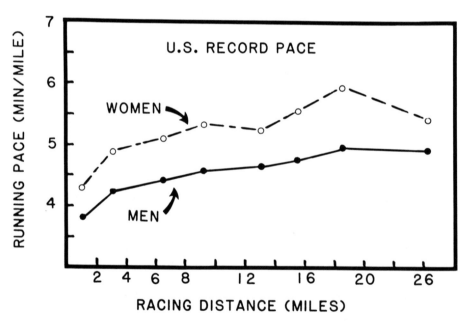

Figure 6-1. Average running pace in minutes per mile for record performances in events of one mile to the marathon. Values are reported for both male and female record holders (ref. 72).

tween men and women are smaller at longer distances, the records do not agree (72). In the ultra-marathon events, the differences between men and women are even greater. Records at 50 and 100 miles are 23 to 20 percent slower for women than men, an average difference in pace of 82 to 93 seconds per mile.

Of course there are many women who are faster than men. Figure 6-2 illustrates the distribution of times of all the men and women in the 9.3-mile 1984 Cincinnati Mini-Marathon. The overlap in performances for the sexes is considerable, indicating that more than 50 percent of the women were faster than 50 percent of the men. It is, however, interesting to note that the overall average time for the men was 68 minutes:54 seconds, compared to 79 minutes:12 seconds for the women—a 15 percent difference, quite similar to the difference in the U.S. records for that distance.

BODY COMPOSITION

The fact that female runners have a higher percentage of body fat than males is likely to account for some of the difference in running performances. As noted in Chapter 1, highly trained male distance runners have been reported to have 4 to 10 percent body fat. Female runners, on the other hand, have been found to have roughly 16 percent body fat, though some individual runners have less than 10 percent. Consequently, female runners carry an average of nine to 12 pounds more body fat than the men. This additional weight requires the expenditure of more energy during running, thereby taxing the oxygen transport system to a greater relative degree when running at set speeds.

To demonstrate the effect of body fat on performance, let us assume that two runners with the same maximal oxygen uptake of 3.30 liters per minute are running at an eight minutes per mile pace, a speed that requires 40 milliliters of oxygen per minute for each kilogram of body weight (ml/kg × min). If the two runners have the same lean body weight of 49.5 kilograms, but differ in body fat by 8 percent, then the cost of running would be 6 percent higher in the fatter runner. The thin runner would be required to use approximately 66 percent of her Vo_2 max, whereas the heavier runner would have to work at nearly 71 percent. Since the ability to maintain a fast pace during competition depends to a large degree on the fractional use of the aerobic capacity, this 5 percent increase would mean that the heavier runner would have to run 20 to 30 seconds slower per mile in order expend the same relative effort.

This information might be taken to mean that every female runner should attempt to drop her body fat to 5 or 6 percent. Such a practice is neither necessary nor healthy. Though a number of the world's best female distance runners have body fat levels below 10 percent, many rec-

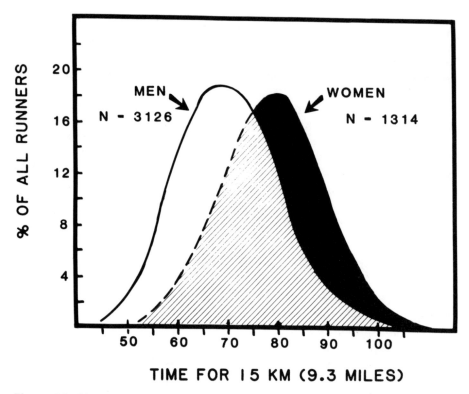

Figure 6-2. The distribution of running times for a 15-kilometer (9.3 mile) race among all male and female participants. The hatched area shows the overlap in performance between the sexes. Thus, a large percentage (more than 50 percent) of the women performed equally as well as many of the men.

ord holders have values above 14 percent. The body fat percentage of highly trained female runners is well below the 25 percent seen in the average untrained female. This difference is, for the most part, the result of heavy training rather than dieting.

Some runners may retain an atypical amount of body fat despite hard training. These individuals should be encouraged to diet during the less intense period of training and competition, since the stress of trying to run while consuming too few calories is certain to impair performance and may lead to a state of chronic fatigue.

MUSCLE COMPOSITION

In early studies with male and female track and field athletes we observed that there was little difference in the muscle fiber composition between the sexes (15). In 1976, Scandinavian investigators reported that among a group of 115 men and women aged 16 years, the mean percentage of slow twitch fibers was 52 percent in both sexes (37). Within the fast twitch fibers, the fast twitch *a* fibers were approximately twice as common as the fast twitch *b* fibers, the mean values being 33 percent and 14 percent, respectively, of the total number of fibers. Similar mean values for the percentage of slow twitch, fast twitch *a* and fast twitch *b* fibers were observed in a study of 54 untrained adult women (51). There is substantial evidence suggesting that there is no difference between men and women with regard to the percentage of slow twitch and fast twitch fibers. Regardless of sex, elite distance runners have a predominance of slow twitch fibers in their leg muscles, ranging from 60 to 98 percent of the muscle.

The only reported difference in muscle composition between the sexes is found in the size of the fibers. Untrained adult men have substantially thicker muscle fibers than untrained females. As shown in Table 6-1, the cross-sectional area (um²) of slow twitch fibers in men, 20 to 30 years of age, are 35 percent larger than those in a similar group of untrained women (61). This difference in fiber areas is somewhat smaller in muscles from 16-year-old males and females. While the men appear to show a 9 percent increase in muscle fiber area from 16 to 30 years of age, the females' muscle cross-sectional area decreases by 8 percent during this same period. At least part of the increase in fiber size seen in the men can be attributed to natural growth. Since females do not grow much after the age of 16, the reduction in their muscle fiber size may be related to less active lifestyles.

This point is supported by the fact that little difference is found between the muscle fiber areas of equally trained male and female distance runners (15). Whereas the muscle fiber area averages 6,331 square micrometers for male middle-distance runners, female runners average 5,856 square micrometers, a difference of only 8 percent. When compared to the muscle fiber size of the untrained women in Table 6-1, it is readily

TABLE 6-1. Fiber cross-sectional area (um²) in the leg muscles of untrained trained men and women (ref. 61).

FIBER TYPE	MALE		FEMALE	
	16 YR	20–30 YR	16 YR	20–30 YR
ST	4,880	5,310	4,310	3,948
FTa	5,500	6,110	4,310	3,637
FTb	4,900	5,600	3,920	2,235
Average	5,066	5,673	4,180	3,273

apparent that physical training has a strong influence on the size of the fibers in females. The female runners have an average fiber area that is 79 percent larger than the 20- to 30-year-old untrained females, and roughly the same size as untrained men.

Since strength and speed are determined in part by muscle mass, the combined size of the muscle fibers is important to the performance of both male and female runners. Here, men have a slight advantage. But there is no evidence to suggest that men have more muscle fibers than women. The fact that well-trained men have only a small advantage in muscle fiber areas and that both sexes appear to have similar leg muscle development suggests that there is no major difference in the number of fibers.

ENERGY SYSTEMS

Delivery of oxygen and fuels to the muscles and removal of wastes depends, in part, on the proliferation of capillaries around each muscle fiber. Female runners have about 4.9 capillaries around each fiber, and male runners have about 5.6 capillaries per muscle fiber. This does not put the female runner at a disadvantage. Since the function of the capillaries is to allow for diffusion of materials into and out of the muscle cells, the size of the area served by each capillary is more important than the number of capillaries. Female runners have somewhat smaller muscle fibers, so the volume of muscle that must be served by each capillary is smaller in women (886 square micrometers per capillary) than in men (1,105 square micrometers per capillary). This means that the exchange of materials between the muscle and the blood should be better in female than in male runners. There is no evidence, however, that this advantage has an impact on performance.

For both sexes there is a close relationship between a runner's Vo_2 max and the average number of capillaries around each leg muscle fiber. Since both factors improve with endurance training, it appears that activity levels are more important than gender with regard to the number of capillaries in the muscle.

The capacity for aerobic energy production depends, in part, on the availability of mitochondria and their associated enzymes. Unfortunately, few data are available to compare the aerobic capacities of muscle in male and female runners. As can be seen in Table 6-2, female runners tend to have somewhat lower aerobic enzyme activities than their male counterparts [17]. Although the precise relation of these enzyme activities to running performance is debatable, we might expect men to have greater endurance than women. This does not appear to be the case. Both the men and women in this study had similar aerobic capacities and were equally good at distances ranging from 10 kilometers to the marathon. Since the

TABLE 6-2. Muscle composition (% slow twitch) and enzyme activities (micromoles/gram/minute) in male and female runners (ref. 15, 17).

GROUP	%ST	SDH	MDH	CPT
Untrained				
Males	52	7.6	48	0.7
Females	51	8.2	50	0.7
Runners				
Males	62	17.7*	71	1.0
Females	61	12.2	72	0.8

SDH = succinate dehydrogenase; MDH = malate dehydrogenase; CPT = carnitine palmityl transferase
*denotes significant difference between men and women.

leg muscles of highly trained men and women have similar aerobic capacities, this factor alone cannot explain the differences in performance between elite men and women.

Some observers have suggested that women might be relatively better in longer events like the marathon because they could burn fat at a greater rate and generally have more fat to burn. This would enable the female runner to spare the use of muscle glycogen, thereby lowering her risk of running out of fuel. We have refuted this theory by measuring the fat-burning capacity of the muscles from highly trained men and women (17). Muscle samples revealed that the men had a significantly greater capacity to use fat than the women, though this fact seemed to have little effect on the body's choice of fuels during exercise. When asked to run for an hour at marathon pace, both sexes derived about 50 percent of their energy from the breakdown of fat. It would appear that there is little or no difference in fat use or performance of highly trained men and women who have similar Vo_2 max values and training backgrounds.

OXYGEN TRANSPORT

The best single determinant for distance running success is the capacity to consume, transport, and use oxygen. Elite female runners have a somewhat lower Vo_2 max values than topflight male runners. As we noted earlier, the difference in performance between male and female distance running records is in the range of 13 to 15 percent. Table 6-3 offers a comparison of Vo_2 max and selected circulatory measurements for men and women. It is interesting to note that on the average, Vo_2 max values for nationally ranked male and female runners differ by 20 to 25 percent. Since women have 6 to 8 percent more body fat than men, Vo_2 max values for male and female runners differ by only 8 to 9 percent

TABLE 6-3. Cardiovascular characteristics of untrained and trained men and women. (Data presented here have been derived from references 4, 17, 33, 55, and 71).

SUBJECTS	$Vo_{2\ max}$	HR_{max}	SV_{max}	Q_{max}	HV	BV
Untrained						
Males	48	192	109	21	785	5.25
Females	40	198	81	16	560	4.07
Runners						
Males	70	187	144	27	930	6.58
Females	59	193	119	23	790	5.67

where $Vo_{2\ max}$ = maximal oxygen uptake (ml/kg × min); HR_{max} = maximal heart rate (beats/min); SV_{max} = stroke volume (ml/beat); Q_{max} = cardiac output (liters/min); HV = heart volume (milliliters); BV = blood volume (liters).

when calculated per kilogram of lean body weight (71).

Cardiac output is by far the single most important determinant of maximal oxygen uptake. The volume of blood that can be pumped by the heart per minute (Q_{max}) is the product of the number of times the heart beats per minute (HR_{max}) and the amount of blood ejected by the heart with each beat (SV_{max}).

Example: 27 liters = (185 beats/min) × (148 ml/beat)

Although both maximum stroke volume and maximum heart volume contribute to maximum volume of blood that can be pumped by the heart per minute, the size of the heart also appears to play a major role in determining the heart's pumping capacity. As noted in Table 6-3, the heart volume (HV) for men and women differs by 140 to 225 milliliters. Of course, heart size is somewhat related to an individual's body size. Measurements of heart volume per kilogram of body weight indicate that the male and female runners shown in Table 6-3 have about the same relative heart volume of 12.3 to 12.7 milliliters per kilogram of body weight. In other research, however, elite male distance runners have been reported to have an average heart volume of 16.4 milliliters per kilogram of body weight, meaning that topflight men have hearts that are nearly 33 percent larger than elite female runners. It appears that a major part of the aerobic advantage held by male runners can be attributed to larger heart volume and its influence on the maximum volume of blood that can be pumped by the heart per minute.

Unfortunately, many of the comparative studies of male and female runners have used elite performers of each sex. Although such comparisons help us to understand the physiological basis for sex differences in running performance, there are few studies that have compared the physiological characteristics of men and women who have performed equally in distance running competition.

Recently, performance-matched female and male runners were studied to compare their physiological characteristics and responses during exercise (54). These men and women had similar training programs and performed equally well in a 15-mile race. In the laboratory, their physiological performances during submaximal and maximal treadmill running were also quite similar (Table 6-4). The two groups used the same amount of oxygen during submaximal running, demonstrating that they had approximately the same running efficiency, which is in agreement with earlier studies (5, 21, 36). The only notable difference between the men and women during exercise was a higher heart rate in females during the submaximal run, reflecting a smaller stroke volume.

As mentioned in Chapter 1, hemoglobin plays a key role in transporting oxygen. Consequently, it is interesting to notice that the female runners described in Table 6-4 had lower hemoglobin concentrations than the males, despite the fact that there was no difference in Vo_2 max values for the two groups. This would suggest that in order to transport the same amount of oxygen per unit of blood, the women must have some means of compensating for their lower hemoglobin concentration. The

TABLE 6-4. Physiological responses during submaximal and maximal treadmill running for performance-matched female and male distance runners. Resting blood samples taken from these runners were analyzed for hemoglobin and 2.3-DPG (2.3 diphosphoglyceric acid). Data adapted from Pate, et al., (54).

MEASUREMENT	FEMALES		MALES
Maximal Exercise			
Vo_2 max (ml/kg $\times$ min)	55.8		55.1
Heart Rate (beats/min)	186		189
Blood Lactate (mmol/l)	7.6		8.8
Submaximal Run (8-min/mile)			
Vo_2 (ml/kg $\times$ min)	43	.	42
Heart Rate (beats/min)	178	*	169
Resting Blood Analyses			
Hematocrit (%)	40.6	*	43.9
Hemoglobin (g/100 ml)	14.1	*	15.7
2.3-DPG/Hb (uM $\times$ g^{-1})	14.2	*	12.2

*Denotes a significant difference (P < .05) between male and female runners.

mechanisms underlying such compensation are not known, though Russ Pate and his colleagues (54) have shown that 2.3 diphosphoglyceric acid, known to facilitate the unloading of oxygen at the muscle, is significantly higher in female than male distance runners (Table 6-4). Though this might enhance the delivery of oxygen, it is only one of the possible mechanisms that might compensate for lower hemoglobin concentrations in female runners.

STRENGTH AND SPEED

Although muscle strength is not considered a critical factor for dis- tance running success, it may affect the runner's speed and mechanics. For that reason, it is interesting to note that women have about one third

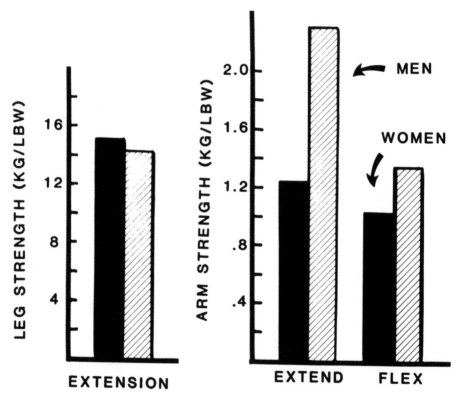

Figure 6-3. Upper and lower body strength for men and women of similar age (20.3 years). Strength has been calculated in terms of maximal force per unit of lean body weight (kilogram of force/kilogram lean body weight). Although there are no differences in leg muscle strength, women are significantly weaker in these measurements of arm strength (ref. 69).

less muscle strength than men. Data from Jack Wilmore (69), have demonstrated that when muscle strength is expressed in terms of total body weight or lean body weight, strength differences between the sexes are reduced.

Figure 6-3 shows the strength differences for the arms and legs of young college men and women (69). Although men have significantly greater strength in the upper body, there is no measurable difference in leg extension strength.

Recent studies have shown that men and women had similar leg strength when they performed isometric knee extensions and relatively slow leg movements of 60 to 150 degrees per second (1). At higher speeds of 180 to 300 degrees per second, however, men were significantly stronger than women. The reason for these differences in leg strength at slow and fast speeds is unknown, although these results suggest that men and women recruit different muscle fibers or that there is some difference in the contractile properties of their muscle fibers. Since we do not know the fiber composition of the subjects used in any of these strength studies, we cannot attribute the differences in upper and lower body strength to variations in the number of fast or slow twitch fibers.

Previous studies have made it clear that the potential for force development is the same in muscle samples taken from both men and women (41, 43). As can be seen in Figure 6-4, arm strength is closely related to the size of the muscle in both men and women. The strength of a single muscle fiber is unaffected by the individual's sex. The major determinant of overall strength is the size of the muscle. The larger muscle has more contractile filaments (actin and myosin) and therefore possesses greater potential for force development when it is activated.

Physiologists have repeatedly demonstrated that strength training produces greater muscle hypertrophy in men than in women (8, 49, 68, 69). In fact, strength training in females seldom produces the muscle bulk commonly seen in men. Muscular hypertrophy is regulated mainly by the hormone testosterone, which is approximately 10 times higher in the blood of men than in women (31, 40).

Since both men and women seem to have approximately the same leg strength per unit of lean body weight, the differences between men and women in distance running performances cannot be explained by a lack of leg strength in the females. Specific leg strength and cross-sectional muscle mass, however, have not been measured in female and male distance runners.

Since sprint runs of 100 and 200 meters require maximal force development in both the upper and lower body, men tend to have a 9 to 10 percent performance advantage in these events. Total body strength may also play a role in determining one's running speed during distance running, though this point remains to be clarified.

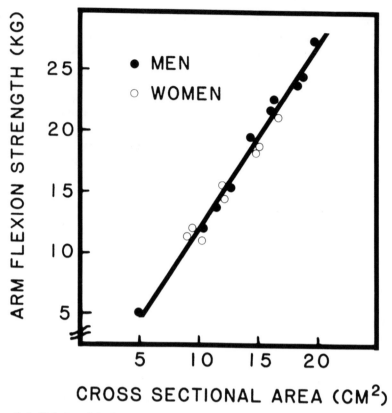

Figure 6-4. Relationship between muscle size (cross-sectional area) and arm flexion strength (43). Note that the values for men and women fall along the same line, indicating that strength is controlled to a large extent by the size of the muscle.

Although men and women have similar leg strength, it is difficult to understand why there is such a marked disparity in upper body muscle development between the sexes. One might anticipate that the hormonal mechanisms responsible for muscle development in the legs would have the same influence on the arm muscles. Apparently this is not the case, which makes it difficult to understand what processes could control the differentiation of fiber growth in the arms and legs. The regulators are most likely associated with the hormonal characteristics of the sexes.

HEAT TOLERANCE

Heat stress offers the greatest single threat to the health of the distance runner. Although training and repeated days of heat exposure provide some tolerance to the heat, there are marked individual variations in the ability to dissipate body heat. While women have significantly more body fat and appear to produce smaller amounts of sweat during exercise than men, they do not run a higher risk of heat injury during distance running. The number of heat-related problems in women during running in hot weather is no greater for women than it is for men.

Few studies have been conducted to assess the tolerance of endurance-trained women to long-term submaximal exercise in the heat. In many cases the women used in studies on heat stress were relatively sedentary, with significantly lower aerobic capacities than the men to whom they were compared. Under these conditions, when both sexes were required to exercise at the same absolute intensity, women had higher heart rates and internal body temperatures.

Since male and female distance runners use about the same percentage of their maximal oxygen uptakes during distance races, it is more appropriate to examine heat tolerance when the subjects are running at the same percent Vo_2 max. When the exercise task is matched to the runner's aerobic capacity, the physiological responses to heat stress are similar for both men and women (27, 28). The only notable differences in their responses to the heat are that men tend to produce more sweat and begin sweating sooner than women (28). Although this may be an advantage during exercise in a hot, dry environment, it also subjects men to a greater rate of dehydration. Despite their lower rates of sweating, trained women are able to dissipate body heat and become acclimatized equally as well as men.

TRAINABILITY

Despite differences in aerobic endurance and muscle strength, men and women appear to adapt to training in much the same way. Females benefit from training just as males do (44).

When men and women train together, their adaptations are nearly identical (23, 28). During regular continuous and interval training, men have been shown to increase their Vo_2 max values 15 percent, while women had a 14.2 percent improvement (28). Heart rate and blood lactate responses during maximal and submaximal exercise did not differ between the sexes or as a result of the style of training.

Male and female cadets at the U.S. Military Academy were studied during their initial training indoctrination (23). The women improved their aerobic capacities by 7.9 percent, whereas the men showed only a 2 percent increase in Vo_2 max values. The smaller improvement in the men were attributed to the fact that they were in better condition than the women at the beginning of the training program (59.4 ml/kg $\times$ min). There have been some suggestions that the mechanisms underlying the improvements in Vo_2 max with training may differ between the sexes

(45). When women are trained at relatively high intensities of 70 and 100 percent Vo_2 max, however, the cardiovascular and respiratory adjustments are similar to those of men (19, 20).

AGING: MATURITY AND PERFORMANCE

The establishment of age categories for distance races is an acknowledgment that growth and aging are among the inherent factors that limit performance. On the average, distance runners tend to achieve their greatest successes during the third and fourth decades of life. An examination of the U.S. records for 10-kilometer and marathon races illustrates the limits of human endurance during various stages of life (72). As shown in Figure 6-5, records for both boys and girls improve rapidly until the ages of 14 to 16, with no difference between the sexes. The best performances seem to occur between 20 and 30 years of age, then they begin to decline at a relatively slow rate. As the runners age, their records for 10-kilometer events slow about 1 percent or 14 seconds per year

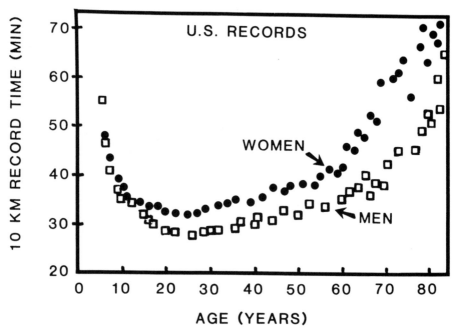

Figure 6-5. U.S. records for 10 kilometers for male and female runners ranging in age from five to 83 years. Note that males and females have similar records until they were approximately 14 or 15 years old, and that the best performances for both sexes are attained between 20 and 30 years of age (ref. 5).

until the age of 60 years. After age 60, the records slow more than a minute or 4 percent per year. These data suggest that decrements in endurance are small during middle age, but begin a rapid decline after the sixth decade of life. Although similar aging patterns can be seen in records for other distance events, it may be a bit misleading to base impressions of aging on the exceptional performances of these record holders. Unfortunately, there have been few opportunities to study a single runner who continued to train intensely for more than a few years.

One exception was the classic case of Clarence DeMar, who won his seventh Boston Marathon at the age of 42, placed seventh at age 50, and was 78th in a field of 153 runners at the age of 65 (25, 50). In all, he ran more than 1,000 distance races, including more than 100 marathons between 1909 and 1957. His performances at the Boston Marathon alone spanned 44 years. DeMar's last race in 1957, at the age of 68, was a 15-kilometer, which he ran despite advanced intestinal cancer and a colostomy. His best pace during the Boston Marathon was 5 minutes:42 seconds per mile (2 hours:29 minutes:42 seconds) at the age of 36. Thereafter, his time gradually slowed to nine minutes per mile (3 hours:58 minutes:37 seconds) at the age of 66, a decline of about 2 percent per year.

It is difficult to draw precise conclusions from DeMar's records since we have only limited knowledge of his training and the status of his health. As runners grow older, few continue to train with the same intensity they had when they were younger. Consequently, it is often difficult to determine whether the decline in performance is due to aging *per se* or reduced training.

Hal Higdon, who has been running competitively for more than 35 years, has sustained his training intensely, showing little decline in performance from the age of 21 to 52. Higdon recorded his lifetime best for the 10-kilometer (30 minutes:6.5 seconds) when he was 24. His best performance in recent years was 31 minutes:8 seconds at the age of 52, representing a two-tenths of 1 percent decline in performance per year over that 28-year period. Between the ages of 27 and 49 years, Higdon's performance in the marathon slowed from 2 hours:21 minutes:55 seconds to 2 hours:29 minutes:27 seconds, again a decline of only two-tenths of 1 percent per year. These data from Higdon and other runners suggest that intense training may slow the rate of decline and the effect of aging on performance.

THE EARLY YEARS

Recreational and competitive sports involve many children under 12 to 13 years old. There are even marathon records for four- to five-year-old boys and girls. Some observers have raised questions concerning the risk of injury or damage to the health of children who attempt to participate in such long-distance events. Current evidence suggests that intense physical training and competition have little effect on normal development, though there may be some changes in bone and muscle growth (70).

Bones. Growth of the long bones, the arms and legs, depends on the growth plates at the ends of the bones. From birth the growth plates add to the bone's length, reaching full development by the time a child is 18 to 20 years of age. While exercise does not appear to influence the growth in length of long bones, it does increase their width, giving them greater strength. Experts generally agree that exercise has a positive influence on bone growth.

Muscle. From birth through adolescence there is a steady increase in the body's muscle mass. At puberty there is a rapid increase in muscle development in boys, which appears to be a direct effect of the sudden rise in their testosterone levels. Girls, on the other hand, do not experience a similar spurt in muscle growth at puberty. Instead, their sexual development is associated with the secretion of the female hormone estrogen, which tends to promote the storage of body fat but has little or no effect on muscle development. Between the ages of 16 and 18 for females and 18 and 22 for males, muscle mass is at its peak unless it is increased further through strength training (70).

Fat. Approximately 80 percent of the body fat is stored in fat cells deposited directly beneath the skin. These cells are formed and begin to store fat well before birth. Some studies have proposed that the number of fat cells is affected by diet and exercise, with overfed individuals developing more fat cells than those who are kept thin during the early years of life. The number of fat cells seem to become fixed sometime during adolescence. Some experts have suggested that it is important to keep the total fat content low during early life to minimize the number of fat cells and reduce the problem of obesity later in life.

There is some evidence in rats, however, which indicates that the number of fat cells can continue to increase throughout life (32). Although heredity may play a role in fat accumulation, diet and exercise can be manipulated either to increase or decrease the fat stores. At birth, fat constitutes 10 to 12 percent of the total body weight. As shown in Table 6-5, normally active girls have significantly more body fat than boys even at seven to nine years of age, which may reflect a difference in physical activity rather than gender.

Oxygen Transport. Since distance running performances are markedly slower in children than in adults (Figure 6-1), we might expect children to have significantly lower aerobic capacities. Surprisingly, the Vo_2

TABLE 6-5. Percentage of body fat in normally active males and females from seven to 60 years of age. Adapted from reference 53.

	PERCENTAGE BODY FAT	
AGE (YR)	FEMALES	MALES
7–9	19.5	14.5
9–11	20.0	17.0
11–13	22.0	16.0
13–15	21.0	13.5
15–17	23.0	11.0
20–30	23.5	12.0
30–40	25.0	17.5
40–50	27.0	22.0
50–60	30.5	23.0

max values for normally active children are not appreciably different from those observed for comparable young adults. Measurements of Vo_2 max levels in normally active boys and girls between seven and 13 years old reveal little difference between the sexes and only small changes in aerobic capacities over this age range (17, 30, 48). The Vo_2 max levels for these children averaged 52.2 ml/kg $\times$ min, similar to those reported for young adult men but somewhat higher than those observed in normally active young women (70).

Likewise, some young trained distance runners, aged 15 to 17, have Vo_2 max values that are not appreciably different from those of elite runners (13, 14, 17, 18, 22, 48). Some years ago we studied a group of 11 high school cross-country runners whose Vo_2 max values averaged 64.8 ml/kg $\times$ min, with three of the runners having values above 70 ml/kg $\times$ min (13). Based on the prediction equations in Chapter 1, runners having these high Vo_2 max values should have been capable of running the two-mile in less than 9 minutes:40 seconds. Surprisingly, the average best performance for these boys was 10 minutes:35 seconds.

Why then are these young runners unable to match the performances of older runners having similar aerobic capacities? The answer appears to be a lack of running efficiency. It costs the young runners substantially more energy to run at a given speed than it does the older runners. Whereas a 20-year-old male or female runner may use oxygen at a rate of 36 to 38 ml/kg $\times$ min while running at eight minutes per mile, a 12-year-old boy may need 50 to 52 ml/kg $\times$ min to run at the same speed (22). This means that it costs the young runner nearly 40 percent more energy to keep pace with the older runner. If both runners had Vo_2 max values of 60 ml/kg × min, then the 12-year-old runner would be working at 85 percent Vo_2 max, while the older runner would use only 62 percent Vo_2 max.

As the young runners age, their running economy improves rapidly. Jack Daniels (22) studied a group of boys every few months from the time they were 12 until they were 14.5 years old. He observed that their maximal oxygen uptake values remained constant over this two-and-one-half-year period (59.5 to 58.8 ml/kg × min), though they gained an average of 20 pounds (9.2 kilograms) and grew 4.4 inches (11.2 centimeters). At the same time, the amount of oxygen they consumed while running at eight minutes per mile decreased from 52.0 ml/kg × min to 45.5. We observed similar changes in Hal Higdon's son Kevin, whom we studied from the age of 12 until he was 23 years old. As can be seen in Table 6-6, Young Higdon's Vo_2 max remained relatively constant from the age of 16 to 23 years, though his running economy improved dramatically.

Initially we might reason that young runners become more efficient as they grow older simply because their legs lengthen and bodies grow rapidly. This is unlikely, since there are many small runners who are highly efficient. Running efficiency seems to be unrelated to leg length or anatomical size. We are more inclined to feel that young runners become more efficient as a consequence of improvements in running skill. These runners improve through experience and repetition. By the age of 18 or 20 years, the patterns of motion needed for smooth, efficient running appear to be fully developed and change little with additional years of training.

Trainability. Are preadolescent boys and girls able to adapt to en-

TABLE 6-6. Changes in oxygen consumption and heart rate (HR) during submaximal and maximal treadmill running for Kevin Higdon from the age of 12 to 23 years.

	12 YR*	15 YR	20 YR	23 YR
Weight (kg)	38.9	60.0	65.8	64.3
% Fat	9.5	7.7	7.5	8.7
Vo_2 max (ml/kg × min)	52.5	72.8	72.8	74.2
HR max (bts/min)	188	185	179	176
8 min/mile				
Vo_2 (ml/kg × min)	52.3	39.5	32.8	33.5
% Vo_2 max	94	54	45	45
HR (beats/min)	176	125	108	113

*At the age of 12 Kevin was not training.

durance training as well as young adults? This question has recently been reviewed by Thomas Rowland (59), who studied the literature dealing with endurance training in prepubescent children (9, 29, 48, 63, 67). Because of limitations in the design of these and other studies, Rowland does not offer a clear answer concerning the trainability of prepubescent children.

Some studies offer the general impression that children between the ages of eight and 13 years adapt to training in much the same manner as adults. Because of their rapid growth, however, it is often difficult to separate the effects of training from the influence of natural growth. Whereas children between the ages of seven and nine years show little improvement in aerobic capacity with training, older boys and girls from 11 to 13 years of age show significant gains in Vo_2 max values with endurance training (29, 30, 34).

The reported variations in response to endurance training among children may be, in part, due to differences in the mode and intensity of training. One study, for example, found no improvement in Vo_2 max with 12 weeks of school physical fitness activities (34). This study, however, did not require the children to exercise with the intensity and for the duration normally followed during training for distance running. Interval and continuous running, on the other hand, has been shown to produce improvements ranging from 10 to 26 percent in Vo_2 max levels.

Table 6-7 presents the findings from a training program conducted with 14 boys who were trained over a period of 32 months that began when they were 11 years old (29). Although Vo_2 max levels improved continually throughout the study, much of this change appeared to parallel the boys' increase in body weight. When Vo_2 max was calculated on the basis of body weight, there appeared to be very little change de-

TABLE 6-7. Changes in body size, heart size, and Vo_2 max in a group of boys who trained for six, 26, or 32 months.

	MONTHS OF TRAINING		
	6	26	32
Height (cm)	+4.0	+13.7	+18.6
Weight (kg)	+2.2	+14.8	+18.7
Heart Volume (ml)	+13	+212	+230
(ml/kg body wt)	−.4	+.8	+.2
Vo_2 max (1/min)	+.33	+.97	+1.23
(ml/kg × min)	+5.5	+1.6	+3.8

spite nearly 2.7 years of training. Similar findings were observed for changes in heart volume, which grew larger throughout the study, but only in proportion to the boys' increase in body size.

It seems doubtful that prepubescent boys and girls are as adaptable to endurance training as adults. Current evidence suggests that children below the age of 10 or 11 years may demonstrate smaller improvements in aerobic capacity than post-adolescent males and females. Since we have observed exceptionally high Vo_2 max values for high school cross-country runners, we believe that the turning point in the adaptability to training must be during or soon after puberty.

The fact that young children are not as trainable as adults should not be interpreted to mean that their health is at risk or that they are incapable of participating in distance running. It simply indicates that the degree of adaptation and level of performance are limited. This may also explain why many athletes experience astounding improvements during the transition from pre- to post-adolescence.

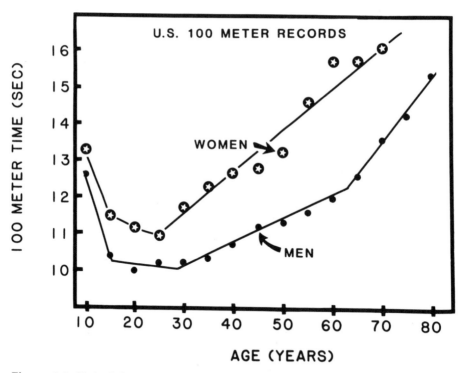

Figure 6-6. United States records for the 100-meter dash for men and women ranging in age from 10 to 80 years (ref. 72). Note that the best performances occur between the ages of 20 and 30 years, followed by a gradual slowing of performance (+1.0 percent per year) until the age of 60.

THE MATURE RUNNER

Whether it be in the 100 meters or the marathon, the record books suggest that the "best years of our lives" are between 20 and 30 years of age (72). Interestingly, the relative rate of decline in performance with aging is independent of the running distance. Performance records for 100 meters, 10 kilometers, and the marathon all slow at about 1 percent per year from the age of 25 to 60 years (Figures 6-5 and 6-6). Aging appears to affect both speed and endurance to about the same degree. The following discussion describes the physiological changes that can be blamed for these age-related decrements in performance.

Factors of Endurance. The first studies of aging and physical fitness were performed by Sid Robinson in the late 1930s (57). He demonstrated that V_{O_2} max values in normally active men declined steadily from 25 to

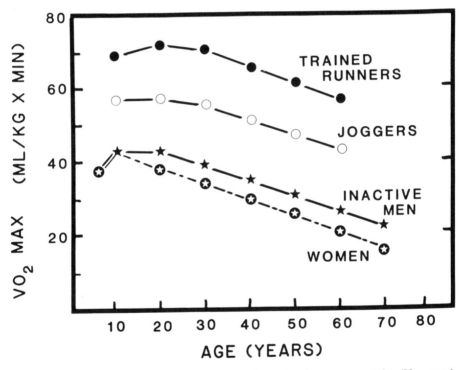

Figure 6-7. Relationship between aging and maximal oxygen uptake (V_{O_2} max) for inactive men and women, joggers, and highly trained runners. These cross-sectional data suggest that after the age of 20 to 25 years V_{O_2} max declines at a steady rate for all adults, regardless of their activity level.

75 years of age. The average values reported by Robinson for different age groups were as follows:

AGE (YEARS)	Vo$_2$ max (ml/kg × min)
25	47.7
35	43.1
45	39.5
52	38.4
63	34.5
75	25.5

A number of investigators have since confirmed these findings in relatively inactive men and women (5, 7, 3). Unfortunately, there have been few opportunities to study runners over a long period of time to determine the impact of lifelong training on Vo$_2$ max levels.

Figure 6-7 illustrates the changes in Vo$_2$ max levels among groups of untrained men and women, joggers, and highly trained runners. Although training offers the runner substantial aerobic advantages, aging appears to induce a similar decline in Vo$_2$ max values during middle age. Some caution must be used in drawing conclusions from these findings, since the older runners and joggers probably do not train with the same intensity and duration as their younger counterparts. At least part of the decline in Vo$_2$ max with age may be related to the nature of training.

We have had the opportunity to test a few runners over a period of 13 to 26 years. In the past 17 years Hal Higdon has on occasion trained with relatively the same intensity as he did when he was 21 to 25 years old. We have measured his Vo$_2$ max since 1968. Although his state of training varied to some degree during that period, his Vo$_2$ max remained

TABLE 6-8. Repeated treadmill tests for Hal Higdon from 36 to 50 years of age.

YEAR	AGE (YR)	WEIGHT (KG)	Vo$_2$ MAX (ML/KG × MIN)	HR MAX (BEATS/MIN)
1968	36	67.5	67.6*	163
1971	39	65.4	62.7	158
1974	43	64.7	64.9	152
1979	48	63.5	65.8	156
1980	49	63.9	64.0	155
1981	50	62.7	63.7	155

*Denotes that Higdon was training for the 1968 Olympic Marathon trial at the time of this test.

relatively constant (Table 6-8). It was also interesting to note that his running economy, or oxygen uptake while running at eight minutes per mile, has remained at 32 to 33 ml/kg × min over this 17-year-period. It is not surprising, therefore, that his performances for the 10-kilometer and marathon distances have declined very little.

Is Higdon an exception? Can other runners reduce the effects of aging on their aerobic endurance by continuing to train intensely? As we will see later in this chapter, middle-aged men and women seem to respond to training in much the same way as individuals in their mid-20s.

In support of the observations with Higdon, let me offer the results from my personal records. Since I was 24 years old, we have regularly measured my Vo$_2$ max levels. Figure 6-8 illustrates those Vo$_2$ max values over a quarter of a century. Between the ages of 24 and 29 years I did not train regularly. Interestingly, my highest Vo$_2$ max values were achieved during periods when I was running 25 to 60 miles per week, or, in recent

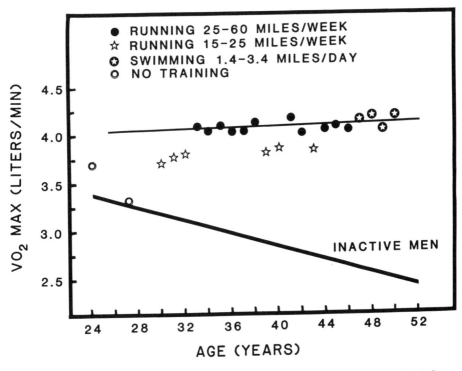

Figure 6-8. Changes in Vo$_2$ max for the author (data points and thin line) from the age of 24 to 50 years. Whereas untrained men (darkest line) show a steady decline in aerobic capacity throughout middle-age, vigorous endurance training (running and swimming) has maintained the author's Vo$_2$ max over this 26-year period.

TABLE 6-9. Best running and swimming performances for the author at different ages. Note that the best performances occur during periods when the volume of training was greatest, which has been greater in recent years.

ACTIVITY	AGE (YR)	TRAINING (MILES/WK)	EVENT	BEST TIME (MIN:SEC)
Running	32	25–28	10 km	43:16
	46	38–44	10 km	40:18
Swimming	22	5.4–7.5	1.5 km	23:31
	50	11–19.2	1.5 km	19:42

years, when I have been swimming 8.5 to 16 miles per week. As can be seen in Table 6-9, all of my best endurance performances (running and swimming) were achieved after I turned 45, in spite of the fact that I trained as a collegiate swimmer until I was 22 years.

One of the most notable long-term studies with distance runners and aging was conducted by Bruce Dill and his colleagues (26) from the Harvard Fatigue Laboratory. Don Lash, world record holder for the two-mile (8 minutes:58 seconds) in 1936, was among those studied by the Harvard group. Although few of the former runners continued to train after leaving college, Lash was still running approximately 45 minutes per day at the age of 49. Despite this activity, his Vo_2 max had declined from 81.4 ml/kg $\times$ min at age 24 years to 54.4 at age 49. As expected, those former runners who did not continue to train during middle age showed much larger declines. On the average, their aerobic capacities declined by about 43 percent from the age of 23 to 50 years (70 to 40 ml/kg $\times$ min). This would suggest that prior training offers no advantage to endurance in later life unless an individual continues to engage in some form of vigorous activity.

Bengt Saltin and Gunnar Grimby (60) have shown that former athletes who have been out of training for more than 10 years still have a 20 percent advantage in Vo_2 max compared to untrained nonathletes. A group of untrained former athletes ranging in age from 50 to 59 years had an average Vo_2 max of 38 ml/kg $\times$ min, while a randomly selected age-matched group of untrained, nonathletes averaged 30 ml/kg $\times$ min. It is impossible, however, to determine whether the former athletes' higher Vo_2 max values are due to their earlier periods of training or to differences in lifestyle or inherited factors or all three.

Since regular physical activity is an important contributor to good health, it is logical to ask, "Does training throughout middle and old age have an effect on longevity?" While it is true that an endurance exercise program may reduce a number of the risk factors associated with cardiovascular disease, there is no direct evidence to prove that you will live longer if you exercise regularly. Even studies using animals have provided conflicting results. One study (35) demonstrated that rats who exercised freely lived roughly 15 percent longer than sedentary animals, but a recent investigation by a group in St. Louis has shown no significant increase in the life span of rats who voluntarily ran on an exercise wheel (42). This later study did report three additional points of interest. First, the incidence of early death was reduced among the animals that exercised. That is, more of the active rats lived to old age, but, on the average, still died at the same age as their sedentary counterparts. Second, the animals chose to reduce their activity levels as they grew older. On the average, the rats ran 24 to 25 miles per week during the first five months of life, but covered only two to four miles per week during the final months of life, an activity pattern common in aging humans. Finally, only the animals that had a restricted food intake and maintained a lower body weight than the freely eating sedentary rats lived significantly more than 10 percent longer. Of course, it is impossible to apply these findings to humans, but it does raise some interesting questions that may be relevant to our health and longevity.

Trainability. Do middle- and older-aged men and women adapt to training as well as younger individuals? There is no doubt that mild running will increase the Vo_2 max and endurance performance of both the young and old (56, 62, 64). Even men above the age of 70 show significant improvements with regular exercise (24, 52). That is not to say that these individuals can perform the same volume or intensity of training as their youthful counterparts, nor do they achieve the same magnitude of improvements with training.

Age takes its toll in some subtle ways. Heart volume, for example, does not increase in response to training in the older individual, although most older runners have hearts that are larger than their sedentary counterparts (10, 60). Unlike younger runners, who demonstrate an increase in heart volume in proportion to the increase in Vo_2 max with training, runners above the age of 40 or 50 years show little increase in left ventricular volume.

Though both young (19 to 21 years) and middle-aged (38 to 55 years) men show similar improvements in maximal cardiac output following endurance training, older (greater than 60 years) men experience little change in maximal cardiac output with training (62). Apparently, these older individuals are able to improve their Vo_2 max values after training by extracting more oxygen from the blood as it passes by the working muscles rather than by delivering more blood (62).

How this adaptation occurs is unclear, but there is substantial evidence to indicate that the muscles of older men remain trainable at least until the age of 75 (52). Although there are some minor improvements in the muscles' enzyme processes during training in older individuals, there appears to be little change in the number of the existing mitochondria or capillaries (2, 47, 62).

There is evidence, however, that some muscle fibers may be lost as the individual ages beyond 60 years (2, 47). Though there is some controversy regarding this matter, there are reports which suggest that some of the fast twitch fibers may be lost as a consequence of disuse. Others have theorized that changes in the neurological controls of the muscles may be one of the first systems affected by aging (47). This point is supported by the fact that the strength decline seen in old age appears before any external changes can be measured in muscle volume. In any event, the decline in muscle strength during old age might not be due solely to muscle fiber atrophy.

FINAL WORDS

This final chapter has again emphasized the individuality of each distance runner. Whether confronted with limitations that are inherited or acquired in the course of aging, nearly everyone is trainable and capable of being a better runner. Differences in performance between men and women and young and old enabled us to better understand the physiological dictates for successful distance running. While we should not dwell on predetermined factors over which we have no control, understanding their limitations and adaptability is important to aid in designing a training program that will help to develop every person's full potential.

BIBLIOGRAPHY

1. Anderson, M. D., R. W. Cote, E. F. Coyle and F. B. Roby. Leg power, muscle strength, and peak EMG activity in physically active college men and women. *Med. Sci. Sports*, 11:81–82, 1979.
2. Aniansson, A. Muscle function in old age with special reference to muscle morphology, effect of training and capacity in activities of daily living. *Dissertation*, Univ. of Goteborg, Goteborg, Sweden, 1980.
3. Astrand, I. Aerobic work capacity in men and women with special reference to age. *Acta Physiol. Scand.*, 49:11, 1960.
4. Astrand, P.-O. and K. Rodahl. *Textbook of Work Physiology*, 184–197, 1977.
5. Astrand, P. O. *Experimental studies of physical working capacity in relation to age and sex*, 121. Copenhagen: Munksgaard, 1952.
6. Avellini, B. A., E. Kamon and J. T. Krajewski. Physiological responses of physical fit men and women to acclimation to humid heat. *J. App Physiol.*, 49:254–261, 1980.
7. Bonjer, F. H. Relationship between working time, physical working capacity and allowable caloric expenditure. *Muskelarbeit und Muskeltraining*, 86–99. Stuttgart, 1968.
8. Brown, C. and J. Wilmore. The effects of maximal resistance training on the strength

and body composition of women athletes. *Med. Sci. Sports*, 6:174–177, 1974.

9. Brown, C. H., J. R. Harrower and M. F. Deeter. The effects of cross-country running on pre-adolescent girls. *Med. Sci. Sport*, 4:1–5, 1972.

10. Child, J. S., R. J. Barnard and R. L. Taw. Cardiac hypertrophy and function in master endurance runners and sprinters. *J. Appl. Physiol: Respirat Environ. Exer. Physiol.*, 57:176–181, 1984.

11. Cohen, J. S. and C. V. Gisolfi. Effects of interval training in work-heat tolerance of young women. *Med. Sci. Sports Exer.*, 14:46–52, 1982.

12. Costill, D. L. Total mileage. *The Runner*, 12:47–48, 1984.

13. Costill, D. L. *Limitations of endurance: With special reference to age*, 1:24. Ball State Univ. Press, 1969.

14. Costill, D. L., G. Branam, D. O. Eddy and K. Sparks. Determinants of marathon running success. *Int. Zeitschift fur angerwandte Physiol.*, 29:249–254, 1971.

15. Costill, D. L., J. Daniels, W. Evans, W. Fink, G. Krahenbuhl and B. Saltin. Skeletal muscle enzymes and fiber composition in male and female track athletes. *J. Appl. Physiol.*, 40:149–154, 1976.

16. Costill, D. L. and J. Miller. Nutrition for endurance sport: Carbohydrate and fluid balance. *Int. J. Sports Med.*, 1:2–14, 1980.

17. Costill, D. L., W. J. Fink, L. H. Getchell, J. L. Ivy and F. A. Witzmann. Lipid metabolism in skeletal muscle of endurance-trained males and females. *J. Appl. Physiol.*, 47:787–791, 1979.

18. Costill, D. L. Metabolic responses during distance running. *J. Appl. Physiol.*, 28:251–255, 1970.

19. Cunningham, D. A. and J. S. Hill. Effect of training on cardiovascular response to exercise in women. *J. Appl. Physiol.*, 39:891–895, 1975.

20. Cunningham, D. A., D. McCrimmon and L. F. Vlach. Cardiovascular response to interval and continuous training in women. *Eur. J. Appl. Physiol.*, 41:187–197, 1979.

21. Daniels, J., G. Krahenbuhl, C. Foster, J. Gilbert and S. Daniels. Aerobic responses of female distance runners to submaximal and maximal exercise. *Ann. N.Y. Acad. Science*, 301:726–733, 1977.

22. Daniels, J. and N. Oldridge. Changes in oxygen consumption of young boys during growth and running training. *Med. Sci. Sports*, 3:161–165, 1971.

23. Daniels, W. L., D. M. Kowal, J. A. Vogel and R. M. Stauffer. Physiological effects of a military training program on male and female cadets. *Aviat. Space Environ. Med.*, 50:562–566, 1979.

24. deVries, H. A. Physiological effects of an exercise training regimen upon men aged 52 to 88. *J. Gerontology*, 25:325–336, 1970.

25. Dill, D. B. Marathoner DeMar: Physiological Studies. *J. Nat. Cancer Inst.*, 35:185–191, 1965.

26. Dill, D. B., S. Robinson and J. C. Ross. A longitudinal study of 16 champion runners. *J. Sports Med. Phys. Fit.*, 7:4–27, 1967.

27. Drinkwater, B. L. Women and exercise: Physiological aspects. *Exercise and Sports Sciences Reviews*, 12:21–51, 1984.

28. Eddy, D. O., K. L. Sparks and D. A. Adelizi. The effects of continuous and interval training in women and men. *Eur. J. Appl. Physiol.*, 37:83–92, 1977.

29. Ekblom, B. Effect of physical training in adolescent boys. *J. Appl. Physiol.*, 27:350–355, 1969.

30. Eriksson, B. O. and G. Koch. Effect of physical training on hemodynamic response during submaximal and maximal exercise in 11 to 13 year old boys. *Acta. Physiol. Scand.*, 87:27–39, 1973.

31. Fahey, T. D., R. M. R. Rolph, J. Nagel and S. Mortara. Serum testosterone, body composition, and strength of young adults. *Med. Sci. Sports*, 8:31–34, 1976.

32. Faust, I. M., P. R. Johnson, J. S. Stern and J. Hirsch. Diet-induced adipocyte number

increase in adult rats: A new model of obesity. *Amer. J. Physiol.*, 235:E279–E286, 1978.

33. Fox, E. L. and D. K. Mathews. *The physiological basis of physical education and athletics.* 348. Philadelphia: W. B. Saunders, 1981.

34. Gilliam, T. B. and P. S. Freedson. Effects of a 12-week school physical fitness program on peak Vo2, body composition, and blood lipids in 7 to 9 year old children. *Int. J. Sports Med.*, 1:73–78, 1980.

35. Goodrick, C. L. Effects of long-term voluntary wheel exercise on male and female Wistar rats. *Gerontology*, 26:22–33, 1980.

36. Hagen, R. D., T. Strathman, L. Strathman and L. R. Gettman. Oxygen uptake and energy expenditure during horizontal treadmill running. *J. Appl. Physiol.*, 49:571–575, 1980.

37. Hedberg, G. and E. Jansson. Skelettmuskelfiberkomposition. *Kapacitet och intresse for olika fysiska aktiviteter bland elever i gymnasieskolan*, 54:1976.

38. Hermansen, L. Oxygen transport during exercise in human subjects. *Acta Physiol. Scand. Suppl.*, 399:1–104, 1973.

39. Hermansen, L. and S. Oseid. Direct and indirect estimation of maximal oxygen uptake in pre-pubertal boys. *Acta Paediat. Scand. Suppl.*, 217:18–23, 1971.

40. Hetrick, G. A. and J. H. Wilmore. Androgen levels and muscle hypertrophy during an eight week weight training program for men and women. *Med. Sci. Sports*, 11:102, 1979.

41. Hettinger, T. *Physiology of Strength.* 1961.

42. Holloszy, J. O., E. K. Smith, M. Vining and S. Adams. Effect of voluntary exercise on longevity of rats. *J. Appl. Physiol.*, 59:826–831, 1985.

43. Ikai, M. and T. Fukunaga. Calculation of muscle strength per unit cross sectional area of human muscle by means of ultrasonic measurements. *Int. Z. Angew. Physiol.*, 26:26–32, 1968.

44. Kilbom, A. Physical training in women. *Scand. J. Clin. Lab. Invest.*, 28:119, 1971.

45. Kilbom, A. and I. Astrand. Physical training with submaximal intensities in women. II. Effect of cardiac output. *Scand. J. Clin. Lab. Invest.*, 28:163–175, 1971.

46. Komi, P. V. and J. Karlsson. Physical performance, skeletal muscle enzyme activities, and fiber types in monozygous and dizygous twins of both sexes. *Acta Physiol. Scand.*, Suppl.:462, 1979.

47. Larsson, L. Morphological and functional characteristics of the ageing skeletal muscle in man. *Acta Physiol. Scand.*, Suppl. 457:36, 1978.

48. Lussier, L. and E. R. Buskirk. Effects of an endurance training regimen on assessment of work capacity in prepubertal children. *Ann. N.Y. Acad. Sci.*, 301:743–747, 1977.

49. Mayhew, J. and P. Gross. Body composition changes in young women and high resistance weight training. *Res. Quart.*, 45:433–440, 1974.

50. Nason, J. The Story of the Boston Marathon. *Boston Globe*, 1966.

51. Nygaard, E. and T. Goricke. Morphological studies of skeletal muscles in women. *Report No. 99.* Copenhagen: August Krogh Inst., 1976.

52. Orlander, J. and A. Aniansson. Effects of physical training on skeletal muscle metabolism and ultrastructure in 70 to 75 year old men. *Acta Physiol. Scand.*, 109:149–154, 1979.

53. Parizkova, J. Body composition and exercise during growth and development. *Physical Activity: Human Growth and Development*, 1974.

54. Pate, R. R., C. Barnes and W. Miller. A physiological comparison of performance-matched female and male distance runners. *Res. Quart. Exer. Sport*, 56:245–250, 1985.

55. Pollock, J. Submaximal and maximal working capacity of elite distance runners. *Ann. N.Y. Acad. Sci.*, 301:310–322, 1977.

56. Pollock, M. L., H. S. Miller, A. C. Linnerud and K. H. Cooper. Frequency of training as a determinant for improvement in cardiovascular function and body composition

of middle-aged men. *Arch. Phys. Med. Rehabil.*, 56:141–145, 1975.

57. Robinson, S. Experimental studies of physical fitness in relation to age. *Arbeitsphysiol.*, 10:251–323, 1938.

58. Rous, J. The cardiovascular system. *Youth and Physical Activity*, 201–230. Brno, Czechoslavakia: Univ. J. E. Purkyme, 1980.

59. Rowland, T. W. Aerobic response to endurance training in prepubescent children; a critical analysis. *Med. Sci. Sports Exer.*, 17:493–497, 1985.

60. Saltin, B. and G. Grimby. Physiological analysis of middle-aged and old former athletes. *Circulation*, 38:1104–1115, 1968.

61. Saltin, B., J. Henriksson, E. Nygaard and P. Andersen. Fiber types and metabolic potentials of skeletal muscles in sedentary man and endurance runners. *Ann. N.Y. Acad. Sci.*, 301:3–29, 1977.

62. Seals, D. R., J. M. Hagbert, B. F. Hurley, A. A. Ehsani and J. O. Holloszy. Endurance training in older men and women. *J. Appl. Physiol.: Respirat. Environ. Exer. Physiol.*, 57:1024–1029, 1984.

63. Shasby, G. B. and F. C. Hagerman. The effects of conditioning on cardiorespiratory function in adolescent boys. *J. Sports Med.*, 3:97–107, 1975.

64. Siegel, W., G. Blomquist and J. H. Mitchell. Effects of a quantitated physical training program on middle-aged sedentary men. *Circulation*, 41:19–26, 1970.

65. Skinner, J. S., O. Bar-Or, V. Bergsteinova, C. W. Bell, D. Royer and E. R. Buskirk. Comparison of continuous and intermittent tests for determining maximal oxygen intake in children. *Acta Paediat. Scand. Suppl.*, 217:24–28, 1971.

66. Sundberg, S. Function and dimensions of the cardiorespiratory system in children and adolescents with different levels of physical activity. *Acta Physiol. Scand. (supplement)*, 1–46, 1983.

67. Vaccaro, P. and D. H. Clarke. Cardiorespiratory alterations in 9 to 11 year old children following a season of competitive swimming. *Med. Sci. Sports Exer.*, 10:204–207, 1978.

68. Wilmore, J. Body composition and strength development. *J. Phys. Educ. Rec.*, 46:38–40, 1975.

69. Wilmore, J. H. *Training for Sports and Activity*, 219–222. Boston: Allyn and Bacon, 1982.

70. Wilmore, J. H. Alterations in strength, body composition and anthropometric measurements consequent to a 10-week weight training program. *Med. Sci. Sport*, 6:133–138, 1974.

71. Wilmore, J. H. and C. H. Brown. Physiological profiles of women distance runners. *Med. Sci. Sports*, 6:178–181, 1974.

72. Young, K. and J. H. Young. *Running Records by Age*, 1:1–85. Tucson: Pub. by authors. 1985.

INDEX

Acidity (pH measurement), *see* Lactic acid
Actin, 163
Adenosine triphosphate (ATP), 59–60, 139
   production of, 37, 38, 86, 88
   sources of, 10
   vitamins and carbohydrate use for, 71
Aerobic energy production, 10–16, 50
   capacity for, 33
   endurance training and, 86
   rates of, 29–30
   see also Vo_2 max
Aerodynamic shadow, 36, 139
Age, 20, 166–178
   body fat and, 168
   bone development and, 168
   cardiovascular health and, 20, 176–177
   muscle development and, 168
   performance impact of, 166–167, 173–174, 175
   running efficiency and, 169–170
   trainability and, 171
   Vo_2 max and, 168–170, 174–177
Air resistance, 26, 139
   at high altitudes, 116
Aldosterone, 74
Altitude, 114–117, 118, 124
   high:
      acclimatization and, 116–117
      overtraining and, 124
      oxygen at, 115
      rate of adaptation at, 116
      running time changes at, 116
      training at, 115–117
Alveoli, 91
Amino acids, *see* Protein
Anaerobic energy production, 10
   interval training and, 101–102
   lactate accumulation in, 34, 48
   strength training and, 89
Anemia, *see* Iron
Anxiety, 124, 131

Ball State University, 129, 141
Blood, 23–25, 48–51, 91–92, 124

anemia in females, 24
cholesterol levels in, 64
enzyme levels of, 25, 50, 124
flow and dehydration, 73
glucose in, 37, 42–43, 50, 60, 64, 67–68, 69, 70
hormones in, 139
lipid profiles of, 24, 64
metabolic functions of, 24
oxygen content of, 91
pH of arterial, 48–49
plasma volume of, 24, 45, 51, 73, 81, 91
red blood cells in, 24, 91, 92
white blood cells of, 125
   see also Hemoglobin, Hematocrit
Blood doping, 92
Blood pressure, 21, 124
Blood vessels, 45
Body fat, 2–4, 155–156
   age and, 168
   effect on performance, 2, 156
   in elite runners, 2
   measurement of, 3
   sex differences in, 2, 155
Boston Marathon, 4, 19, 167
British Commonwealth Games (1962), 17–18
Bruce Physical Fitness Index, 21

Caffeine, 68
Calcium, 73–74
Capillaries, 86, 87, 158, 178
   detraining effects on, 145
   sex differences in, 158
Carbohydrates, 10, 37–39, 59–68, 81–82
   blood glucose and, 37, 60, 67
   cholesterol formation and, 64
   feedings during exercise, 69
   glycogen replacement and, 61, 141
   in sports drinks, 75–77
   intake of, 63, 67, 71–73
   percentages in diet, 60, 61, 62, 71, 149
   solution absorption of, 69

Glycogen, *continued*
storage and endurance training, 60–65, 86, 88
Glycolysis, 89
Grimby, Gunnar, 176

Hansen, O., 39, 60
Harvard Fatigue Laboratory, 176
Harvard Step Test, 21
Head colds, 124
Heart, 16–21, 92–93
disease of:
diet and, 64
running and, 20, 24
sex differences in, 160
size of, 17–19, 92–93, 160
volume of, 93, 160, 177
see also Cardiac output, Heart rate, Stroke volume
Heart rate, 20–21, 45–46, 92–93, 100, 102
determination of, 46
effect on performance, 20, 21
heat acclimatization and, 111
ideal standards for, 46
interval training and, 98–102
maximal, 93
monitoring for stress, 46
overtraining and, 124, 129
percent of maximal, 20, 21
racing pace and, 138
sex differences in, 161
Heat, *see* Environmental conditions
Heat acclimatization, 51–54, 74
adjustments in, 111, 112
characteristics of, 111
dehydration and, 113–114
effects on rectal temperatures, 111, 112
electrolyte loss, 74–78, 80
sex differences in, 165
sweating and, 111–112
Heat, body, *see* Temperature, body
Heat exhaustion, 54, 73, 111, 113–114
Heat stroke, 111, 113–114
prevention of, 53
symptoms of, 53
Height, 4
Hematocrit(s), 45
effect of intense training on, 91
runners and, 23
Hemodilution, 91
Hemoglobin, 23–24, 45, 80–81
blood doping and, 92
concentration at high altitudes, 116

iron in, 80
sex differences in, 161–162
training effects on, 81, 91, 92
Heparin, 68
Higdon, Hal, 18, 167, 174–175
Higdon, Kevin, 170
Humidity, 52, 53
Hyperglycemia, 64
Hypoglycemia, *see* Blood, glucose in
Hypothalamus, 51, 52

Insulin, 69, 70
carbohydrate intake and elevation of, 67
International Olympic Committee, 68
Iron, 72, 82
deficiency of, 80–81
females and, 81, 82
supplementation, 81
Irritability, 124

Karpovich, Peter, 137
Kidneys, 24, 50
electrolyte management in, 74, 82
function during exercise, 74
Kilocalories:
consumption of, 29–30, 72
surplus of, 73
see also Diet
Kuipers, Harm, 142

Lactate, *see* Lactic acid
Lactate dehydrogenase (LDH), 25, 124–125
Lactic acid (lactate), 16, 89, 99–102, 107, 130
accumulation of, 34–35, 48, 89, 126–130, 137–138
detraining and levels of, 145–146
effects of elevations in, 48–50
interval training and, 99–102
muscle soreness and, 50
production at high altitudes, 116
removal of, 50, 102, 107, 145
Lash, Don, 176
Limburg, University of, 142
Lipids, *see* Fats (as fuel)
Lipoproteins, 24
Liver, 66–68
glucose production in, 42–43, 50, 60, 68
glycogen stores in, 60, 66–67
lactate removal and, 50
vitamin storage in, 78
Lungs, 21–23, 46–48, 91

maintaining Vo_2 max and, 134
muscular strength and, 135
plan for, 135–136
Temperature, body, 51–54, 73–75
elevation:
dangers of, 52–54
cardiac output and, 45
fluid intake and, 75
sweating response and, 51, 52, 73, 111
body water losses in, 73
distance running and, 74
ionic concentration of sweat, 73–74, 76
sex differences in, 165
see also Heat acclimatization, Heat exhaustion, Heat stroke
10-kilometer races, 43, 46–47, 52, 53, 100, 135, 149
age and performance in, 166–167
preparation for, 97–98, 101, 103, 105, 106–108
running pace in, 137
tapering for, 136
Terrain, 35–36
Testosterone, 163, 168
Thirst, 77–78
Training, 36, 85–118, 147, 148–150, 165
age influences on, 172, 173–178
electrolyte loss and, 80
intervals, 97–105
aerobic, 97–99
aerobic-anaerobic, 99–101
anaerobic, 101–103
optimal adaptations to, 95–96, 104, 148–149
program design of, 117–118
progression of, 96, 104, 118, 134, 148–149
purpose of, 94
reductions in, 96, 134–137, 149
sex differences in, 165–166
specificity, 32, 108, 110, 111, 117, 147
stress assessment and, 132–134
see also Detraining, Endurance training, Overtraining, Retraining
Treadmill tests, 12–13, 16, 17, 21, 33, 37–39, 43
sex differences in, 161
varied paces and, 137–138
Triglycerides, 37, 43–44, 50, 68
breakdown to fatty acids, 43, 50
elevations of, 64, 68
plasma and, 24
Tuttle, Gary, 2
Vastus lateralis, 36, 40–41
Vital capacity, *see* Lungs
Vitamins, 71–72, 78, 82
A, 78, 80
B complex, 71, 78, 80
C, 71, 78, 80
D, 78, 80
deficiencies, 78
E, 72, 78, 80
folic acid, 78
function of, 71
K, 78
pantothenic acid, 78
RDA consumption by runners, 71, 78
supplements, 71, 80, 82
table, 79
Vo_2 max, 12–16, 147, 176
age differences and, 169–170, 171–172, 176
blood doping and, 92
capillarization and, 158
distances, levels at, 50, 138
elite runners and, 13–15, 34, 159
energy needs and, 31–34, 39
estimates of, 15–16
high altitudes and, 116–117
improvements in, 93, 94–95, 103, 104, 165
maintenance of, 134, 145–146
overtraining and, 129
percentage used, 16, 33–34, 35, 39, 50, 133–134, 138, 155
performance and, 13–15, 33
red blood cell count and, 91
sex differences in, 159–161
stress assessments and, 132–134
terrain variations and, 35–36

Waitz, Grete, 2, 16, 17, 30, 34
Warm-down, 107–108
Warm-up, 101, 107, 149
Water, 75, 76, 77–78, 82
Weightlifting, 89, 110
Weight loss:
high altitudes and, 116
muscle-liver glycogen stores and, 66–67, 81
overtraining and, 124
performance and, 2, 81
race preparation and, 81
Western Hemisphere Marathon (1962), 96
Weston, Edward Payson, 29

X ray, 1, 13, 18